T0338289

International Valuation Standards

International Valuation Standards

A Guide to the Valuation of Real Property Assets

David Parker

Library of Congress Cataloging-in-Publication data applied for

A catalogue record for this book is available from the British Library.

ISBN: 9781118329368

Cover image: Getty Images © piccerella

Set in 10/13pt Trump Mediaeval by SPi Global, Pondicherry, India
Printed and bound in Malaysia by Vivar Printing Sdn Bhd

1   2016

To my twins, Elliot and Victoria.
May the future recompense for that foregone.

Contents

Foreword

International Valuation Standards (IVSs) are essential to measuring the performance of investment funds consistently and transparently across the globe. All fund managers have a duty to invest clients' money responsibly, and for me this means adherence to IVS.

This book is therefore timely, with no other analysis of the content and application of IVSs available to the property industry and property profession worldwide. This scholarly work does not simply describe IVSs but analyses them in detail, drawing together the context of globalisation with the historic and central concept of market value.

The book's focus on the instruction, implementation and reporting of valuation as an interconnected process is enlightening, as is the use of the RICS Red Book Global Edition to illustrate the application of IVSs. The Red Book transcends national differences and shows how IVSs can be adopted and applied by professionals active in many countries across the world.

David Parker is a recognised authority on property valuation theory and practice, with roles both in academia and practice. If property investors, property lenders and property valuers around the world followed his pithy maxim "say what you are going to do, do it and say what you have done", many of the problems so commonly arising in valuation could be avoided.

Martin Brühl FRICS
Managing Director, Union Investment Real Estate GmbH
Germany

About the Author

David Parker is an internationally recognised property industry expert on both the theory and practice of valuation and a highly regarded property academic, being a director and adviser to property investment groups including listed real estate investment trusts, unlisted funds and private property businesses (www.davidparker.com.au).

Professor Parker is currently the inaugural Professor of Property at the University of South Australia, a Visiting Professor at University Tun Hussein Onn in Malaysia, a Visiting Fellow at the University of Ulster and an Acting Valuation Commissioner of the Land and Environment Court of New South Wales.

With over 25 years of experience in all aspects of valuation, property fund management, portfolio management, asset management and property management, Professor Parker previously held senior executive positions with Richard Ellis, Schroders Property Fund and ANZ Funds Management.

Holding BSc, MComm, MBA, MPhil and PhD degrees, Professor Parker is a Fellow of the Royal Institution of Chartered Surveyors, the Australian Institute of Company Directors, the Australian Institute of Management and the Australian Property Institute and a Senior Fellow of the Financial Services Institute of Australasia. He is a member of the Society of Property Researchers, the American Real Estate and Urban Economics Association and the European, American, Asian and Pacific Rim Real Estate Societies.

The author of numerous papers published in academic and industry journals, Professor Parker is a regular conference presenter around the world, Editor of the *Pacific Rim Property Research Journal* and Editorial Board Member for the highly ranked *Journal of Property Research* and *Property Management*.

David Parker may be contacted by email at davidparker@davidparker.com.au.

Preface

Having evolved over half a century, *International Valuation Standards* are a shining example of what may be achieved when nations work together for the common global good.

With a source in the ruins of the 1974 UK property crash, valuation standards evolved through Europe and then to the world following the stock market crash of 1987 and the global property downturn of the early 1990s.

The exponential growth of globalisation in business has reduced the significance of national and political borders and increased the significance of economic integration. The interconnectedness of the world's major economies was glaringly apparent during the Global Financial Crisis towards the end of the first decade of the twenty-first century, when problems arising in the US property, banking and finance markets rapidly became problems for the property, banking and finance markets of each of the world's major economies.

Recognition of globalisation through *International Financial Reporting Standards*, designed to provide a common basis of measurement in order to foster international business and the global flow of capital, together with the increasing prevalence of cross-border secured lending necessitates a common basis of value measurement for real property assets.

International Valuation Standards provide that common basis and are now prevalent in many of the world's major economies offering standardisation of concepts and terminology while leaving scope for flexibility in methodology and application to suit differing countries and differing circumstances.

With *International Valuation Standards* starting to take precedence over harmonised national valuation standards, an analysis of their application is timely. As it may be daunting to start at the beginning of the most recent published edition of *International Valuation Standards* and keep reading until the end is reached, this book seeks to group elements of *International Valuation Standards* together with explanation through application to the real world of business.

Accordingly, both of the principal forms of real property assets, being investment property and owner occupied property, are considered together with both of the principal purposes for valuation, being for financial reporting and for secured lending. Similarly, the valuation process, through the key stages of instruction, implementation and reporting, is dissected and analysed in the context of the relevant provisions of *International Valuation Standards*.

Caution is, however, required given the dynamic nature of *International Valuation Standards* which are regularly amended and updated, such that primary reliance should always be placed on the most recent *International Valuation Standards* which may be found at www.ivsc.org.

David Parker
Adelaide, February 2016

Acknowledgements

The author gratefully acknowledges the general contribution of the Royal Institution of Chartered Surveyors and of delegates at American, European and Pacific Rim Real Estate Society Conferences over the past few years in providing feedback to research papers, together with the specific contribution, through review of draft chapters, by Chris Thorne, former Technical Director for the International Valuation Standards Council.

Introduction

International Valuation Standards are now accepted as the basis for the measurement of the value of real property assets in most of the world's major economies. Through an evolutionary process of harmonisation, the national valuation standards issued by the professional bodies, regulators or governments of many countries in the world are now aligned with *International Valuation Standards*.

It is, therefore, timely for a scholarly work to analyse and explain *International Valuation Standards* in the context of application to global business. Drawing on the author's 25 years of experience in property valuation and extensive academic study of the valuation process, this book seeks to provide an understanding of the key aspects of *International Valuation Standards* and their interrelationship with *International Financial Reporting Standards* and *International Accounting Standards*.

Placing *International Valuation Standards* in the context of globalisation, the book focuses on the central concept of market value, reconciling a conceptual basis for valuation with economic theory and capital market theory. Distinguishing the definitions of value, cost and price, other key definitions are analysed and the principal approaches to valuation within *International Valuation Standards* identified.

Having examined the market approach to valuation, the book continues to examine the income approach to valuation in the context of investment property and the cost approach to valuation in the context of owner occupied property, both for the purposes of financial reporting and for the purposes of secured lending.

International Valuation Standards: A Guide to the Valuation of Real Property Assets, First Edition. David Parker.
© 2016 John Wiley & Sons, Ltd. Published 2016 by John Wiley & Sons, Ltd.

The book also describes and analyses those elements of *International Valuation Standards* that are of relevance to the three principal stages of the real property valuation process, being the instruction of the valuer, undertaking the valuation and reporting the valuation which should be seamlessly integrated in valuation practice.

Like the global businesses and property markets within which real property assets for valuation sit, *International Valuation Standards* are continuously changing, being regularly updated and amended, such that primary reliance should always be placed on the most recent *International Valuation Standards* which may be found at www.ivsc.org.

1

Market Value

1.0 Introduction

In the context of the valuation of real property assets, this book provides an analysis of the International Valuation Standards (IVS), International Accounting Standards (IAS) and International Financial Reporting Standards (IFRS) which, being dynamic, are regularly updated and/or replaced. Accordingly, readers should not rely upon this book as a current statement of an IVS, IAS or IFRS publication and should visit www.ifrs.org and/or www.ivsc.org to find the most recent version.

This chapter seeks to outline the emergence of globalisation, the role of IFRS and the evolution of valuation standards setting, the role of the International Valuation Standards Council (IVSC) and IVSs and an analysis of market value, being the central concept of IVSs, with an overview of other IVSs relevant to the valuation of businesses and business interests, intangible assets and financial instruments.

Chapter 2 will then develop a conceptual framework for valuation based on economic theory, align this framework with finance and capital market theory, examine the definition of the market and distinguish definitions of cost and price from defined concepts of value before reconciling these to the conceptual framework for valuation.

Chapter 3 will consider various aspects of valuation standard definitions within IVSs, discuss the definitions of other relevant contextual terms and identify the principal approaches to valuation within IVSs including a focus on the market approach to valuation.

International Valuation Standards: A Guide to the Valuation of Real Property Assets,
First Edition. David Parker.
© 2016 John Wiley & Sons, Ltd. Published 2016 by John Wiley & Sons, Ltd.

Chapter 4 will describe and analyse those elements of IVSs that are of relevance to the three principal stages of the real property valuation process, being the instruction of the valuer, undertaking the valuation and reporting the valuation.

Chapter 5 will consider IVSs in the context of the valuation of investment property, with particular reference to IAS 40 *Investment Property* and the income approach to valuation, including an examination of IVSC TIP 1 *Discounted Cash Flow*.

Finally, Chapter 6 will focus on IVSs in the context of the valuation of owner occupied property held by operating businesses, with particular reference to IAS 16 *Property, Plant and Equipment* and the cost approach to valuation, including an examination of IVSC TIP 2 *The Cost Approach to Tangible Assets*.

In many countries around the world, national and local valuation professional bodies adopt IVSs and supplement them with national or local valuation practice guidance which may expand upon IVSs in a national or local context for the benefit of their membership. However, only the Royal Institution of Chartered Surveyors (RICS) produces global valuation practice guidance that adopts and expands upon IVSs but is not country specific, comprising mandatory professional standards and valuation practice statements and non-mandatory practice guidance applications and practice guidance notes for use by members globally – generally referred to as the RICS Red Book Global (RICS 2013). Accordingly, this book refers to the RICS Red Book Global for the purposes of considering how a professional body interprets IVSs for application by its members worldwide but without a country-specific application.

This book is based upon International Valuation Standards 2013 (IVSC, 2013) and International Financial Reporting Standards 2013 (IFRS, 2013). Given their nature, IVSs, IAS's and IFRSs are dynamic, being regularly updated and with the most recently published versions replacing previously published versions. Accordingly, readers should not rely upon this book as a current statement of an IVS, IAS or IFRS publication and should visit www.ifrs.org and/or www.ivsc.org to find the most recent version.

1.1 Globalisation and valuation

This section seeks to outline the emergence of globalisation and the role of IFRS, with the following sections considering the evolution of valuation standards setting, the role of IVSC and IVSs and an analysis of market value, being the central concept of IVSs, with an overview of other IVSs relevant to the valuation of businesses and business interests, intangible assets and financial instruments.

1.1.1 Globalisation

Globalisation has increasingly gained pace since the end of the Second World War, with the Bretton Woods Agreement on international monetary policy, commerce and finance, the emergence of container shipping and the growth in international air travel as examples of global developments facilitating increasing international integration in trade and commerce. The late twentieth-century developments in communications, computing and the advent of the internet facilitated even greater globalisation in banking, finance and investment contributing to the current very high level of interconnectedness between the world's major economies.

The establishment of the International Monetary Fund, World Bank and Basel Committee on Banking Supervision provide examples of the impact of globalisation in the financial markets, with groups such as the G20 providing an example of governmental globalisation. The creation of the European Union led to the free movement of labour and capital across Europe and a common currency, with the fall of the Berlin Wall leading to the creation of independent eastern European states which further enhanced European movement of labour and capital.

A series of bilateral and later regional trade agreements between countries, the formation of GATT and the World Trade Organisation have each fostered the development of international trade and the growth of multinational corporations such as HSBC and Airbus, making it economically feasible for a European based company to manufacture goods in China or India and sell to world markets in the USA or Africa, either directly through the supply chain leading to the world's shopping centres or indirectly through fulfilment of internet orders.

The increasing impact of globalisation has the effect of reducing the significance of national and political borders and increasing the significance of economic integration. The interconnectedness of the world's major economies was glaringly apparent during the Global Financial Crisis towards the end of the first decade of the twenty-first century, when problems arising in the US property, banking and finance markets rapidly became problems for the property, banking and finance markets of each of the world's major economies.

In the context of property, the growth in multinational corporations has significantly increased the amount of property in other countries held by businesses for the purposes of operations. As a result of globalisation, such multinational corporations as HSBC and Airbus have become significant property owners and occupiers in a vast number of countries around the world. Similarly, property investment has rapidly globalised in the last 25 years with the emergence of sovereign wealth funds in the 1970s building diversified global property portfolios and many pension funds, superannuation funds, real estate investment trusts (REITs) and other property fund managers seeking to invest outside their country of origin, resulting in many of the major office, shopping centre, hotel and warehouse properties of large cities around the world now being owned by foreign investors.

The globalisation of property has been mirrored by the globalisation of property services groups, with the UK Richard Ellis merging with the US Coldwell Banker to become CBRE and the UK Jones Lang Wootton merging with the US LaSalle Partners in 1999 to become Jones Lang LaSalle or JLL, with 30,000 staff in 750 locations in 60 countries (Babawale, 2012a).

Consistent with trends in other parts of the economy worldwide, the emergence of both multinational corporations and international property investors has created the demand for international valuation services and the merger of major national firms into international property services groups has created the supply of international valuation services.

1.1.2 International Financial Reporting Standards

In an increasingly global marketplace, international comparability of information is essential to enable the effective allocation of scarce resources. Accordingly, global businesses require a common basis for company accounts that is understandable, comparable, reliable and relevant for internal and external users across different countries.

As globalisation evolved, it became apparent that national accounting standards would be both inadequate for and complicate international business and investment. The apparent need for international accounting standards led to the formation of the International Accounting Standards Committee (IASC) in 1973 by accounting bodies from Australia, Canada, France, Germany, Mexico, the Netherlands, the United Kingdom, Ireland and the United States. The aim of the IASC was to achieve consistency internationally in definitions, measurement and treatment of transactions in the course of business or investment to enable financial reporting that permitted cross country comparability and appreciation. (Dugeri et al., 2012) Those standards issued by the IASC between 1973 and 2001 comprise the International Accounting Standards (IAS's).

From 2001, the International Accounting Standards Board (IASB) succeeded the IASC and assumed the full standard setting role for the accountancy profession worldwide, with those standards issued by the IASB from 2001 comprising the IFRS (Dugeri et al., 2012). The objectives of the IASB are:

- to develop, in the public interest, a single set of high quality, understandable, enforceable and globally accepted financial reporting standards based on clearly articulated principles;

- to promote the use and rigorous application of those standards;
- to take account of the needs of a range of sizes and types of entities in diverse economic settings; and
- to promote and facilitate the adoption of IFRS through the convergence of national accounting standards and IFRS's (IFRS, 2013, para 6, page A10).

The IASB achieves its objectives primarily by developing and publishing IFRS's and promoting their use (IFRS, 2013, para 7, page A10). IFRS's set out recognition, measurement, presentation and disclosure requirements dealing with transactions and events that are important in general purpose financial statements (IFRS, 2013, para 8, page A11), prepared by the entity (IAS 1, para 2, page A541) on the going concern assumption (IAS 1, para 25, page A547).

Those IAS's and IFRS's of principal relevance to the valuation of real property assets include:

IAS 16	*Property, Plant and Equipment*
IAS 17	*Leases*
IAS 36	*Impairment of Assets*
IAS 40	*Investment Property*
IFRS 5	*Non-Current Assets Held for Sale and Discontinued Operations*
IFRS 13	*Fair Value Measurement*

Currently, around 100 countries have adopted IFRS including the European Union, Australia, Canada, Montenegro and Nepal. However, major economies such as the USA, Japan and India are yet to require IFRS for listed companies.

The benefits of IFRS, as a common basis for accounting worldwide, includes the provision of high quality, transparent and comparable information in financial reporting to help investors, other participants in the various capital markets of the world and other users of financial information make economic decisions (IFRS, 2013). Such transparency and comparability aids the global flow of capital between countries, supports national economies and improves international competitiveness as well as reducing financial reporting costs, improving the quality of financial reporting and providing more useful information to decision makers.

Therefore, for such multinational corporations as HSBC and Airbus and for international property investors such as sovereign wealth funds, pension funds, superannuation funds, REITs and other property fund managers, who have become significant property owners and occupiers in a vast number of countries around the world, IFRS effectively provide one common basis for accounting worldwide facilitating the ultimate 'apples with apples' comparison for the purpose of decision making.

1.1.3 Valuation

While IFRS effectively provide one common basis for accounting worldwide, in order for IFRS to provide a reliable decision-making basis in the context of property, the provision of those inputs concerning property valuation also need to be undertaken on one common basis worldwide.

The global client base driving the adoption of international standards in accounting and banking also required the same for valuation, given that valuation is the basis for lending decisions, financial reporting of multinational companies, cross border property investment, securitisation of real estate and so forth (Babawale, 2012b):

> In the emerging globalised world, valuations that would be relied upon internationally can therefore be produced only by a valuation profession that conforms to international standards of professional education, competence and practice. (Babawale, 2012a)

Essentially, the principal drivers for the introduction and adoption of international valuation standards may be identified as:

- the requirement of Governments for valuations of publicly owned assets for the purpose of accountability, measurement of performance and financial transparency;
- the trend towards the privatisation of Government enterprises;
- the development of international accounting standards;
- emerging economies with no established skill or depth in real estate appraisal;
- the Basel Committee on bank lending;
- world trade agreements, designed to balance world trade practices;
- the move towards a fair value accounting model;
- the activities of the United Nations Conference on Trade and Development, which is working towards the harmonisation of accounting and other professional practices; and
- the need for performance measurement of both investment property and owner occupied property to contribute to the measurement of property, portfolio and company management performance (Edge, 2001).

While the principal benefit of converging valuation regulation internationally with accounting regulation may be contended to be the efficient and effective functioning and stability of global capital and debt markets, several further benefits of global regulatory convergence may be identified:

- improving the comparability of financial information, with consistent valuation practices supporting the transparency and credibility of valuations in financial reporting globally, so increasing the potential mobility of capital across national borders and providing all decision makers with consistent, high quality, reliable information with which to make informed investment, resource and policy decisions;

- improving the auditability of financial statements, with adoption and application of globally consistent valuation standards providing auditors with clear benchmarks to assess whether valuations included in financial statements are reasonably founded;
- reducing the effects of systemic risk, with a reduction in the threats to the global financial systems of such behaviours as over confidence in rising markets and extreme risk aversion in falling markets which may heighten systemic risk in globally connected markets such as banking, insurance and securities;
- reducing information costs, with multinational companies and global property investors being able to measure assets consistently in different countries which reduces the cost of preparing financial statements and the need to reconcile differing valuation approaches;
- decreasing the opportunities for regulatory arbitrage by removing opportunities for pricing differentials that do not have a basis in economic fundamentals but instead arise from different valuation practices;
- providing an underpinning for a global regulatory system, through which global bodies such as the G20 can develop global solutions to address global issues with regulatory convergence facilitating intergovernmental co-operation, greater institutional linkages and international policy integration; and
- providing additional benefits for developing and emerging economies, through the adoption and implementation of existing high-quality, internationally accepted standards recognised by international bodies, governments, investors, corporations, lenders and so forth (IVSC, 2014).

The development of international valuation standards that are consistent with IFRS contributes to achieving such benefits and provides investors, regulators, and users of valuations with that which they seek, being consistency, clarity, reliability and transparency in valuation reporting worldwide (Edge, 2001), as:

> Clients need to understand that a valuation produced in Massachusetts, Manchester, Melbourne, Moscow or Matabeleland is reliable in its standards and its methodologies. (Gilbertson, 2002)

Like the journey to achieve one common basis for accounting worldwide through IFRS, the journey to achieve one common basis for valuation worldwide was an evolutionary process spanning almost half a century.

1.2 Evolution of valuation standard setting

The previous section sought to outline the emergence of globalisation and the role of IFRS, with this section seeking to consider the evolution of valuation standards setting and the role of IVSC and IVSs, with the following sections then seeking to analyse market value, being the central concept of IVSs and to provide an overview of other IVSs relevant to the valuation of businesses and business interests, intangible assets and financial instruments.

The challenge facing international valuation standard setters may be summarised as follows:

> Deals happen. There is not a perfect market. This imperfection makes a valuer's task very difficult. The valuer has to interpret where the market is going. A valuation is like a snapshot in time.
>
> Imagine a photograph containing a ball in flight. Is it actually going up or down? That's what the client wants to know. He would really like to know where that ball will be after an agreed period of time, but that is probably too difficult for all but the crystal ball gazers.
>
> Valuers have to reflect, not make, the market. A valuation could be a surrogate pricing process. Whereas, worth is what the purchaser is prepared to pay. What is value? Does value exist? Can value really be measured or is it ethereal?
>
> Does a valuer work in the property market, or measure the market in property? (Gilbertson, 2002)

with this challenge exacerbated by the booms and busts of independent and interdependent cyclical national property markets worldwide.

1.2.1 Principal phases

The journey to achieve one common basis for valuation worldwide has been an evolutionary process spanning almost half a century, which may be contended to comprise the following principal phases (Babawale 2012a, 2012b; Banfield, 2014; Dugeri et al., 2012; Edge, 2001; French, 2003; IVSC, 2015a; Mackmin, 1999; Mallinson and French, 2000):

- **initial development of valuation standards in the UK:**
  Arising from the 1970s UK recession and the 1974 UK property crash which precipitated a loss of credibility for the valuation profession, RICS established a joint working party with the Institute of Chartered Accountants in England and Wales in 1973 to report on the valuation of property assets, followed by the formation of the Asset Valuation Standards Committee in 1974 which developed guidance notes;

Following Greenwell's (1976) criticism of traditional capitalisation of income methods as incorrect, illogical and by deduction, leading to inaccurate valuations, RICS responded by establishing a research programme into valuation methods and published *Guidance Notes on the Valuation of Assets* in 1976, the original RICS Red Book, being endorsed by the Bank of England, London Stock Exchange, City Panel on Takeovers and Mergers, banking associations and others; The Red Book has been regularly updated since, including reflection of the RICS-initiated Trott Report (1980, 1986), Mallinson Report (1994) (incorporated in the 1996 RICS Red Book) and Carsberg Report (2002);

- **followed by development of regional European valuation standards:**
  The European Group of Valuers of Fixed Assets (TEGOVOFA) was created in 1977, now The European Group of Valuer Associations (TEGoVA), which created a set of regional European valuation standards published in 1981 as the Blue Book or Guide Bleu;

- **and development of valuation standards internationally:**
  The International Assets Valuation Committee (TIAVSC) was created in 1981/82 which metamorphosed into the International Valuation Standards Committee in 1996 and the International Valuation Standards Council (IVSC) in 2008, having published the first International Valuation Standards in 1985;

  Since 2000, IVSC published IVSs reviewed in accordance with IFRS, reflecting international regulatory convergence, with the process coming full circle as the 2003 edition of the RICS Red Book adopted and supported IVSs; and

  In 2014, IVSC Trustees commissioned an independent assessment 'to ensure the organisation is equipped for the next phase of its development' (IVSC, 2015a). A Review Group was created which assessed the governance, financial stability, processes and outputs of IVSC and made recommendations for improvements which are currently in the process of evaluation and implementation.

Therefore, valuation standards developed out of valuation practice rather than out of valuation theory, having evolved independently of economic theory, finance theory and capital market theory, the effect of which will be considered in greater detail in Chapter 2. Significantly, the development of valuation standards worldwide was initially undertaken by national valuation professional bodies independently or in association and then internationally for around 30 years, but in a property vacuum until 2000 when convergence with the common basis for accounting worldwide was undertaken, reflecting the demands of globalisation and leading to the evolution of one common basis for valuation worldwide.

1.2.2 Role of IVSC

The IVSC is an independent, non-profit organisation incorporated in the USA which has two principal functions:

- to develop and promulgate globally recognised financial standards, acceptable to the world's capital market organisations, regulators and market participants; and
- to act as a global focus for the valuation profession;

which came into sharp focus following the Global Financial Crisis from 2007 when G20 leaders called for standard setters to improve valuation principles and to achieve clarity and consistency worldwide (IVSC, 2009).

The objective of the IVSC is to build confidence and public trust in the valuation process by creating a framework for the delivery of credible valuation opinions by suitably trained valuation professionals acting in an ethical manner (IVSC, 2013).

In its policy paper on *Global Regulatory Convergence and the Valuation Profession*, IVSC succinctly stated:

> With many corporations and financial institutions now operating globally, convergence of the diverse systems of national regulation of the financial markets is essential for both effective regulation and to facilitate economic growth.
>
> Consistent and effective regulation is important in promoting the comparability of financial information, minimising the effects of systemic economic risks, and helping to create a level playing field for international competition.
>
> For the valuation profession, regulatory convergence includes the global adoption and implementation of high-quality internationally accepted standards for the undertaking and reporting of those valuations that are relied upon by investors and regulators of the global financial markets. (IVSC, 2014)

Acting in the public interest, IVSC contends that valuation is a key input into financial information relied upon by investors and used to support decisions in financial markets, such as financial reporting, managing the solvency of financial institutions, supporting lending or other investment decisions and pricing units in collective investment schemes, that each have a direct impact on the public interest and that each will benefit from global regulatory convergence (IVSC, 2014).

IVSC operates by consulting with valuation users to identify their concerns, working with professional valuers to identify issues and projects and then developing and promoting solutions (such as standards, valuation applications or technical information papers) following an established process of public exposure and consultation. Enforcement of compliance with IVSs is, however, not undertaken by IVSC but by those regulators and national valuation professional organisations adopting the IVSs (IVSC, 2012a).

1.2.3 Role of IVSs

The two components of the role of IVSC, being to develop and promulgate international valuation standards and to act as a global focus for the valuation profession, are effectively intertwined. IVSC is required to develop standards at a conceptual or principle level that are capable of implementation internationally and which require both enforcement of implementation by national bodies or regulators and development of complementary and consistent national standards, where necessary, by national bodies or regulators.

1.2.3.1 Structure of IVSs

IVSs, by definition, are of international application, with the role of regional and national standards considered in the following section. It is through application that IVSs gain their status as, when a statement is made that a valuation has been undertaken in accordance with IVSs, it is implicit that all relevant standards are complied with and due account is taken of any supporting guidance issued by IVSC (IVSC, 2013, page 3). Accordingly, unlike some national and regional standards issued by valuation professional organisations for their valuer members, IVSs are not mandatory on valuers unless they state that they are undertaking a valuation in accordance with the IVSs.

The objective of the IVSs is to increase the confidence and trust of users of valuation services by establishing transparent and consistent valuation procedures (IVSC, 2013, page 2). An IVS is intended to do one or more of the following:

- identify or develop globally accepted principles and definitions;
- identify and promulgate procedures for the undertaking of valuation assignments and the reporting of valuations;
- identify specific matters that require consideration and methods commonly used for valuing different types of asset or liability; and/or
- identify appropriate valuation procedures for the major purposes for which valuations are required (IVSC, 2013, page 2).

An IVS contains either:

- requirements that have to be followed in order to produce a valuation that is compliant with the standards; or

- information or guidance that does not direct or mandate any particular course of action but which is intended to assist the development of better and more consistent valuation practice or that helps users better understand a valuation on which they intend to rely (IVSC, 2013, page 2).

While IVSs may be applied to assets or liabilities, this book only considers IVSs in the context of assets, specifically real property assets. The IVSs are arranged as a Framework, General Standards, Asset Standards, Valuation Applications and Technical Information Papers.

Further, it should be noted that, rather than necessarily adopting dictionary definitions or commonly used interpretations of terms, IVSs define and construe terms in a particular manner for the purpose of consistency in application and users should be aware of such definitions and constructions in order to appropriately apply IVSs. Within this book, a reference to a term as defined by IVSs is italicised, such that, for example, *market value* refers to the term 'market value' as it is defined in IVSs.

1.2.3.1.1 IVS Framework

The IVS Framework provides, as the name suggests, a framework or scaffolding within which the General Standards, Asset Standards, Valuation Applications and Technical Information Papers sit, setting forth generally accepted valuation principles and concepts that are to be followed in the application of each but not including any procedural requirements (IVSC, 2013, page 2).

The IVS Framework is principally considered in Chapter 2 in the context of valuation concepts and valuation approaches.

1.2.3.1.2 IVS General Standards

The IVS General Standards comprise:

- IVS 101 *Scope of Work*;
- IVS 102 *Implementation*; and
- IVS 103 *Reporting*;

which are considered in detail in Chapter 4. IVS General Standards set forth the requirements for the conduct of all valuation assignments (except as modified by an Asset Standard or a Valuation Application), being designed to be capable of application to valuations of all types of assets for any valuation purpose to which the IVSs apply (IVSC, 2013, page 2).

1.2.3.1.3 IVS Asset Standards

The IVS Asset Standards include:

- IVS 220 *Plant and Equipment*;
- IVS 230 *Real Property Interests*; and
- IVS 233 *Investment Property Under Construction*;

which are considered in detail in Chapters 5 and 6 plus others not directly concerning real property assets which are considered in section 1.4, below.

IVS Asset Standards include *Requirements* and *Commentary*, with *Requirements* setting forth any additions to or modifications of the requirements in the General Standards with illustrations of application. The *Commentary* provides background information on the characteristics of each asset type that influence value and identifies the common valuation approaches and methods used (IVSC, 2013, page 2).

As referred to in section 1.0, above, IVSs are dynamic, being regularly updated and/or replaced. Currently, IVS 230 and IVS 300 may be amended, IVS 233 may be retired and a generic guidance paper on the valuation of property in the course of development may be introduced. Accordingly, as stated above, readers should not rely upon this book as a current statement of an IVS, IAS or IFRS publication and should visit www.ifrs.org and/or www.ivsc.org to find the most recent version.

1.2.3.1.4 IVS Valuation Applications

The IVS Valuation Applications include:

- IVS 300 *Valuations for Financial Reporting*; and
- IVS 310 *Valuations of Real Property Interests for Secured Lending*;

which are considered in detail in Chapters 5 and 6.

IVS Valuation Applications address common purposes for which valuations are required, each including *Requirements* and *Guidance*, with *Requirements* setting forth any additions to or modifications of the requirements in the General Standards with illustrations of application. The *Guidance* provides background information on:

- the valuation requirements of internationally applicable regulations or standards issued by other bodies, such as IFRS;
- other commonly accepted requirements for valuations for that purpose; and
- appropriate valuation procedures to meet these requirements (IVSC, 2013, page 3).

1.2.3.1.5 Technical Information Papers

The Technical Information Papers (TIP's) include:

- TIP 1 *Discounted Cash Flow* (considered in Chapter 5);
- TIP 2 *The Cost Approach to Tangible Assets* (considered in Chapter 6);
- TIP 3 *The Valuation of Intangible Assets* (considered in section 1.4.2, below); and
- TIP 4 *Valuation Uncertainty* (considered in Chapter 4).

Technical Information Papers support the application of the requirements in other standards by:

- providing information on the characteristics of different types of asset that are relevant to value; and/or
- providing information on appropriate valuation methods and their application; and/or
- providing additional detail on matters identified in another standard; and/or
- providing information to support the judgement required in reaching a valuation conclusion in different situations (IVSC, 2013, page 3).

TIP's are neither a text book nor an academic discussion and are not intended to provide training or instruction to inexperienced valuers. While TIP's provide guidance, they do not prescribe or mandate the use of a particular approach but present information to an experienced valuer to assist in the selection of the most appropriate course of action to take (IVSC, 2013, page 3).

1.2.3.2 International, Regional and National Valuation Standards

Having considered the development of IVSs, the other component of the role of IVSC is to promulgate international valuation standards and to act as a global focus for the valuation profession. This is largely operationalised by IVSC through engagement with valuation professional organisations (VPOs), regulators and other groups around the world who enforce implementation and who may also develop complementary and consistent regional and/or national standards.

IVSC further describes its role as to promote and advance the global regulatory convergence agenda through the independent development of high-quality, internationally accepted valuation standards, provision of support for their adoption and implementation and engagement with member valuation professional bodies to promote consistent competency and ethical standards (IVSC, 2014):

> We serve the public interest by promoting consistent compliance with, and implementation of, high-quality, internationally accepted standards in the preparation and presentation of valuations around the world. (IVSC, 2015b)

Through the signing of a memorandum of understanding, IVSC has formalised its relationship with 20 VPOs to foster adoption of IVSs, with IVSC having engaged with 50 VPOs spanning geographically from the Norges Takseringsforbund to the Property Institute of New Zealand and from the China Appraisal Society to the Colombian Registro Nacional de Avaluadores. (IVSC, 2015b).

Such VPOs are generally the national valuation professional body for their country who advance the adoption and implementation of IVSs in that country, act to regulate individual valuers either through self-regulation or shared regulation with government and promote the benefits of IVSs to their government and regulators (IVSC, 2014).

With IVSC producing international standards, being a limited number of high level, principle based requirements which are supported with guidance and of common applicability across countries, it is then up to member VPOs to produce regional or national standards or guidance, as may be required for that jurisdiction, consistent with the provisions of the IVSs (IVSC, 2014):

> ... valuation rules are no longer national standards existing in isolation. The standards of various countries have to harmonise with each other, and to do that there must be a strong, single benchmark of common standards to which all our states can relate. This is the role that the IVSC fulfils. (Edge, 2001)

By each member VPO's standards and guidance harmonising with IVSs, they effectively harmonise with each other and so achieve the IVSC policy goal of global regulatory convergence. Such convergence may be further extended where the VPO, regulator or government of developing countries, that lack their own national standards, choose to adopt IVSs as their de facto national standards.

In a national context such as Great Britain, for example, RICS is the national VPO which engages with IVSC and adopts IVSs in the RICS Red Book (UK Version) which is binding on RICS members acting in Great Britain and who are, therefore, required to follow IVSs. The RICS Red Book includes mandatory professional standards (PS), mandatory valuation practice statements (VPS) and advisory (not mandatory) valuation practice guidance applications (VPGA), with the UK version then also including RICS UK Valuation Standards (UKVS), RICS UK Appendices and RICS UK Valuation Practice Guidance Notes (VPGN) to cover specific statutory or regulatory requirements in the jurisdiction of Great Britain while being consistent with IVSs (Banfield, 2014).

1.3 Market value

The previous sections sought to outline the emergence of globalisation, the role of IFRS, the evolution of valuation standard setting and the role of IVSC and IVSs, with this section seeking to analyse market value, being the central concept of IVSs, with the following sections then seeking to provide an overview of other IVSs relevant to the valuation of businesses and business interests, intangible assets and financial instruments.

The concept of market value evolved in an early Australian High Court decision, *Spencer v Commonwealth* (1907) 5 CLR 418, which enunciated several of the key elements found in today's definition of *market value* by the IVSC that is now adopted globally though not, necessarily, fully integrated with economic theory, finance theory and capital market theory as will be considered further in Chapter 2.

1.3.1 Spencer concept of market value

A significant early development in the evolution of the concept of market value was the decision of the Australian High Court in *Spencer v Commonwealth* (1907) 5 CLR 418 (*Spencer*). Following the cessation of colonial status with the creation of the Commonwealth of Australia upon Federation on 1 January 1901 and separation from Great Britain, the High Court of Australia was only four years old when three judges heard an appeal on a compulsory acquisition matter. The bench was particularly notable, comprising Griffith CJ who was generally claimed to be the principal author of the Constitution of Australia and the first Chief Justice of Australia, Barton J who had previously been the first Prime Minister of Australia from 1901 to 1903 and Isaacs J who became the first Australian born Governor General of Australia in 1930.

The appeal concerned the acquisition by the Commonwealth of 6 acres, 1 rood and 2 perches of land in North Fremantle for the construction of a fort, being described as follows:

> The land consists of sand-hummocks overlooking the Indian Ocean. It has no grass; and it is useless in its present condition for any purpose of production.

with Mr Spencer claiming compensation of £10,000 and the High Court awarding the sum of £3,000, being that which had previously been admitted and paid into Court.

The significance of the decision lies in the way in which the judges constructed the concept of market value:

> In my judgement, the test of value of land is to be determined, not by inquiring what price a man desiring to sell could actually have obtained for it on a given day, ie, whether there was in fact on that day a willing buyer, but by inquiring "What would a man desiring to buy the land have had to pay for it on that day to a vendor willing to sell it for a fair price but not desirous to sell?" It is, no doubt, very difficult to answer such a question, and any answer must be to some extent conjectural. The necessary mental process is to put yourself as far as possible in the position of persons conversant with the subject at the relevant time, and from that point of view to ascertain what, according to then current opinion of land values, a purchaser would have had to offer for the land

to induce such a willing vendor to sell it, or, in other words, to inquire at what point a desirous purchaser and a not unwilling vendor would come together. (Griffiths CJ)

And I should say, in view of the many authorities cited and upon the sense of the matter, that a claimant is entitled to have for his land what it is worth to a man of ordinary prudence and foresight, not holding his land for merely speculative purposes, nor, on the other hand, anxious to sell for any compelling or private reason, but willing to sell as a business man would be to another such person, both of them alike uninfluenced by any consideration of sentiment or need. (Barton J)

To arrive at the value of the land on that date, we have, as I conceive, to suppose it sold then, not by means of a forced sale, but by voluntary bargaining between the plaintiff and a purchaser, willing to trade, but neither of them so anxious to do so that he would overlook any ordinary business consideration. We must further suppose both to be perfectly acquainted with the land, and cognizant of all circumstances which might affect its value, either advantageously or prejudicially, including its situation, character, quality, proximity to conveniences or inconveniences, its surrounding features, the then present demand for land, and the likelihood, as then appearing to persons best capable of forming an opinion, of a rise or fall for what reason soever in the amount which one would otherwise be willing to fix as the value of the property. (Isaacs J)

together with:

In order that any article may have an exchange value, there must be presupposed a person willing to give the article in exchange for money and another willing to give money in exchange for the article. (Griffiths CJ)

… value implies the existence of a willing buyer as well as of a willing seller… (Griffiths CJ)

Prosperity unexpected, or depression, which no man would ever have anticipated, if happening after the date named, must be alike disregarded. (Isaacs J)

… the all important fact on that day is the opinion regarding the fair price of the land, which a hypothetical prudent purchaser would entertain, if he desired to purchase it for the most advantageous purpose for which it was adapted. The plaintiff is to be compensated; therefore he is to receive the money equivalent to the loss he has sustained by deprivation of his land, and that … cannot exceed what such a prudent purchaser would be prepared to give him. (Isaacs J)

Within the judges' construction of the concept of market value, the following elements may be identified:

- an estimated amount: *could actually have obtained for it, have had to pay* (Griffith CJ), *value of the land, the fair price of the land* (Isaacs J);

- an exchange: *a man desiring to buy the land have had to pay for it... to a vendor willing to sell, may have an exchange value* (Griffith CJ), *willing to trade* (Isaacs J);
- a valuation date: *on a given day, on that day* (Griffith CJ), *on that date, prosperity unexpected, or depression,... if happening after the date named* (Isaacs J);
- a willing buyer: *a man desiring to buy the land, a desirous purchaser, willing buyer* (Griffith CJ), *voluntary bargaining, willing to trade, hypothetical prudent purchaser* (Isaacs J);
- a willing seller: *a vendor willing to sell it for a fair price, a not unwilling vendor* (Griffith CJ), *voluntary bargaining, willing to trade* (Isaacs J);
- a knowledgeable and prudent buyer and seller: *to a man of ordinary prudence and foresight, willing to sell as a business man would be to another such person* (Barton J), *perfectly acquainted with the land, hypothetical prudent purchaser* (Isaacs J);
- an absence of compulsion: *but not desirous to sell* (Griffith CJ), *nor, on the other hand, anxious to sell for any compelling or private reason, uninfluenced by any consideration of sentiment or need* (Barton J), *not by means of a forced sale, overlook any ordinary business consideration* (Isaacs J); and
- an assumption of highest and best use: *the most advantageous purpose for which it was adapted* (Isaacs J).

Accordingly, at the beginning of the last century within the judgements in *Spencer*, the key elements of the concept of market value may be identified. It should, however, be noted that the judgements were in the context of a vacant block of land on the coast of Western Australia in 1907 such that, while as a concept it is still of relevance today, care is required in the interpretation of language in this century – for example, *perfectly acquainted with the land* should be interpreted relative to a vacant coastal block in 1907 rather than in the context of the application of the efficient market hypothesis to a high rise office investment property in 2015.

Significantly, as will be considered further in Chapter 2, the judgements in *Spencer* contribute to the development of valuation theory through the provision of a legal construct of supply, demand, price, market and participants for a specific statutory purpose.

1.3.2 IVS definition of market value

The definition of market value is both fundamental for and central to IVSs:

> *Market value* is the estimated amount for which an asset or liability should exchange on the *valuation date* between a willing buyer and a willing seller in

an arm's length transaction, after proper marketing and where the parties had each acted knowledgably, prudently and without compulsion. (IVSC, 2013, page 8; IVSC, 2013, para 29, page 18; RICS, 2013, page 9)

The definition includes most elements identified above from the concept of market value in *Spencer*, being:

- an estimated amount;
- an exchange;
- a valuation date;
- a willing buyer;
- a willing seller;
- a knowledgeable and prudent buyer and seller; and
- an absence of compulsion,

but does not explicitly include an assumption of highest and best use, though this is fundamental to the proper application of the definition and will be considered further, below.

However, the IVS definition also adds the following to the concept of market value in *Spencer*:

- an arm's length transaction; and
- a period of marketing.

Significantly, neither the IVS definition of *market value* nor the judgements in *Spencer* explicitly address an assumption concerning transaction costs, which will also be considered further below.

Reflecting the fundamental nature and centrality of the definition of *market value* to IVSs, extensive instruction concerning interpretation and application is provided by IVSC:

> The definition of *market value* shall be applied in accordance with the following conceptual framework: (IVSC, 2013, para 30, page 18)

with nine elements addressed, each of which are considered in the following subsections. Application of the definition of *market value* in this way is mandatory (*shall*), being obligatory not optional, with application otherwise not providing an assessment of *market value*. As a *conceptual framework*, the elements are proposed as a series of overarching principles or scaffolding for the valuation process, capable of interpretation and application to different types of property interests in different countries at different times, thus being an effective example of principles based standard setting for international application.

1.3.2.1 Estimated amount
The *conceptual framework* states:

> (a) "the estimated amount" refers to a price expressed in terms of money payable for the asset in an arm's length market transaction. *Market value* is the most probable price reasonably obtainable in the market on the *valuation date* in keeping with the *market value* definition. It is the best price reasonably obtainable by the seller and the most advantageous price reasonably obtainable by the buyer. This estimate specifically excludes an estimated price inflated or deflated by special terms or circumstances such as atypical financing, sale and leaseback arrangements, special considerations or concessions granted by anyone associated with the sale, or any element of *special value*; (IVSC, 2013, para 30(a), page 18)

The use of the term *estimated* reinforces that a valuation is a matter of opinion rather than a matter of fact, with the *estimated amount* being an assessment of *price* or *most probable price*. Effectively, *price* or *most probable price* is the intersection between the hypothetical purchaser's assessment of worth (*most advantageous price*) and the hypothetical vendor's assessment of worth (*best price*).

The specification of *arm's length market transaction* adds the element of separation and independence of the parties to the concept expressed in *Spencer*, while the *market transaction* confirms the estimated amount to be an amount in exchange in a given market.

For both hypothetical parties, the *price* or *most probable price* is *reasonably obtainable*, requiring an assumption of reasonableness by the parties in the price-setting process. Effectively, this is consistent with the hypothetical purchaser's *most advantageous price* and the hypothetical vendor's *best price*, being that price obtainable without being unreasonable.

However, the *price* or *most probable price* is assumed to not be influenced by issues that may make the hypothetical purchaser's *most advantageous price* and the hypothetical vendor's *best price* assessments of worth which may be unlikely to converge, such as special terms, financing, leaseback or concessions. It is challenging, given the assumption of hypothetical parties and the absence of a *special purchaser*, to understand how any element of *special value* may arise. Effectively, a 'plain vanilla' or 'normal' transaction, presumably with 'typical' financing, is to be assumed with no abnormal or unusual features that may affect the pricing of the transaction, though that which may be 'plain vanilla' or 'normal' may differ between property sectors and property markets around the world.

1.3.2.2 An asset should exchange
The *conceptual framework* states:

> (b) "an asset should exchange" refers to the fact that the value of an asset is an estimated amount rather than a predetermined amount or actual sale price. It is the price in a transaction that meets all the elements of the market value definition at the *valuation date*; (IVSC, 2013, para 30(b), page 18)

The use of the phrase *should exchange* rather than 'would' is consistent with the hypothetical nature of the transaction and the *estimated amount*, reflecting the notion of the hypothetical purchaser's *most advantageous price* and the hypothetical vendor's *best price* assessments of worth coming together at a point of agreement that satisfies (*meets*) all (not most or some) of the assumptions of *market value* on a specified date.

1.3.2.3 On the valuation date
The *conceptual framework* states:

> (c) "on the *valuation date*" requires that the value is time-specific as of a given date. Because markets and market conditions may change, the estimated value may be incorrect or inappropriate at another time. The valuation amount will reflect the market state and circumstances as at the *valuation date*, not those of any other date; (IVSC, 2013, para 30(c), page 18)

The assessment of value is temporal, being reflective of market conditions at that time and only applicable on the *valuation date* thus requiring care when market conditions may be changing rapidly either upwards or downwards and even greater care when market conditions may be at an inflection point.

Consistently, if a valuation is being prepared retrospectively, care is required concerning regard to proximate changes in market conditions or the happening of a reasonably anticipated event subsequent to the *valuation date* or to evidence of transactions at the *valuation date* that emerge subsequently.

1.3.2.4 Between a willing buyer
The *conceptual framework* states:

> (d) "between a willing buyer" refers to one who is motivated, but not com-pelled to buy. This buyer is neither over eager nor determined to buy at any price. This buyer is also one who purchases in accordance with the realities of the current market and with current market expectations, rather than in

relation to an imaginary or hypothetical market that cannot be demonstrated or anticipated to exist. The assumed buyer would not pay a higher price than the market requires. The present owner is included among those who constitute "the market"; (IVSC, 2013, para 30(d), page 18)

The characterisation of the willing buyer as *motivated, but not compelled,* not *over eager nor determined to buy at any price* is consistent with the rational investor assumption that underlies capital market theory and finance theory, but inconsistent with the behavioural characteristics often observed in property transactions when parties become emotionally involved with buyers rarely, if ever, being unmotivated. Effectively, the definition requires the assumption of a willing buyer who is both rational and emotionally detached.

While the buyer is not explicitly stated to be hypothetical and so may be actual (such as the *present owner*), care is required to avoid infecting the assumption of *willing* with the characteristics of a specific party. While the buyer may be hypothetical, the market in which they are assumed to be transacting is real, both in terms of current conditions and expectations of that which may happen in the foreseeable future. Accordingly, it is not some form of normalised market or long-term average market, but the actual market as at the *valuation date.*

Further, the impermissibility of an *imaginary or hypothetical market* requires a focus on that market which exists with those buyers who exist. Accordingly, in a depressed market when debt financing is generally unavailable, a market of equity funded buyers could be assumed and the participation of debt funded buyers could not be assumed unless it could be *demonstrated or anticipated to exist.*

Consistent with economic theory, there will always be a price at which a market will clear. As Banfield (2014) notes:

> For there to be a sale there has to be a purchaser and in reality whatever the state of the market there is always a figure at which somebody will deal – remember the present owner is included among those who constitute the market. (Banfield, 2014, page 122)

1.3.2.5 *And a willing seller*
The *conceptual framework* states:

> (e) "and a willing seller" is neither an over eager nor a forced seller prepared to sell at any price, nor one prepared to hold out for a price not considered reasonable in the current market. The willing seller is motivated to sell the asset at market terms for the best price attainable in the open market after proper marketing, whatever that price may be. The factual circumstances of the actual

owner are not a part of this consideration because the willing seller is a hypothetical owner; (IVSC, 2013, para 30(e), page 19)

The characteristics of the *willing seller* mirror those of the *willing buyer*, being *neither over eager nor a forced seller, nor one prepared to hold out for a price not considered reasonable.* Effectively, the definition requires the assumption of a willing seller who is also both rational and emotionally detached, consistent with a willingness to sell *for the best price attainable, whatever that price may be, after proper marketing.*

Similarly, the market is assumed to be the *current market*, consistent with the assumptions for the *willing buyer*. Further, the conditions and circumstance of the actual owner are assumed irrelevant as the hypothetical scenario requires a focus on what a hypothetical owner would do as a *willing seller.*

1.3.2.6 *In an arm's length transaction*

The IVS definition adds the assumption of *in an arm's length transaction* to the concept of market value in *Spencer* with the *conceptual framework* stating:

> (f) "in an arm's length transaction" is one between parties who do not have a particular or special relationship, eg parent and subsidiary companies or landlord and tenant, that may make the price level uncharacteristic of the market or inflated because of an element of *special value*. The *market value* transaction is presumed to be between unrelated parties, each acting independently; (IVSC, 2013, para 30(f), page 19)

Summarised in the last sentence, the *arm's length transaction* assumption concerns each party being assumed to be independent or not related and operating in isolation. More obvious examples of a lack of independence would be if the parties were assumed to have some form of relationship or connection that may lead to paying more or less than the price level of the market, with the extreme being if the purchaser was a *special purchaser* such that *special value* may arise.

Effectively, the parties are assumed to be standalone market participants engaging in a unique transaction which is consistent with the assumption of parties acting rationally but inconsistent with the nature of the property market where parties may be likely to transact with each other on multiple occasions over time and so not operate in isolation.

1.3.2.7 *After proper marketing*

The IVS definition adds the assumption of *after proper marketing* to the concept of market value in *Spencer* with the *conceptual framework* stating:

> (g) "after proper marketing" means that the asset would be exposed to the market in the most appropriate manner to effect its disposal at the best price reasonably

obtainable in accordance with the *market value* definition. The method of sale is deemed to be that most appropriate to obtain the best price in the market to which the seller has access. The length of exposure time is not a fixed period but will vary according to the type of asset and market conditions. The only criterion is that there must have been sufficient time to allow the asset to be brought to the attention of an adequate number of market participants. The exposure period occurs prior to the *valuation date*; (IVSC, 2013, para 30(g), page 19)

Significantly, the transaction is assumed to occur *after* marketing and such marketing is assumed to be *proper*, being marketing that is *the most appropriate manner to effect its disposal at the best price reasonably obtainable*. Accordingly, the *proper* marketing for a large office property investment for sale by tender may differ from that for a large manufacturing facility for sale by auction, but each is assumed to have occurred before the *valuation date*.

Both the marketing and the method of sale are to be *most appropriate* to achieve the *best price*, such that it may be prudent, in the case of larger or unusual properties, for the valuer to state the assumed form of marketing and method of sale in the valuation report.

The duration of the marketing period may vary depending on the nature of the property, the state of the market and the profile of market participants, being of greatest significance for large or unusual properties in declining or depressed markets or for properties for which market participants are challenging to identify. Conversely, with properties for which there are very few but easily identifiable market participants, an *adequate number* may be canvassed in a short period. As above, it may be prudent, in such cases, for the valuer to state the assumed duration of the marketing period in the valuation report.

1.3.2.8 *Where the parties had each acted knowledgably, prudently*
The *conceptual framework* states:

(h) "where the parties had each acted knowledgably, prudently" presumes that both the willing buyer and the willing seller are reasonably informed about the nature and characteristics of the asset, its actual and potential uses and the state of the market as of the *valuation date*. Each is further presumed to use that knowledge prudently to seek the price that is most favourable for their respective positions in the transaction. Prudence is assessed by referring to the state of the market at the *valuation date*, not with benefit of hindsight at some later date. For example, it is not necessarily imprudent for a seller to sell assets in a market with falling prices at a price that is lower than previous market levels. In such cases, as is true for other exchanges in markets with changing prices, the prudent buyer or seller will act in accordance with the best market information available at the time; (IVSC, 2013, para 30(h), page 19)

Acting knowledgably and prudently is not explicitly defined but may be implied to be related to information. Knowledge would appear to be awareness of the information and prudence would appear to be the use of that information to seek an optimal price, which is generally consistent with the notion of prudence as carefulness and risk aversion.

The phrase *acted knowledgably, prudently* is limited to both parties being assumed to be *reasonably informed* (which is somewhat less than fully informed) about only three nominated issues, being:

- the nature and characteristics of the asset;
- its actual and potential uses; and
- the state of the market as of the valuation date

which may be contended to be a much lower level of knowledge than may be possessed by an actual major investor or major occupier prior to making a decision on a property transaction.

Significantly, the assessment of prudence is temporal, being in the context of the state of the market at the *valuation date* and disregarding anything that may have happened thereafter. Accordingly, that which may be considered prudent at the peak of a property boom just before the collapse may not be judged to have been prudent retrospectively six months after the collapse, but this should be disregarded. The assessment of prudence by the willing parties is, therefore, a snapshot rather than a video.

1.3.2.9 And without compulsion

The *conceptual framework* states:

> (i) "and without compulsion" establishes that each party is motivated to undertake the transaction, but neither is forced or unduly coerced to complete it. (IVSC, 2013, para 30(i), page 19)

The use of the term *and* firmly links *without compulsion* to the definition as a requirement for both parties, being consistent with the notion of *willing* and the reference to *motivated*. While this qualification removes such scenarios as forced sales or pressure to buy/sell from third parties, the reference to undue coercion also potentially precludes reflection of some common property market behavioural characteristics such as peer pressure.

Having considered the principal elements stated in the IVS definition of *market value*, the following sections consider assumptions which are not stated in the IVS definition, being the highest and best use assumption and the transaction costs assumption.

1.3.3 *Highest and best use assumption*

The assumption of highest and best use is identified as an element in the concept of market value in the judgements in *Spencer* and is implicit in the IVS definition of *market value.*

In the *IVS Framework*, highest and best use is addressed as follows:

> The *market value* of an asset will reflect its highest and best use. The highest and best use is the use of an asset that maximises its potential and that is possible, legally permissible and financially feasible. The highest and best use may be for continuation of an asset's existing use or for some alternative use. This is determined by the use that a market participant would have in mind for the asset when formulating the price that it would be willing to bid. (IVSC, 2013, para 32, page 20)

and:

> The highest and best use of an asset valued on a stand-alone basis may be different from its *highest and best use* as part of a group, when its contribution to the overall value of the group must be considered. (IVSC, 2013, para 33, page 20)

The assumption of highest and best use is fundamental to the concept of *market value*, as it excludes limitation to a sub-optimal use, consistent with the rational hypothetical buyer who would seek to optimise the use of a property to the maximum of its potential and, therefore, to optimise the value of the property. Such optimal use may be the existing use or may be an alternative use, with potential alternative uses constrained to those that meet the following three criteria:

> The determination of the highest and best use involves consideration of the following:
>
> (a) to establish whether a use is possible, regard will be had to what would be considered reasonable by market participants,
> (b) to reflect the requirement to be legally permissible, any legal restrictions on the use of the asset, eg zoning designations, need to be taken into account,
> (c) the requirement that the use be financially feasible takes into account whether an alternative use that is physically possible and legally permissible will generate sufficient return to a typical market participant, after taking into account the costs of conversion to that use, over and above the return on the existing use. (IVSC, 2013, para 34, page 20)

The interpretation of *possible* focuses on that use which *would be considered reasonable by market participants,* requiring consideration of such physical issues as being capable of real-world creation given such constraints as the location, size and topography of the land. Similarly, the interpretation of *legally permissible* focuses on planning aspects (such as use, nature of development, density, height and so forth) but may also include permissibility within the form of title held which is particularly significant for leasehold interests, licenses and other forms of title that are not freehold title. Further, the interpretation of *financially feasible* focuses on acceptability of return as a relative measure (being relative to the *existing use*) rather than as an absolute measure, consistent with the assumption of the rational hypothetical buyer.

It should be noted that all three constraints are applicable to an assessment of highest and best use, such that a proposed use which is possible and legally permissible may not be the highest and best use if it is not financially feasible. Effectively, the IVSs require the assumption of highest and best use to reflect a real-world scenario that could actually occur, rather than a hypothetical scenario that would be unlikely to or would not occur in reality.

The highest and best use assumption is linked to *aggregation* (considered further in Chapter 2) which may be a significant issue in the valuation of owner occupied property (considered further in Chapter 6). Where a property to be valued forms part of a group, such as a dilapidated warehouse in the middle of a major manufacturing facility, in terms of highest and best use its value as a renovated warehouse may vary from its value as a site for extension of the manufacturing facility, reflecting the difference in highest and best use between consideration as a standalone asset and as part of a group of assets.

Significantly, the assessment of highest and best use is through the eyes of a *market participant*, usually being the assumed rational hypothetical buyer, who reflects all aspects of the assessment of highest and best use in the price it would attribute to the property. However, such assumed rational hypothetical buyer is not necessarily a single party (which would potentially invoke aspects of *investment value* or *special value*) but is indicative or representative of a small group of assumed rational hypothetical buyers as will be considered in further detail in Chapter 2.

1.3.4 Transaction costs assumption

An assumption concerning transaction costs may not be found in either the IVS definition of *market value* or the judgements in *Spencer*, but is addressed in the *IVS Framework* as follows:

> *Market value* is the estimated exchange price of an asset without regard to the seller's costs of sale or the buyer's costs of purchase and without adjustment for any taxes payable by either party as a direct result of the transaction. (IVSC, 2013, para 35, page 20)

1 Market Value

Accordingly, transaction costs may be interpreted to include:

- *costs of sale* and *costs of purchase* – being such costs as agency fees, marketing costs, legal fees and so forth for the seller and due diligence costs, legal fees and so forth for the buyer; and
- *any taxes payable by either party as a direct result of the transaction* – being such commonly levied taxes as stamp duty on transfer, title registration fees and so forth,

as being excluded from the estimated exchange price of an asset, though such costs and taxes may be included as inputs in some valuation methods such as discounted cash flow and the residual method.

While the exclusion of *costs of sale* and *costs of purchase* may be applied commonly and consistently to all purchaser groups, the exclusion of *taxes payable* requires greater care. Some purchaser groups (such as institutions, REITs and so forth) may be liable for taxes directly resulting from the transaction whereas other purchaser groups (such as charities, public bodies and some religious groups) may be exempt and other purchaser groups (such as private individuals) may receive concessional treatment. Accordingly, where the assumed rational hypothetical buyer is identifiable as a specific group, the exclusion of taxes may be anticipated to have a common effect on price formation. However, where the assumed rational hypothetical buyer is identifiable as potentially being one or more specific groups with differing tax status, the distinction between *market value* and *investment value* may require greater attention.

1.3.5 Market value in practice

The concept and definition of *market value* is fundamental to IVSs and may be initially challenging to grasp. The RICS Red Book Global provides a succinct description of market value as follows:

> It describes an exchange between parties that are unconnected and are operating freely in the marketplace and represents the figure that would appear in a hypothetical contract of sale, or equivalent legal document, at the *valuation date*, reflecting all those factors that would be taken into account in framing their bids by market participants at large and reflecting the highest and best use of the asset. (RICS, 2013, para 1.2.2, page 53)

> It ignores any price distortions caused by *special value* or *synergistic value*. It represents the price that would most likely be achievable for an asset across a wide range of circumstances. (RICS, 2013, para 1.2.3, page 53)

> [and reflecting] the actual market state and circumstances as of the effective *valuation date*. (RICS, 2013, para 1.2.4, page 53)

with Banfield (2014) explaining:

> Market value represents the price that would most likely be achievable for a property across a wide range of circumstances. In essence the definition, if applied correctly, should produce a price that the asset or liability should be expected to sell at a specific date in an unrestricted marketplace following proper marketing appropriate for the type of asset. The definition of necessity has to include certain assumptions but these only reflect the normal workings of the marketplace and should produce the most probable price reasonably obtainable. (Banfield, 2014, page 106)

The contributory elements to *market value* will be considered further in Chapter 2, with particular reference to their difference to the contributory elements to *investment value, synergistic value, fair value* and *special value.*

1.4 Businesses and business interests, intangible assets and financial instruments

The previous sections sought to outline the emergence of globalisation, the role of IFRS, the evolution of valuation standard setting and the role of IVSC and IVSs and to provide an analysis of market value, being the central concept of IVSs, with this section seeking to provide an overview of other IVSs relevant to the valuation of businesses and business interests, intangible assets and financial instruments.

1.4.1 Businesses and business interests

IVS200 *Businesses and Business Interests* is an IVS Asset Standard that applies to the valuation of businesses and business interests, being defined as:

> A business is a commercial, industrial, service or investment activity. A valuation of a business may either comprise the whole of the activity of an entity or a part of the activity. (IVS 220, para C2, page 41)

noting that it is important to distinguish between the value of a business entity and the value of the individual assets or liabilities of that entity (IVS 220, para C2, page 41).

IVS200 provides *Commentary* on the need for clarity concerning ownership rights in the valuation process and the care required in consideration of information received from management, noting the *market approach* and *income approach* to be likely to be the most suitable valuation approaches with extensive commentary provided thereon.

1.4.2 Intangible assets

For some of world's biggest multinational corporations, such as Coca-Cola and Microsoft, intangible assets may be of vastly greater value to the entity than tangible assets. Goodwill, brand names, trademarks, web addresses, customer lists and so forth may all be of value. For some entities, the only assets of value may be their name, reputation and the ideas of their employees which are all intangible assets (Gilbertson and Preston, 2005).

IVS 210 *Intangible Assets* is an IVS Asset Standard that applies to the valuation of intangible assets, being defined as:

> An intangible asset is a non-monetary asset that manifests itself by its economic properties. It does not have physical substance but grants rights and economic benefits to its owner. (IVS 210, para C1, page 49)

noting that it is important to clearly identify an *intangible asset* by reference to its type and the legal right or interest in that asset (IVS 220, para 2, page 47).

IVS 210 provides *Commentary* on the principal types of intangible assets, including goodwill and the following principal classes:

- marketing related *intangible assets* such as trademarks, trade names, unique trade design, internet domain names and non-compete agreements;
- customer or supplier related *intangible assets* such as service or supply agreements, licensing or royalty agreements, order books, employment agreements and customer relationships;
- technology related *intangible assets* such as patented technology, unpatented technology, databases, formulae, designs, software, processes or recipes; and
- artistic related *intangible assets* such as royalties from artistic works including plays, books, films and music and from non-contractual copyright protection,

noting that the *market approach, income approach* and *cost approach* to valuation may all be applied to *intangible assets* with extensive commentary provided thereon (IVS 220, para C4–C40, pages 49–55).

Extensive guidance on the principal recognised approaches and methods that are used for valuing intangible assets is provided in TIP3 *The Valuation of Intangible Assets* (IVSC, 2012b).

1.4.3 Financial instruments

IVS 250 *Financial Instruments* is an IVS Asset Standard that applies to the valuation of financial instruments, being defined as:

> A financial instrument is a contract that creates rights or obligations between specified parties to receive or pay cash or other financial consideration, or an equity instrument. The contract may require the receipt or payment to be made on or before a specific date or be triggered by a specified event. An equity instrument is any contract that creates a residual interest in the assets of an entity after deducting all of its liabilities. (IVS 250, para C1, page 79)

noting that valuation reporting should have regard to issues of materiality, uncertainty, complexity, comparability and the underlying assets for those *financial instruments* subject to valuation (IVS 250, para 5, page 77).

IVS 250 provides *Commentary* on the distinction between 'cash instruments' and 'derivative instruments', the market for *financial instruments*, issues associated with credit risk, liquidity and market activity, the role of a control environment and the application of the *market approach, income approach* and *cost approach* to the valuation of *financial instruments* with extensive commentary provided thereon (IVS 250, para C3–C36, pages 79–87).

1.5 Summary and conclusions

This chapter sought to outline the emergence of globalisation, the role of IFRS and the evolution of valuation standard setting, the role of IVSC and IVSs and an analysis of market value, being the central concept of IVSs, with an overview of other IVSs relevant to the valuation of businesses and business interests, intangible assets and financial instruments.

Increasingly gaining pace since the end of the Second World War, fostered by greater international economic cooperation through trade and commerce during the latter part of the twentieth century and accelerated by the digital revolution of this century, globalisation has contributed to multinational corporations such as HSBC and Airbus and sovereign wealth funds, pension funds, superannuation funds, REITs and other property fund managers holding vast property portfolios spread across the globe.

As globalising multinational corporations sought a common basis for company accounts that was understandable, comparable, reliable and relevant for internal and external users across different countries for decision making and the allocation of scarce resources, the IASC was formed and then succeeded by the IASB leading to the development and implementation of IFRS for financial reporting in many countries around the world but currently excepting the major economies of the USA, Japan and India.

In order for IFRS to provide a reliable decision-making basis in the context of property, the provision of those inputs concerning property valuation also needed to be undertaken on one common basis worldwide. Starting with RICS in the UK, then expanding across Europe, valuation standard setting became more homogenised with the creation of TIAVSC in 1981/82 leading to the publication of international valuation standards in 1985, the creation of IVSC and the convergence of IVSs with IAS's and IFRS's since 2000. The development of IVSs for assets such as real property and plant and equipment and for purposes such as financial reporting and secured lending facilitated not only convergence with IFRS but also the opportunity for harmonisation with the standards and guidance notes developed by IVSC member valuation professional organisations around the world. Reflecting the valuation of assets and liabilities generally rather than just property, IVSC also developed IVSs for the valuation of business and business interests, intellectual property and financial instruments which are also convergent with IFRS.

The concept and definition of *market value* is the centrepiece of IVSs, being essentially an assessment of what a property should hypothetically transact for on a given date if assumptions are made about the parties, marketing, information, willingness, transaction costs and taxes. The concept of market value evolved in an early Australian High Court decision, *Spencer v Commonwealth* (1907) 5 CLR 418, which enunciated several of the key elements found in today's definition of *market value* by the IVSC that is now adopted globally though not, necessarily, fully integrated with economic theory, finance theory and capital market theory.

The next chapter will develop a conceptual framework for valuation based on economic theory, align this framework with finance and capital market theory, examine the definition of the market and distinguish definitions of cost and price from defined concepts of value before reconciling these to the conceptual framework for valuation.

Chapter 3 will then consider various aspects of valuation standard definitions within IVSs, discuss the definitions of other relevant contextual terms and identify the principal approaches to valuation within IVSs including a focus on the market approach to valuation.

Chapter 4 will describe and analyse those elements of IVSs that are of relevance to the three principal stages of the real property valuation process, being the instruction of the valuer, undertaking the valuation and reporting the valuation.

Chapter 5 will consider IVSs in the context of the valuation of investment property, with particular reference to IAS 40 *Investment Property* and the income approach to valuation, including an examination of IVSC TIP 1 *Discounted Cash Flow*.

Finally, Chapter 6 will focus on IVSs in the context of the valuation of owner occupied property held by operating businesses, with particular reference to IAS 16 *Property, Plant and Equipment* and the cost approach to valuation, including an examination of IVSC TIP 2 *The Cost Approach to Tangible Assets*.

References

Babawale, G.K. (2012a) Paradigm Shift in Investment Property Valuation Theory and Practice: Nigerian Practitioners' Response, *Mediterranean Journal of Social Sciences*, **Vol. 3**, No. 3.

Babawale, G.K. (2012b) An Assessment of the Current Standard of Real Estate Valuation Practice in Nigeria, *Social Science*, **Vol. 47**.

Banfield, A. (2014) *A Valuer's Guide to the RICS Red Book 2014*, RICS, London.

Dugeri, T.T., Gambo, Y.L. and Ajayi, C.A. (2012) Internalising International Valuation Standards: Relevance and Applicability Issues in the Nigerian Context, *ATBU Journal of Environmental Technology*, **Vol. 5**, No. 1.

Edge, J.A. (2001) The Globalization of Real Estate Appraisal: A European Perspective, *The Appraisal Journal*, January.

French, N. (2003) The RICS Valuation and Appraisal Standards, *Journal of Property Investment and Finance*, **Vol. 21**, No. 6.

Gilbertson, B. (2002) Valuation or Appraisal: An Art or a Science?, *Australian Property Journal*, February.

Gilbertson, B. and Preston, D. (2005) A Vision for Valuation, *Journal of Property Investment and Finance*, **Vol. 23**, No. 2.

Greenwell, W. (1976) A Call for New Valuation Methods, *Estates Gazette*, **238**: 481.

International Financial Reporting Standards (2013) *International Financial Reporting Standards 2013*, International Accounting Standards Board, London.

International Valuation Standards Council (2009) *Setting the Standard*, IVSC, London.

International Valuation Standards Council (2012a) *Raising the Bar for the Valuation Profession*, Roundtable Discussion, IVSC, London.

International Valuation Standards Council (2012b) *TIP3 – The Valuation of Intangible Assets*, IVSC, London.

International Valuation Standards Council (2013) *International Valuation Standards 2013*, IVSC, London.

International Valuation Standards Council (2014) *Global Regulatory Convergence and the Valuation Profession*, IVSC, London.

International Valuation Standards Council (2015a) *IVSC Review Group Report – Engagement Paper*, IVSC, London.

International Valuation Standards Council (2015b) *IVSC Annual Report 2014–2015*, IVSC, London.

Mackmin, D. (1999) Valuation of Real Estate in Global Markets, *Property Management*, **Vol. 17**, No. 4.

Mallinson, M. and French, N. (2000) The Nature and Relevance of Uncertainty and How It Might Be Measured and Reported, *Journal of Property Investment and Finance*, **Vol. 18**, No. 1.

Royal Institution of Chartered Surveyors (2013) *RICS Professional Standards, Global and UK 2014*, RICS, London.

2

Concepts

2.0 Introduction

In the context of the valuation of real property assets, this book provides an analysis of the International Valuation Standards (IVS), International Accounting Standards (IAS) and International Financial Reporting Standards (IFRS) which, being dynamic, are regularly updated and/or replaced. Accordingly, readers should not rely upon this book as a current statement of an IVS, IAS or IFRS publication and should visit www.ifrs.org and/or www.ivsc.org to find the most recent version.

Chapter 1 outlined the emergence of globalisation, the role of IFRS and the evolution of valuation standard setting, the role of IVSC and IVSs and an analysis of *market value*, being the central concept of IVSs, with an overview of other IVSs relevant to the valuation of businesses and business interests, intangible assets and financial instruments.

This chapter seeks to develop a conceptual framework for valuation based on economic theory, align this framework with finance and capital market theory, examine the definition of the market and distinguish definitions of cost and price from defined concepts of value before reconciling these to the conceptual framework for valuation.

Chapter 3 will then consider various aspects of valuation standard definitions within IVSs, discuss the definitions of other relevant contextual terms and identify the principal approaches to valuation within IVSs including a focus on the market approach to valuation.

Chapter 4 will describe and analyse those elements of IVSs that are of relevance to the three principal stages of the real property valuation process,

International Valuation Standards: A Guide to the Valuation of Real Property Assets,
First Edition. David Parker.
© 2016 John Wiley & Sons, Ltd. Published 2016 by John Wiley & Sons, Ltd.

being the instruction of the valuer, undertaking the valuation and reporting the valuation.

Chapter 5 will consider IVSs in the context of the valuation of investment property, with particular reference to IAS 40 *Investment Property* and the income approach to valuation, including an examination of IVSC TIP 1 *Discounted Cash Flow*.

Finally, Chapter 6 will focus on IVSs in the context of the valuation of owner occupied property held by operating businesses, with particular reference to IAS 16 *Property, Plant and Equipment* and the cost approach to valuation, including an examination of IVSC TIP 2 *The Cost Approach to Tangible Assets*.

In many countries around the world, national and local valuation professional bodies adopt IVSs and supplement them with national or local valuation practice guidance which may expand upon IVSs in a national or local context for the benefit of their membership. However, only the Royal Institution of Chartered Surveyors (RICS) produces global valuation practice guidance that adopts and expands upon IVSs but is not country specific, comprising mandatory professional standards and valuation practice statements and non-mandatory practice guidance applications and practice guidance notes for use by members globally – generally referred to as the RICS Red Book Global (RICS 2013). Accordingly, this book refers to the RICS Red Book Global for the purposes of considering how a professional body interprets IVSs for application by its members worldwide but without a country specific application.

This book is based upon International Valuation Standards 2013 (IVSC, 2013) and International Financial Reporting Standards 2013 (IFRS, 2013). Given their nature, IVSs, IAS's and IFRSs are dynamic, being regularly updated and with the most recently published versions replacing previously published versions. Accordingly, readers should not rely upon this book as a current statement of an IVS, IAS or IFRS publication and should visit www.ifrs.org and/or www.ivsc.org to find the most recent version.

2.1 Conceptual framework

This section seeks to develop a conceptual framework for valuation based on and consistent with economic theory, through a consideration of the concepts of supply, demand, price, market and participants. The following sections will then seek to align the conceptual framework for valuation with finance and capital market theory and examine the definition of market with the final section seeking to distinguish the definitions of cost and price from defined concepts of value, before reconciling these to the conceptual framework for valuation.

A significant challenge in developing a conceptual framework for valuation within which IVSs may be accommodated is that valuation theory is only partially developed, being relatively incomplete and relatively incoherent compared to economic theory, finance theory and capital market theory, with the further challenge that the current content of IVSs is reflective of their evolution rather than being grounded in a robust and coherent theory of value.

As discussed in Chapter 1, IVSs are the product of a century of evolution from a foundation in the concepts of supply, demand, price, market and participants derived from long established economic theory. At the turn of the last century, the Australian High Court decision in *Spencer v Commonwealth* (1907) 5 CLR 418 contributed to the development of valuation theory through the provision of a legal construct of supply, demand, price, market and participants for a specific statutory purpose. During the Great Depression, academics including Bonbright (1937) contributed to the development of valuation theory through the application of the concept of utility from economic theory. The introduction of planning after the Second World War impacted valuation theory through the introduction of a supply constraint which limited practical utility relative to the theoretical concept promoted by Bonbright (1937).

For the latter part of the last century, valuation theory evolved independently of economic theory, finance theory and capital market theory as the valuation profession developed its own terminology with some similarities between countries, as discussed in Chapter 1. Following a series of late twentieth-century property market collapses in different countries, various valuation professional bodies revisited their adopted terminology and started codification through the independent development of valuation standards and guidance notes.

At the beginning of this century, globalisation then drove a move towards standardisation of valuation standards and guidance notes internationally, drawing on those already published by different professional bodies around the world, leading to the development of those IVSs that are the subject of this book. Accordingly, while no criticism is intended, IVSs are a product of their evolution rather than being grounded in a defined conceptual framework for valuation based on a coherent theory of value but, perversely, through their deep consideration of the theoretical aspects of valuation, they make a significant contribution to the development of valuation theory.

While finance theory and capital market theory evolved out of economic theory, valuation theory did not and so is not necessarily aligned with such theory. Therefore, while IVSs are not necessarily fully aligned with valuation theory, neither are they necessarily fully aligned with economic theory, finance theory and capital market theory leading to occasional anomalies. Such anomalies potentially become an issue when the corporate world, accounting world, finance world, funds management world and similar business worlds, which generally operate consistent with economic theory, finance theory and capital market theory, come into contact with the property world with valuation often being that point of contact.

It may, therefore, be contended to be helpful to develop a conceptual framework for valuation that is consistent with economic, finance and capital market theory and within which IVSs may be accommodated.

2.1.1 Approaching IVSs through economic theory

As noted above, IVSs have a foundation in the concepts of supply, demand, price, market and participants from long-established economic theory. Generally, for supply and demand to interact and result in price, it is necessary to have a market and participants in that market. Further, the nature of a market and the participants in that market will usually be linked. As Gilbertson (2002) observes:

> Does a valuer work in the property market, or measure the market in property?

In the context of property, it may be contended that the property market comprises an amalgam of markets in property which may be considered to include all sectors (residential, commercial, retail, industrial, etc. – the property market), an individual sector (such as retail – a general market), a sub-sector (such as super-regional shopping centres – a sub-market) or an individual property (such as a kiosk – a unique market).

Consistent with the concept of the property market, it may be contended that participants in such markets may be considered to include all participants (such as for the market for property comprising all sectors), a large group (such as for the market for property comprising a sector generally, such as retail property), a small group (such as for the market for property comprising a sub-sector or sub-market, such as super-regional shopping centres) or an individual (such as for the market for property comprising an individual property or unique market, such as a kiosk).

Generally, it may be contended that IVSs are unlikely to be applied in the context of that property market comprising all sectors and all participants, being more likely to be applied to a market in property at a sector, sub-sector or individual level. Effectively, therefore, assuming a single vendor, a market in property may comprise a large group of purchasers in a general market (such as the market in property for retail property), a small group of purchasers in a sub-market (such as the market in property for super-regional shopping centres) or a single purchaser in a unique market (such as the market in property for a kiosk), as illustrated in Figure 2.1.

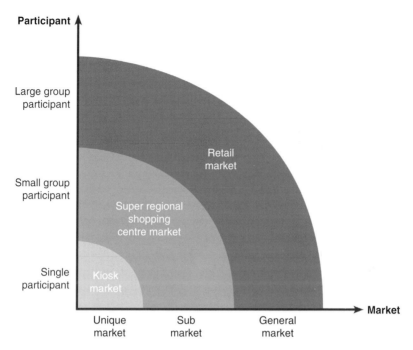

Figure 2.1 Conceptual framework – participants and markets.

As Figure 2.1 shows, the unique market is within or a sub-set of the sub-market which, in turn, is within or a sub-set of the general market and each comprises participants who are actual and capable of being identified or nominated.

Therefore, for the purposes of developing a conceptual framework for valuation, let such a single participant market be referred to as a 'nominated unique market' (NUM), a small group of participants market be referred to as a 'nominated sub-market' (NSM) and a large group of participants market be referred to as a 'nominated general market' (NGM) as illustrated in Figure 2.2.

For example, in the case of a nominated general market such as the retail property market, participants may include nominated participants such as individuals, small funds, large funds and so forth. For a nominated sub-market such as the super-regional shopping centre market, participants may include one such group of nominated participants such as large funds while, for a nominated unique market such as the kiosk market, there may only be one vendor and one purchaser being nominated individuals.

Therefore, for the purposes of developing a conceptual framework for valuation, let a single participant be referred to as a 'nominated unique participant' (NUP), a small group of participants be referred to as a 'nominated

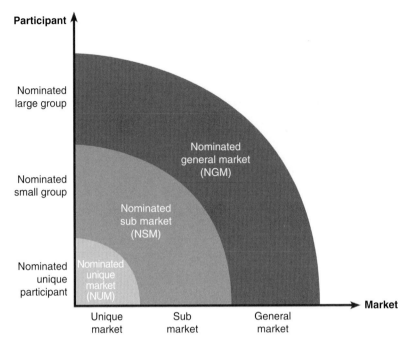

Figure 2.2   Conceptual framework – nominated participants and markets.

small group' (NSG) and a large group of participants be referred to as a 'nominated large group' (NLG) as illustrated in Figure 2.2.

Figures 2.1 and 2.2 illustrate a scenario of actual markets where the participants in the markets are known to exist and may be nominated. However, the same theoretical principles may also apply to hypothetical markets where the participants in a postulated market are known to exist and so may be postulated but may not, necessarily, be nominated. While it is possible to hypothesise a postulated general market and a postulated sub-market, each of which may be known to include a range of postulated participants but who may not, necessarily, be nominated, it is challenging to hypothesise such a unique market as, for such a market to exist, the participant must, by its nature, be both known and capable of nomination.

The addition of postulated markets and postulated participants may be illustrated in Figure 2.3, which extends the concept of the market from the actual to the hypothetical, with the hypothetical market being close to but apart from the actual or nominated market.

Therefore, for the purposes of developing a conceptual framework for valuation, let the 'postulated small group' (PSG) of participants market be referred to as a 'postulated sub-market' (PSM) and the 'postulated large group' (PLG) of participants market be referred to as a 'postulated general

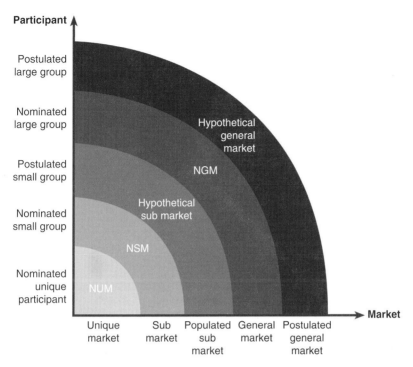

Figure 2.3 Conceptual framework – postulated participants and postulated markets.

market' (PGM), creating a 'hypothetical submarket' (HSM) and a 'hypothetical general market' (HGM), respectively, as summarised in Figure 2.4.

It may, therefore, be contended that Figure 2.4 summarises a conceptual framework for valuation within which both actual (nominated) and postulated (hypothetical) participants and actual (nominated) and postulated (hypothetical) markets may be theoretically accommodated.

2.1.2 Concept of exchange

As noted above, IVSs have a foundation in the concepts of supply, demand, price, market and participants from long-established economic theory. Generally, for supply and demand to interact and result in price, it is necessary to have a market and participants in that market. Further, the nature of a market and the participants in that market will usually be linked and, as also noted above, markets and participants may either be actual (nominated) or postulated (hypothetical).

Consistent with the concepts of supply, demand, price, market and participants from economic theory is the concept of exchange, whereby supply, demand and participants come together in a market and price is that point

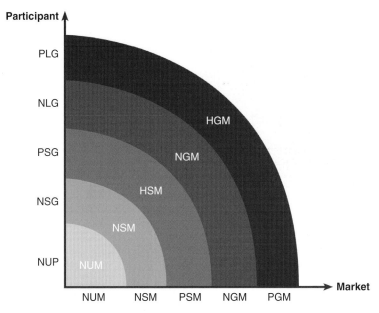

Figure 2.4   Conceptual framework – postulated participants and hypothetical markets.

at which exchange occurs. Effectively, consistent with economic theory, this is the concept of an exchange occurring within or upon a market, being an 'on market exchange'.

The concept of on market exchange is a fundamental theoretical concept for both IVSs and the development of a conceptual framework for valuation, with many aspects of IVSs being built on the assumption of actual or hypothetical participants making an actual or hypothetical exchange in an actual or hypothetical market, as illustrated in Figure 2.5.

On market exchange has, by definition, two conceptual elements being the concept of on market and the concept of exchange. For the purposes of developing a conceptual framework, it is contended to be relevant to consider relaxation of these two conceptual elements through a consideration of the concepts of off market and no exchange. Central to on market exchange is the offer of a property widely and openly to a market (which may be nominated or postulated) that comprises the most likely buyer group (which may be unique, small group or large group) and from which a transaction eventuates being of principal relevance to the successful vendor and the successful purchaser.

Relaxing the concept of exchange leads to combining the concept of on market with the concept of no exchange, being a scenario where actual or hypothetical participants come together in an actual or hypothetical market but no exchange occurs. Central to on market, no exchange is the offer of a

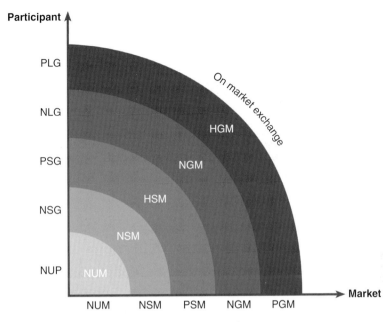

Figure 2.5 Conceptual framework – on market exchange.

property widely and openly to a market (which may be nominated or postulated) that comprises the most likely buyer group (which may be unique, small group or large group) but from which no transaction eventuates being of principal relevance to unsuccessful potential purchasers.

Relaxing the concept of on market leads to combining the concept of exchange and the concept of off market, being a scenario where actual or hypothetical participants make an actual or hypothetical exchange directly rather than in an actual or hypothetical market. Central to an off market exchange is the offer of a property selectively and on a closed basis to a market (which may be nominated or postulated) that comprises the most likely buyer group (which may be unique, small group or large group) and from which a transaction eventuates being of principal relevance to the successful vendor and the successful purchaser.

Relaxing the concept of on market and relaxing the concept of exchange leads to combining the concept of off market and the concept of no exchange, being a scenario where actual or hypothetical parties do not make an exchange directly rather than in an actual or hypothetical market. Central to an off market no exchange is the offer of a property selectively and on a closed basis to a market (which may be nominated or postulated) that comprises the most likely buyer group (which may be unique, small group or large group) but from which no transaction eventuates being of principal relevance to unsuccessful purchasers.

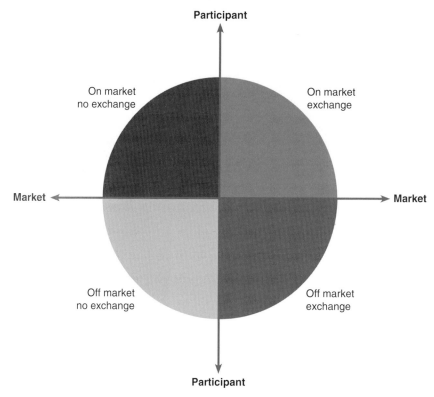

Figure 2.6   Conceptual framework – on/off market and exchange/no exchange.

The concepts of on market, off market, exchange and no exchange may be contended to be mirror images of each other in a continuum, as shown in Figure 2.6.

Further, the concepts of nominated and postulated markets and nominated and postulated participants may be combined with the concepts of on market/off market and exchange/no exchange in a conceptual framework for valuation as shown in Figure 2.7.

2.1.3 *Conceptual framework – summary*

From the starting point of long-established economic theory, the concepts of supply, demand, price, market and participants may be developed to propose a conceptual framework for valuation that is consistent with economic theory, with that proposed conceptual framework illustrated in Figures 2.4 and 2.7 and which may be characterised as a continuum as illustrated in Figure 2.8.

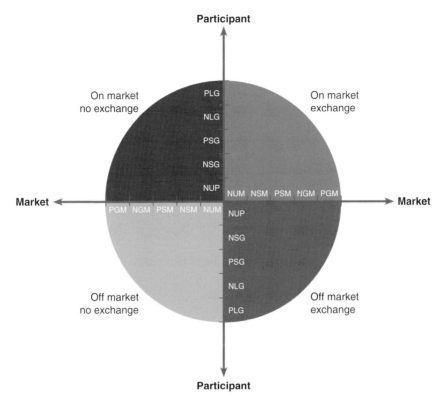

Figure 2.7 Conceptual framework – participants, market, on/off market, exchange/no exchange.

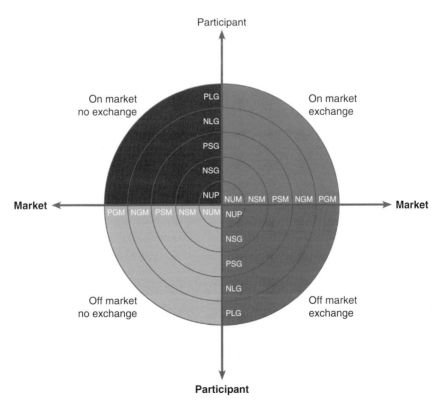

Figure 2.8 Conceptual framework – participants, market, on/off market, exchange/no exchange.

This section sought to develop a conceptual framework for valuation based on economic theory, with the next section seeking to align this framework with finance and capital market theory and the following sections then seeking to examine the definition of the market and to distinguish definitions of cost and price from concepts of value before reconciling these to the conceptual framework for valuation.

2.2 Reconciliation with capital market theory

The previous section sought to develop a conceptual framework for valuation based on and consistent with economic theory, through a consideration of the concepts of supply, demand, price, market and participants, with this section seeking to align the conceptual framework for valuation with finance and capital market theory and the following section seeking to examine the definition of market with the final section seeking to distinguish the definitions of cost and price from defined concepts of value, before reconciling these to the conceptual framework for valuation.

Finance theory and capital market theory posit, among other things, that the rate of return on an asset is linked to the risk of an asset, with the lowest risk attracting the lowest rate of return and the highest risk attracting the highest rate of return. Given a common cash flow, capitalisation or discounting will result in a lower rate of return producing a higher initial capital sum and a higher rate of return producing a lower initial capital sum. To this extent, alignment may be identified between valuation theory, finance theory and capital market theory.

Similarly, in finance theory and capital market theory, long-term government bonds are generally considered to offer the lowest level of risk, with increasingly risky assets attracting increasingly large risk premiums, such that the rate of return for assets becomes linked to the interest rate structure of an economy. This is reflected by participants in the property markets and so by valuers attempting to reflect the actions of market participants in the valuation process. Again, to this extent, alignment may be identified between valuation theory, finance theory and capital market theory.

Significantly, from the viewpoint of the conceptual framework for valuation developed above, finance theory and capital market theory include an explicit consideration of the components of risk, using the aggregation of influences on return at various levels to classify types of risk and so providing the foundation for modern portfolio theory. Such influences may result in positive or negative variation of return, with positive effects commonly considered influences on growth and negative effects commonly considered influences on risk.

Though continuously evolving in finance, capital market and property research, the influences on return which, through their variation, become influences on growth or risk may be contended to comprise:

- **Systematic Influences**
  Economy wide, asset class wide and sector wide influences of a descending hierarchical character, common to all assets in an asset class, pervasive and beyond control at an individual asset level. In the context of property, systematic influences may include economic influences (such as the rate of inflation) and government influences (such as taxation) which commonly affect all property sectors;
- **Unsystematic Influences**
  Sector wide and asset specific influences of a descending, hierarchical nature limited to either individual assets or groups of assets and so pervasive only at the sector level and potentially within partial control at an individual asset level. In the context of property, unsystematic influences may include such influences as evolving workspace utilisation and green building preference which commonly affect all assets in the office sector; and
- **Idiosyncratic (Specific) Influences**
  Influences idiosyncratic to a specific asset which may be addressed by diversification in a multi asset portfolio but which are significant at the individual asset level. In the context of property, idiosyncratic influences may include location and building quality which commonly vary between individual assets.

While systematic risk is common to all assets in an asset class, unsystematic risk and idiosyncratic risk may be managed, reduced or eliminated through diversification in a multi asset portfolio comprising an appropriate number of assets with a low, non-existent or negative correlation of returns.

While finance theory and capital market theory consider systematic, unsystematic and idiosyncratic influences in the context of asset classes and assets, the principles may also be capable of application to markets and to participants so facilitating alignment with the conceptual framework for valuation.

Systematic influences are common to all assets and so may be expected to be pervasive for both a nominated and postulated large group and a nominated and postulated small group of participants and/or a nominated or postulated large market and a nominated or postulated sub-market and so may be of particular relevance for the assessment of *market value* within IVSs.

Further, it may be contended that unsystematic influences may be likely to be significant for a nominated small group of participants and/or a nominated sub-market or for a postulated small group of participants and/or postulated sub-market and so may be of particular relevance for the assessment of *investment value* and *market value* within IVSs.

Similarly, it may be contended that idiosyncratic influences may be likely to be of significance for a nominated unique participant and/or a nominated unique market and so may be of particular relevance for the assessment of *special value* and *fair value* within IVSs.

It may, therefore, be contended that, in addition to concepts of risk-return, the conceptual framework developed for valuation may also be aligned, in principle, with the concepts of systematic, unsystematic and idiosyncratic influences within finance and capital market theory.

Having a conceptual framework for valuation based on economic theory, this section sought to align this framework with finance and capital market theory with the next section seeking to examine the definition of the market and the final section then seeking to distinguish definitions of cost and price from defined concepts of value before reconciling these to the conceptual framework for valuation.

2.3 Definition of the market

The previous sections sought to develop a conceptual framework for valuation based on and consistent with economic theory, through a consideration of the concepts of supply, demand, price, market and participants and to align the conceptual framework for valuation with finance and capital market theory, with this section seeking to examine the definition of market and the final section then seeking to distinguish the definitions of cost and price from defined concepts of value, before reconciling these to the conceptual framework for valuation.

The definitions of the market in IVSs will be examined through a consideration of what is a market for the purposes of IVSs, who are the participants in such a market, what is the role of market activity and what is an asset.

2.3.1 What is a market?

The general conceptual definition of a market in IVSs is broadly consistent with economic theory:

> A market is the environment in which goods and services trade between buyers and sellers through a price mechanism. The concept of a market implies that goods or services may be traded among buyers and sellers without undue restriction on their activities. Each party will respond to supply-demand relationships and other price-setting factors as well as to their own understanding of the relative utility of the goods or services and individual needs and desires. (IVSC, 2013, para 10, page 13)

However, as well as concepts of numerous participants, a transaction and a price, the definition introduces the concepts of 'without undue restriction' and 'understanding of relative utility' and the behavioural economics concept of 'individual needs and desires'. Accordingly, users should be wary of markets with only one buyer or with unusual levels of restriction (which may be regulatory, financial, etc.) and be conscious in their consideration of participants that each may have a different perception of the utility of a property and so exercise judgement while being influenced by personal characteristics which may be rational or irrational but will impact how they respond to supply-demand and price settings.

Further, the market is assumed to be directly related to the asset which may be local or international and may comprise many or few participants:

> The concept of *market value* presumes a price negotiated in an open and competitive market where the participants are acting freely. The market for an asset could be an international market or a local market. The market could consist of numerous buyers and sellers, or could be one characterised by a limited number of market participants. The market in which the asset is exposed for sale is the one in which the asset being exchanged is normally exchanged. (IVSC, 2013, para 31, page 20)

Consistently, the particular definition of a property market in IVSs provides specific, limiting constraints:

> Unless otherwise clear from the context, references in IVS to the market mean the market in which the asset or liability being valued is normally exchanged on the *valuation date* and to which most participants in that market, including the current owner, normally have access. (IVSC, 2013, para 13, page 14)

Accordingly, IVSs do not consider a general market to be relevant, but instead consider the particular sub-market for the asset being valued to be the relevant market for consideration. This is qualified as being that sub-market in which the current owner and most participants would be transacting as at the valuation date, being the sub-market and small group participants referred to in Figure 2.4.

The user should, therefore, take care to identify the relevant sub-market and small group participants for consideration in the valuation process and give consideration to the depth of the sub-market through the number of small group participants. Users should note, however, that a sub-market is not necessarily local and for some assets (such as high rise office towers) it may be national and for some (such as airports) it may be international where there may be only one potential purchaser locally but a small group of potential purchasers nationally or internationally:

> In order to estimate the most probable price that would be paid for an asset, it is of fundamental importance to understand the extent of the market in which that asset would trade. This is because the price that can be obtained will depend upon the number of buyers and sellers in the particular market on the *valuation date*. To have an effect on price, buyers and sellers must have access to that market. A market can be defined by various criteria. These include:
>
> (a) the goods or services that are traded, eg the market for motor vehicles is distinct from the market for gold,
> (b) scale or distribution restraints, eg a manufacturer of goods may not have the distribution or marketing infrastructure to sell to end users and the end users may not require the goods in the volume at which they are produced by the manufacturer,
> (c) geography, eg the market for similar goods or services may be local, regional, national or international. (IVSC, 2013, para 11, pages 13–14)

While the small group participants must be more than one, it may not necessarily be more than two. However, the user should take care to consider the implications on transaction price of a market with a limited number of purchasers relative to that in a market with a greater pool of purchasers, particularly in the context of relative utility and behavioural influences as referred to above.

Various other aspects of economic, finance and capital market theory are echoed in the IVSs, including that markets are neither perfect nor efficient, exhibiting imperfections in supply/demand responses at given points in time and pricing effects due to information constraints:

> Markets rarely operate perfectly with constant equilibrium between supply and demand and an even level of activity, due to various imperfections. Common market imperfections include disruptions of supply, sudden increases or decreases in demand or asymmetry of knowledge between market participants. Because market participants react to these imperfections, at a given time a market is likely to be adjusting to any change that has caused disequilibrium. A valuation that has the objective of estimating the most probable price in the market has to reflect the conditions in the relevant market on the *valuation date,* not an adjusted or smoothed price based on a supposed restoration of equilibrium. (IVSC, 2013, para 14, page 14)

Users should note that the market in IVSs is conceptualised as that which it is at the valuation date, rather than that which it was at some point in the past or that which it may be at some point in the future. This is particularly significant at points of market disequilibrium such as collapses or booms when it is the current state of the market that requires reflection rather than that state which might apply should the market return to that state which is perceived by the user to be normal.

While theoretically correct over the long term, some aspects of economic theory underlying IVSs have limitations in the context of property:

> However, although at any point in time a market may be self-contained and be little influenced by activity in other markets, over a period of time markets will influence each other. For example, on any given date the price of an asset in one state may be higher than could be obtained for an identical asset in another. If any possible distorting effects caused by government trading restrictions or fiscal policies are ignored, suppliers would, over time, increase the supply of the asset to the state where it could obtain the higher price and reduce the supply to the state where the price was lower, thus bringing about a convergence of prices. (IVSC, 2013, para 12, page 14)

Users should be aware that the heterogeneity of property, locational specificity of property and extent of regulatory differences mean that convergence of prices between markets may be a long and slow process. Therefore, in markets where distorting effects may exist which impact on transaction price relative to other markets, users should be very cautious if having regard to the possible impact on value of any change in such effects.

2.3.2 Who are the participants in a market?

As noted in the previous section, the user should take care to identify the relevant sub-market and small group participants for consideration in the valuation process. However, care should be taken to focus on the entire small group participants rather than on an individual member of a small group:

> References in IVS to market participants are to the whole body of individuals, companies or other entities that are involved in actual transactions or who are contemplating entering into a transaction for a particular type of asset. The willingness to trade and any views attributed to market participants are typical of those of buyers and sellers, or prospective buyers and sellers, active in a market on the *valuation date*, not to those of any particular individual or entity. (IVSC, 2013, para 18, page 15)

For example, if the relevant small group participants comprise office equity REITs, then the willingness to trade and views that are typical of that entire small group are relevant for consideration rather than those of one particular office equity REIT. While not articulated, typical may be contended to include the characteristics of willingness to trade and of views that are common to multiple small group participants.

This is especially important when a user is considering the small group participants in a market-based valuation where both the vendor and potential purchasers are hypothetical, being postulated not nominated:

> In undertaking a market-based valuation, matters that are specific to the current owner or to one particular potential buyer are not relevant because both the willing seller and the willing buyer are hypothetical individuals or entities with the attributes of a typical market participant. These attributes are discussed in the conceptual framework for *market value*. The conceptual framework also requires the exclusion of any element of *special value* or any element of value that would not be available to market participants generally. (IVSC, 2013, para 19, page 15)

> The factors that are specific to a particular buyer or seller and not available to market participants generally are excluded from the inputs used in a market-based valuation. Examples of entity specific factors that may not be available to market participants include the following:

> (a) additional value derived from the creation of a portfolio of similar assets,
> (b) unique synergies between the asset and other assets owned by the entity,
> (c) legal rights or restrictions,
> (d) tax benefits or tax burdens,
> (e) an ability to exploit an asset that is unique to that entity. (IVSC, 2013, para 20, pages 15–16)

The exclusion of focus on an individual participant in market-based valuations is fundamental to IVSs, with the focus on an individual participant being a key feature of other bases of value such as investment value, fair value, synergistic value and special value.

While not exhaustive, the IVSs provide five examples of 'factors' that may differ for an individual participant compared to typical participants in a small group. An individual participant that may benefit from a 'factor' to a greater extent than a typical participant may be prepared to offer a higher price which is consistent with the assumptions underlying investment value, special value and fair value but inconsistent with the assumptions underlying market-based valuations.

2.3.3 What is the role of market activity?

In the same way that any notion of a normalised market was excluded, above, with the focus being on the actual market as at the valuation date, IVSs also exclude any notion of a normalised level of activity in a market with the focus being on the actual level of activity in a market at the valuation date:

> The degree of activity in any market will fluctuate. Although it may be possible to identify a normal level of activity over an extended period, in most markets there will be periods when activity is significantly higher or lower than this norm. Activity levels can only be expressed in relative terms, eg the market is more or less active than it was on a previous date. There is no clearly defined line between a market that is active or inactive. (IVSC, 2013, para 15, page 14)

Users should, therefore, take care during periods of relatively high and low activity (which are becoming increasingly easily identifiable as published data on aggregated transaction levels becomes more commonly available in various parts of the world) concerning the interplay between assumptions about marketing period and market value. For example, in an inactive market, an assumed marketing period of three months may result in a different assessment of market value to an assumed marketing period of six months.

It may be contended that there is a difference between 'less active' and 'inactive' for which the user should take care. A market that is 'less active' may still have transactions, albeit fewer, as evidence to which to have regard, such that a market approach valuation remains an exercise in assessing relativity. However, in an 'inactive' market, there may no transactions to which to have regard, such that a market approach valuation becomes an exercise in assessing the level at which a market may clear and an asset may transact.

Further, in a falling market, users should take care with the interpretation of comparable sales transactions as not all sales in a falling market are necessarily 'forced sales' and it should similarly not be assumed that all buyers are voraciously opportunistic:

> Price information from an inactive market may still be evidence of *market value*. A period of falling prices is likely to see both decreased levels of activity and an increase in sales that can be termed 'forced'. However, there are sellers in falling markets that are not acting under duress and to dismiss the evidence of prices realised by such sellers would be to ignore the realities of the market. (IVSC, 2013, para 17, page 15)

The complexity of the interplay between participants in a property market and the level of activity in a property market is succinctly summarised in the IVSs:

> When demand is high in relation to supply, prices would be expected to rise which tends to attract more sellers to enter the market and therefore increased activity. The converse is the case when demand is low and prices are falling.

However, different levels of activity may be a response to price movements rather than the cause of them. Transactions can and do take place in markets that are currently less active than normal and, just as importantly, prospective buyers are likely to have in mind a price at which they would be prepared to enter the market. (IVSC, 2013, para 16, page 15)

This links to the economic concept of utility and the behavioural finance concepts referred to above, as differing levels of activity may generate different responses by different market participants. Accordingly, users should take care in identifying the small group participants which may change or evolve at market inflection points. Further, particular care is required in less active markets to distinguish between the price at which typical small group participants may enter the market consistent with the assumptions underlying market value and the price at which a particular participant may enter the market as this may be an expression of investment value or special value.

2.3.4 What is an asset?

Having identified the market for the purposes of IVSs to be a sub-market and the participants to be small group participants, it is important for the purposes of IVSs to identify whether the asset under consideration is independent or linked to a group of assets as the latter may give rise to *synergistic value*, as considered in detail in section 2.4.3.3, below:

The value of an individual asset is often dependent upon its association with other related assets. Examples include:

(a) offsetting assets and liabilities in a portfolio of financial instruments,
(b) a portfolio of properties that complement each other by providing a prospective buyer with either a critical mass or a presence in strategic locations,
(c) a group of machines in a production line, or the software required to operate a machine or machines,
(d) recipes and patents that support a brand,
(e) interdependent land, buildings, plant and other equipment employed in a business enterprise. (IVSC, 2013, para 23, page 16)

Examples (b) and (e) may commonly arise in property valuation and require careful consideration in the context of IVSs by the user. As will be considered further in Chapter 4, clarity of instruction and reporting are essential to explicitly describe the status of the asset being valued:

Where a valuation is required of assets that are held in conjunction with other complementary or related assets, it is important to clearly define whether it is the group or portfolio of assets that is to be valued or each of the assets individually. If the latter, it is also important to establish whether each asset is assumed to be valued:

(a) as an individual item but assuming that the other assets are available to a buyer, or
(b) as an individual item but assuming that the other assets are not available to a buyer. (IVSC, 2013, para 24, pages 16–17)

Whether such factors are specific to the entity or would be available to others in the market generally is determined on a case-by-case basis. For example, an asset may not normally be transacted as a stand-alone item but as part of a group. Any synergies with related assets would transfer to market participants along with the transfer of the group and therefore are not entity specific. (IVSC, 2013, para 21, page 16)

The interplay between aggregation and synergistic value for an individual asset and a group of assets is complex and great care by the user is required to clearly define that which is being assessed and for what. Further, the typical small group participant purchaser needs to be borne in mind by the user to avoid any influence of investment value or special value that may arise from undue focus upon or consideration of an individual or particular purchaser.

2.3.5 *Definition of the market – summary*

While IVSs general conceptual definition of a market is broadly consistent with economic theory, the particular definition of a property market focuses on the sub-market and small group participants. Significantly, for IVSs, the market is conceptualised as that which actually exists with a resulting level of market activity at the valuation date rather than that which the user may consider normal and the small group participants conceptualised as typical rather than as individual, with care required concerning possible incursion into investment value or special value. Further, clarity is required by the user regarding the identification of the asset being valued as independent or part of a group with care also required concerning possible incursion into synergistic value.

Having developed a conceptual framework for valuation based on economic theory and aligned this framework with finance and capital market theory, this section sought to examine the definition of the market with the next section seeking to distinguish definitions of cost and price from defined concepts of value before reconciling these to the conceptual framework for valuation.

2.4 Value vs. cost vs. price

Definitions of cost and price will be distinguished from defined concepts of value, including market value, investment value, synergistic value, fair value and special value, prior to a discussion of the relative contributions of each to value and then the reconciliation of each to the conceptual framework for valuation.

2.4.1 Price

The conceptual distinction between price, cost and value and then between the various bases of value that follow there from is a fundamental principle underlying IVSs. Distinct from value which is a matter of opinion, price is a matter of fact, being the outcome of a contemplated or actual transaction:

> Price is the amount asked, offered or paid for an asset. Because of the financial capabilities, motivations or special interests of a given buyer or seller, the price paid may be different from the value which might be ascribed to the asset by others. (IVSC, 2013, para 6, page 13)

Price indicators may occur at any point during the negotiation of a transaction, effectively being a signpost, as well as an actuality at the conclusion of a transaction and may reflect the characteristics of the individual vendor and purchaser rather than the market as a whole and so not be generalisable across a market. Accordingly, in considering price as evidence of value, users should investigate the vendor and purchaser's financial capabilities, motivations or special interests to determine the likelihood of replication by others in the market. While an observation of price in a single transaction may be of very limited use, multiple consistent observations of price in a series of transactions may be indicative of a market level.

2.4.2 Cost

Like price, cost is conceptually distinguishable from value in IVSs, being also a matter of fact rather than a matter of opinion. Further, like price, cost is observable but that may be the extent of the useful information contributed with potentially limited insight provided into value:

> Cost is the amount required to acquire or create the asset. When that asset has been acquired or created, its cost is a fact. Price is related to cost because the price paid for an asset becomes its cost to the buyer. (IVSC, 2013, para 7, page 13)

The parameters of the amount required to acquire an asset are not specified and may include acquisition costs such as legal fees, due diligence costs and so forth. Similarly, the parameters of the amount required to create an asset are not specified and may include such costs to create an asset as profit and risk margin, debt costs and so forth. The complexities of determining the cost to create an asset will be considered further in Chapter 6.

As with price, the financial capabilities, motivations or special interests of particular parties are not controlled and may result in a different acquisition cost or cost to create than would arise from typical market participants and so not be generalisable across a market.

2.4.3 Value

Within the IVSs, value can only be a judgement of one of two things, being either the most probable price in exchange or the economic benefits of ownership, broadly according with concepts of market value and concepts of investment value, respectively.

Further, as noted above, this principle is extended consistently in the IVSs to *basis of valuation*:

A *basis of valuation* can fall into one of three principal categories:

(a) The first is to indicate the most probable price that would be achieved in a hypothetical exchange in a free and open market. *Market value* as defined in these standards falls into this category.
(b) The second is to indicate the benefits that a person or an entity enjoys from ownership of an asset. The value is specific to that person or entity, and may have no relevance to market participants in general. *Investment value* and *special value* as defined in these standards fall into this category.
(c) The third is to indicate the price that would be reasonably agreed between two specific parties for the exchange of an asset. Although the parties may be unconnected and negotiating at arm's length, the asset is not necessarily exposed in the market and the price agreed may be one that reflects the specific advantages or disadvantages of ownership to the parties involved rather than the market at large. *Fair value* as defined in these standards falls into this category. (IVSC, 2013, para 27, page 17)

with a fourth basis of value being categories other than the three principal categories particular to a specific purpose of valuation, such as statutory, regulatory (including IFRS) or by some form of documented agreement.

Having regard to the assumptions that underlie a valuation, including the form of the transaction, the participants to the transaction and market exposure, Table 2.1 compares principal categories (a), (b) and (c), manifest as market value, investment value/special value and fair value, respectively.

As will be discussed in greater detail later in this section, the *basis of valuation* as defined by IVSs does not appear entirely consistent with the

2 Concepts

Table 2.1 Bases of value – assumptions

Fundamental assumption	Principal category (a) market value	Principal category (b) investment value, special value	Principal category (c) fair value
Form of transaction	Hypothetical exchange	No exchange – benefits enjoyed by owner	Exchange
Participants to transaction	Two participants	One participant perspective	Two participants
Market exposure	Free and open market	No market exposure	Off market

Source: Author

conceptual framework for valuation developed in section 2.1 which focused on the concepts of the market, participant, exchange and on/off market as illustrated in Figure 2.7 and which may be characterised as a continuum as illustrated in Figure 2.8.

Accordingly, it may be contended to be helpful to frame a discussion of the following definitions of value adopted by IVSs in the context of the conceptual framework for valuation through the lenses of market, participant, exchange and on/off market:

2.4.3.1   Market value;
2.4.3.2   Investment value;
2.4.3.3   Synergistic value;
2.4.3.4   Fair value; and
2.4.3.5   Special value

before considering the relative contribution of each to value in section 2.4.3.6.

2.4.3.1 Market value

While the definition of *market value* was considered at length in Chapter 1, it may be contended to be helpful to consider it within the conceptual framework for valuation that was developed based on economic, finance and capital market theory and relative to the definitions of other *bases of value* considered above:

> **Market value** is the estimated amount for which an asset or liability should exchange on the *valuation date* between a willing buyer and a willing seller in an arm's length transaction, after proper marketing and where the parties had each acted knowledgably, prudently and without compulsion. (IVSC, 2013, page 8; IVSC, 2013, para 29, page 18; RICS, 2013, page 9)

As noted above, *market value* as defined by IVSs falls into the first of three principal categories of *basis of valuation*, being that which indicates the

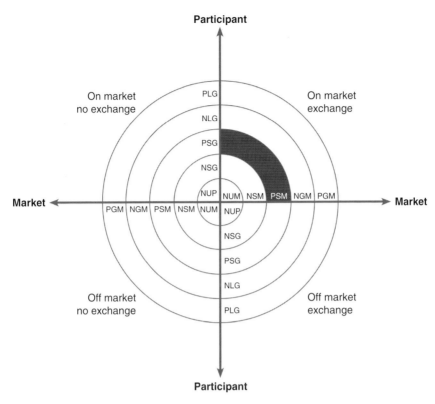

Figure 2.9 Conceptual framework – market value.

most probable price that would be achieved in a hypothetical exchange in a free and open market, so within the exchange–on market quadrant of the contextual framework for valuation.

The hypothetical willing buyer is, by definition, postulated rather than nominated. Further, as discussed in Chapter 1, the postulated willing buyer comprises a member of a group most likely to buy the subject property, being a postulated small group participant likely to be operating in a postulated sub-market.

Accordingly, *market value* represents the intersection of a postulated small group participant and a postulated sub-market within the conceptual framework for valuation, as illustrated in Figure 2.9.

Market value may be distinguished from investment value, synergistic value, fair value and special value by its adoption of a postulated market and postulated participants, being grounded in a hypothetical on market exchange.

The definition of *market value* in IVSs may be contended to more closely and fully align with economic, finance and capital market theory than the other definitions of investment value, synergistic value, fair value and special value within the IVSs. As the product of over a century's evolution, which was considered in detail in Chapter 1, the definition of *market value* has benefited from a depth of analysis and level of intellectual rigour not yet afforded to the other definitions which may be expected to occur over time in the future and potentially lead to closer and fuller alignment.

The challenge for the user remains, of course, the extent to which reality may be mirrored through the effective and appropriate application of the assumptions underlying *market value* concerning the postulated small group participant, the postulated sub-market, the nature of the marketing and the nature and extent of information. While the effective and appropriate application may result in a valuation outcome that would closely mirror observable price should a transaction occur, the range of assumptions suggests that a range of valuation outcomes is more likely. For example, mixing blue and yellow paint will provide an outcome of green paint, but the extent to which blue paint is emphasised relative to yellow paint could result in a range of outcomes from very dark green paint to very light green paint.

2.4.3.2 Investment value

Historically, Commonwealth valuation practice used the term 'worth' and US valuation practice used the term 'investment value' to describe the same concept. The IVSs adopt the term 'investment value' though it may be contended that 'worth' more effectively expresses the concept of the value of an asset to a particular participant or group, as in the phrase 'the asset is worth $x to y'.

Interestingly, the RICS Red Book Global (RICS, 2013) provides an addition to the IVS definition of *investment value*:

> **Investment value** is the value of an asset to the owner or a prospective owner for individual investment or operational objectives (IVSC, 2013, page 8; IVSC, 2013, para 36, page 20)

being:

> The value of an asset to the owner or a prospective owner for individual investment or operational objectives. (May also be known as worth). (RICS, 2013, page 8)

As noted above, *investment value* as defined by IVS falls into the second of three principal categories of *basis of valuation*, being that which indicates the benefits that a person or an entity enjoys from ownership of an asset.

It may be contended that such ownership may be either actual or prospective, so including both a vendor and one or more potential purchasers, where a property is offered for sale widely and openly on a market, a public marketing period ensues, offers from potential purchasers are received and evaluated, one purchaser's offer is selected and a transaction occurs. The successful purchaser may be contended to be within the on market–exchange quadrant of the contextual framework for valuation, whereas the unsuccessful potential purchasers may be within the on market–no exchange quadrant.

Further, if a vendor was to offer a property off market, being on a closed basis to selective potential purchasers rather than widely and openly on market and without a public marketing period, receiving and evaluating offers from potential purchasers and selecting one purchaser with a transaction occurring, the successful purchaser may be contended to be within the off market–exchange quadrant of the contextual framework for valuation, whereas the unsuccessful potential purchasers may be within the off market–no exchange quadrant.

The off market–no exchange quadrant would also be relevant where *investment value* is applied in the context of property portfolio analysis:

> This is an entity specific *basis of value*. Although the value of an asset to the owner may be the same as the amount that could be realised from its sale to another party, this *basis of value* reflects the benefits received by an entity from holding the asset and, therefore, does not necessarily involve a hypothetical exchange. *Investment value* reflects the circumstances and financial objectives of the entity for which the valuation is being produced. It is often used for measuring investment performance. Differences between the *investment value* of an asset and its *market value* provide the motivation for buyers or sellers to enter the marketplace. (IVSC, 2013, para 37, page 21)

> If the objective of the valuation is to determine the value to a specific owner, entity specific factors are reflected in the valuation of the asset. Situations in which the value to a specific owner may be required include the following examples:

> (a) supporting investment decisions,
> (b) reviewing the performance of an asset. (IVSC, 2013, para 22, page 16)

The final sentence of the first paragraph, above, would appear broadly consistent with finance theory whereby vendors and purchasers seek to identify what they consider to be mis-priced assets in the market, being assets where the potential transaction price will result in a risk-return outcome that exceeds the investors target risk-return outcome leading to a buy/sell decision.

Concerning the use of *investment value* for performance measurement, Banfield (2014) notes:

> Investment value is an estimate of value of a property to a particular owner or purchaser who may wish to analyse the potential performance against certain investment criteria, for example, a target rate of return, as opposed to those generally prevailing in the market. (Banfield, 2014, pages 108–109)

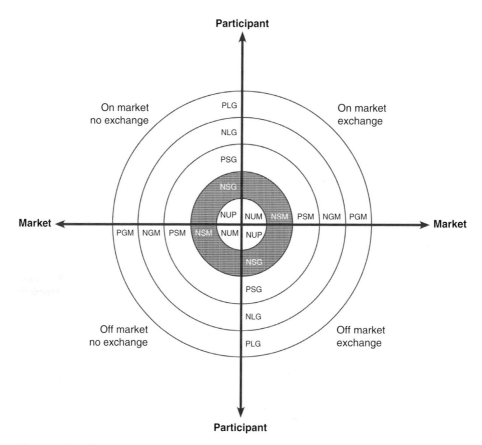

Figure 2.10   Conceptual framework – investment value.

Given that the 'individual investment or operational objectives' are central to an assessment of *investment value*, users should take care to clearly articulate and define these as they provide the underlying conditions upon which *investment value* may be assessed.

The vendor and potential purchasers are, by definition, nominated rather than postulated and may be contended, consistent with the concept of *investment value* reflecting value attributable to individual investment or operational objectives, to be a small group rather than a large group active in a sub-market rather than a general market.

Accordingly, *investment value* represents the intersection of a nominated small group participant and a nominated sub-market within the contextual framework for valuation, as illustrated in Figure 2.10.

Investment value may be distinguished from *market value* through its basis in the actual (nominated) rather than the hypothetical (postulated). Further, *investment value* may be distinguished from synergistic value through the requirement for an exchange to occur in order for synergistic value to manifest.

Investment value may be distinguished from *fair value* through its dependence on multiple prospective purchasers rather than on a unique participant. Further, concerning *special value*, it may be contended that *investment value* may be distinguished by the absence of a nominated unique party, being the special purchaser.

2.4.3.3 *Synergistic value*

Related to, but distinct from, the concept of special value in IVSs is the concept of *synergistic value*:

> **Synergistic value** is an additional element of value created by the combination of two or more assets or interests where the combined value is more than the sum of the separate values. (IVSC, 2013, page 8; RICS, 2013, page 10)

While the example often used for *synergistic value* is that value created by the combination of a freehold and long leasehold interest, it may potentially arise from any combination of two or more assets for any purpose and so requires careful distinction by the user from concepts of aggregation in the IVSs.

While the value created by the combination of a freehold and long leasehold interest has traditionally been known as marriage value in Commonwealth jurisdictions, such marriage value does not entirely align with the definition of *synergistic value* adopted by IVSs which includes the possibility of two unrelated participants rather than a related lessor and lessee. It is, therefore, unhelpful that the RICS Red Book Global (RICS, 2013) uses the same definition for *marriage value* as for *synergistic value* (RICS, 2013, page 10).

It may be contended that for *synergistic value* to be manifest, a transaction needs to occur placing *synergistic value* within the exchange quadrants of the contextual framework for valuation. In the event of no transaction occurring, it would be challenging to distinguish *synergistic value* from *investment value*.

Such exchange may be contended to occur on market, where a property is offered for sale widely and openly and a transaction occurs, or off market, where a property is offered on a closed basis to selective potential purchasers leading to a transaction. While that manifested by the successful purchaser may be *synergistic value*, that which is manifested by the unsuccessful purchasers, in an on or off market–no exchange scenario, may be contended to be *investment value*.

Significantly, for *synergistic value* to arise, there must be more than one market participant, otherwise it may be special value that arises:

> If the synergies are only available to one specific buyer then it is an example of *special value*. (IVSC, 2013, para 47, page 22)

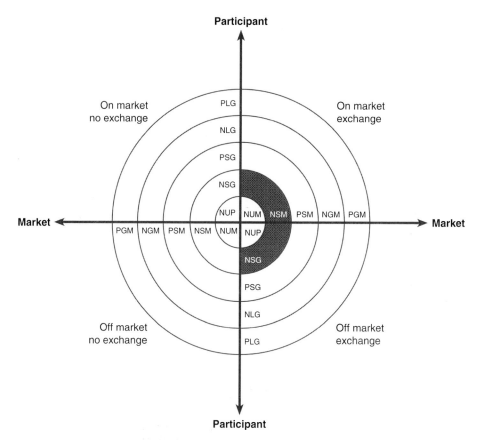

Figure 2.11   Conceptual framework – synergistic value.

The vendor and potential purchasers are, therefore, nominated rather than postulated and may be contended to be a small group participant, rather than a unique participant, active in a sub-market within which the subject property and others similar to it transact.

Accordingly, *synergistic value* represents the intersection of a nominated small group participant and a nominated sub-market within the contextual framework for valuation, as illustrated in Figure 2.11.

Synergistic value may be distinguished from *market value* through its basis in the actual (nominated) rather than in the hypothetical (postulated). Further, *synergistic value* may be distinguished from *investment value* by its requirements for an exchange to occur in order to manifest.

Concerning *fair value, synergistic value* may be distinguished through its dependence on multiple prospective purchasers rather than an unique participant. Further, *synergistic value* may be distinguished from *special value* by the absence of a special purchaser.

2.4.3.4 *Fair value*

The concept of fair value is the centrepiece of IFRS and a fundamental building block for consistent financial reporting internationally. However, IVSs also use the term fair value but define it differently and on the basis that it does not apply to financial reporting:

> **Fair value** is the estimated price for the transfer of an asset or liability between identified knowledgeable and willing parties that reflects the respective interests of those parties.[1] (IVSC, 2013, page 7; IVSC, 2013, para 38, page 21; RICS, 2013, page 7). ([1] This does not apply to valuations for financial reporting – see IVS 300). (IVSC, 2013, page 7)

Consistently, as noted above, *fair value* as defined by IVS falls into the third of three principal categories of *basis of valuation*, being that which indicates the price that would be reasonably agreed between two specific parties for the exchange of an asset.

Accordingly, reflecting the transfer or exchange of an asset places *fair value* within the exchange quadrants of the contextual framework for valuation. In the event of no transaction occurring, it would be challenging to distinguish *fair value*, which reflects the respective interests of the parties, from *investment value*.

Such exchange may be contended to occur on market, where a property is offered for sale widely and openly and a transaction occurs, or off market, where a property is offered on a closed basis to a selective potential purchaser leading to a transaction.

The vendor and purchaser are, by definition, nominated rather than postulated and may be contended to be a unique participant and operating in a unique market focusing on a specific asset.

Accordingly, *fair value* represents the intersection of a nominated unique participant and a nominated unique market within the contextual framework for valuation, as illustrated in Figure 2.12.

Fair value may be distinguished from *market value* through its basis in the actual (nominated) rather than the hypothetical (postulated). Further, *fair value* may be distinguished from *investment value* through its dependence on an unique participant rather than multiple prospective purchasers.

Concerning *synergistic value*, *fair value* may be distinguished through its dependence on a unique participant rather than multiple prospective purchasers. Further, special value may be distinguished from *fair value* through the absence of a requirement for a special purchaser.

Fair value is, by far, the most intellectually challenging *basis of value* in IVSs, both in terms of its conceptual overlap with other *bases of value* and its apparently limited application in property valuation practice.

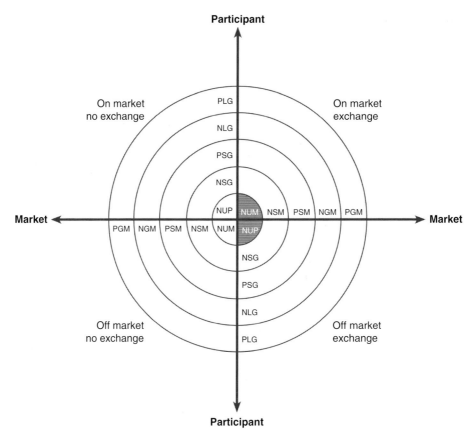

Figure 2.12   Conceptual framework – fair value.

While the definition of *fair value* includes elements of *market value* (estimated price, knowledgeable and willing parties), it also includes elements of *investment value* (identified parties, respective interests of those parties):

> For purposes other than use in financial statements, *fair value* can be distinguished from *market value*. *Fair value* requires the assessment of the price that is fair between two identified parties taking into account the respective advantages or disadvantages that each will gain from the transaction. It is commonly applied in judicial contexts. In contrast, *market value* requires any advantages that would not be available to market participants generally to be disregarded. (IVSC, 2013, para 40, page 21)

Examples of the use of *fair value* include:

(a) determination of a price that is fair for a shareholding in a non-quoted business, where the holdings of two specific parties may mean that the price that is fair between them is different from the price that might be obtainable in the market,

(b) determination of a price that would be fair between a lessor and a lessee for either the permanent transfer of the leased asset or the cancellation of the lease liability. (IVSC, 2013, para 42, page 21)

As a hybrid definition, it is challenging to identify situations where an assessment of *fair value* may be required in property valuation practice with the IVSs suggesting 'judicial contexts', presumably being those unusual circumstances where statute adopts but does not define the term fair value, together with that in (b) which appears to be similar to *synergistic value* in a property context.

Accordingly, therefore, *fair value* within IVSs is potentially most significant for what it is not, being neither *market value* under IVSs nor fair value under IFRS:

> *Fair value* is a broader concept than *market value*. Although in many cases the price that is fair between two parties will equate to that obtainable in the market, there will be cases where the assessment of *fair value* will involve taking into account matters that have to be disregarded in the assessment of *market value*, such as any elements of *special value* arising because of the combination of interests. (IVSC, 2013, para 41, page 21)

Concerning *fair value* within IVSs not being the same as fair value under IFRS, the footnote to the IVS definition is critical:

> The definition of fair value in IFRS is different from the above. The IVSB considers that the definitions of fair value in IFRS are generally consistent with *market value*. The definition and application of fair value under IFRS are discussed in IVS 300 *Valuations for Financial Reporting*. (IVSC, 2013, para 39, page 21)

> The commentary in IFRS 13 and, in particular, the reference to market participants, an orderly transaction, the transaction taking place in the principal or most advantageous market and to the highest and best use of an asset, make it clear that fair value under IFRSs is generally consistent with the concept of *market value* as defined and discussed in the IVS *Framework*. For most practical purposes, therefore, *market value* under IVS will meet the fair value measurement requirement under IFRS 13 subject to some specific assumptions required by the accounting standard such as stipulations as to the unit of account or ignoring restrictions on sale. (IVS 300, para G2, pages 94–95)

For the benefit of the valuation practitioner, the RICS Red Book Global (RICS, 2013) clearly distinguishes definitions of fair value:

> There are two distinct definitions, and great care must be exercised in selecting and specifying the correct definition according to the valuation context.

2 Concepts

1. The price that would be received to sell an asset, or paid to transfer a liability, in an orderly transaction between market participants at the measurement date. (IFRS 13)
2. (being the IVS definition given above) The estimated price for the transfer of an asset or liability between identified knowledgeable and willing parties that reflects the respective interests of those parties. (IVS 2013) This does not apply to valuations for financial reporting – see IVS 300. (RICS 2013, page 7)

noting that the reference to market participants and sale in IFRS 13 make it clear that, for most practical purposes, the IFRS concept of *fair value* is consistent with that of IVS *market value* and so there would be no difference between them in terms of the valuation figure reported (RICS VPS4, para 1.5.3, page 56).

In March 2014, IVSC and IFRS agreed upon and published a statement of protocols acknowledging that interacting and exchanging information on how to measure fair value would be relevant and helpful in developing standards and guidelines on fair value measurement.

2.4.3.5 *Special value*
Special value is defined in IVSs as:

> **Special value** is an amount that reflects particular attributes of an asset that are only of value to a *special purchaser*. (IVSC, 2013, page 8; IVSC, 2013, para 43, page 22; RICS, 2013, page 9)

with special purchaser defined in IVSs as:

> **A special purchaser** is a particular buyer for whom a particular asset has *special value* because of advantages arising from its ownership that would not be available to other buyers in (a/the) market. (IVSC, 2013, para 44, page 8, page 22; RICS, 2013, page 9)

While not specifically considered or excluded, it may be contended that a vendor (being the other participant in *special value*) is not necessarily special, generally being a rational market participant seeking to optimise its interests.

As noted above, *special value* as defined by IVS falls into the second of three principal categories of *basis of valuation*, being that which indicates the benefits that a person or entity enjoys from ownership of an asset. However, it may be contended that, in the context of *special value*, the definition of *basis of valuation* in IVSs does not appear to be entirely consistent with the conceptual framework for valuation developed in section 2.1.

Primarily, it may be contended that for a *special purchaser* to manifest *special value*, a transaction needs to occur, being within the exchange quadrants of the contextual framework for valuation. In the event of no exchange occurring, it would be challenging to distinguish *special value* from *investment value*.

Secondarily, such exchange may be contended to occur on market, where a property is offered for sale widely and openly and a transaction occurs, or off market, where a property is offered on a closed basis to a selective potential *special purchaser* leading to a transaction.

The vendor and *special purchaser* are, by definition, nominated rather than postulated and further, by definition, the *special purchaser* is unique:

> *Special value* can arise where an asset has attributes that make it more attractive to a particular buyer than to any other buyers in a market. These attributes can include the physical, geographic, economic or legal characteristics of an asset. *Market value* requires the disregard of any element of *special value* because at any given date it is only assumed that there is a willing buyer, not a particular willing buyer. (IVSC, 2013, para 45, page 22)

Accordingly, therefore, *special value* may be contended to represent a unique combination of market and participant in an on or off market exchange, which is unlikely to be replicated by any other combination of market and participant, in the context of a specific asset with identifiable advantageous idiosyncratic attributes.

It may be contended that *special value* represents the core of the intersection of a nominated unique participant and a nominated unique market within the contextual framework for valuation, as illustrated in Figure 2.13.

Special value may be distinguished from *market value* through its basis in the actual (nominated) rather than in the hypothetical (postulated). Further *special value* may be distinguished from *investment value*, *synergistic value* and *fair value* through the requirement for a *special purchaser*.

Reflecting the unique circumstances giving rise to *special value*, which may distort consideration of *market value*, IVSs require *special value* to be reported and distinguished when identified:

> When *special value* is identified, it should be reported and clearly distinguished from *market value*. (IVSC, 2013, para 46, page 22)

Given the unique circumstances under which *special value* may arise, great care is required by users in the analysis of such transactions or in the assessment of same which may be, potentially, somewhere between challenging and impossible to undertake.

2 Concepts

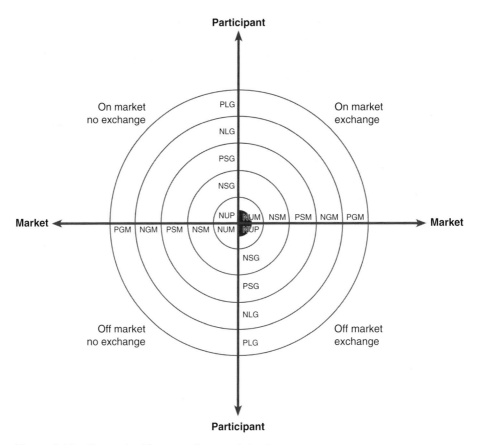

Figure 2.13   Conceptual framework – special value.

2.4.3.6 *Relative contribution to value*

How the relative contributions to value of each of the *bases of value* may compare is a particularly challenging aspect of IVSs, stemming in part from the evolution of *bases of value* and their previous lack of grounding within a conceptual framework for valuation, with a range of opinions on interpretation prevailing within the valuation profession and standard setting community.

It may be contended that the foundation of *market value* in the hypothetical (postulated) renders *market value* the base level of price likely to be achievable in a market. If it may further be contended that if a hypothetical vendor and a hypothetical purchaser may exchange an asset for *market value*, then it is conceptually unlikely that such an asset would be exchanged for less and conceptually possible that it may be exchanged for more in the event of differing assumptions.

How much more may be contended to be dependent on the characteristics and number of actual (or nominated, rather than hypothetical) potential purchasers. For a pool of actual potential purchasers with general similarity of individual investment or operational objectives, an additional amount above *market value* may be anticipated to be paid by the successful purchaser reflecting its individual investment or operational objectives, which vary slightly from those of similar purchasers in the pool, with such an additional amount being manifest as *investment value*.

Where an actual purchaser from such a pool of potential purchasers can derive benefit from adding the subject property to a portfolio of properties (or other combination of interests), such an actual purchaser may be anticipated to pay more than its opinion of *investment value* to recognise the value of the benefits achievable, with such an additional amount being manifest as *synergistic value*.

Alternatively, where there is one, unique actual purchaser and one, unique actual vendor, an additional amount above *investment value* may be anticipated to be paid by the purchaser reflecting its interests in association with those of the vendor, with such an additional amount being manifest as *fair value*.

At the other end of the spectrum to *market value* is the scenario where one, unique actual purchaser identifies attributes of an asset that are only of value to it and not to any other potential purchasers and so may be anticipated to pay an additional amount above *investment value* to reflect such particular attributes, with such an additional amount being manifest as *special value*.

Reflecting such theoretical proportionality in a general sense, rather than practically and specifically, such relative contributions to value may be illustrated diagrammatically in Figure 2.14. However, it should be noted that the height of bars is only indicative of a general relativity between the different *bases of value* and is not an expression of likely quantum of value difference.

2.4.4 Reconciliation to the conceptual framework for valuation

Distinguishing between concepts of value, cost and price is fundamental to an understanding and application of IVSs. With price and cost conceptually being matters of fact as the outcome of a contemplated or actual transaction and an observable outcome, respectively, they are fundamentally distinguishable from value which is a matter of opinion.

Value is considered within IVSs through the definitions of *market value, investment value, synergistic value, fair value* and *special value*. While *market value* may be distinguished from other definitions of value by its adoption of a postulated rather than nominated participant and market, each of the other definitions of value may be mutually distinguishable by the number of participants and requirement for exchange to occur.

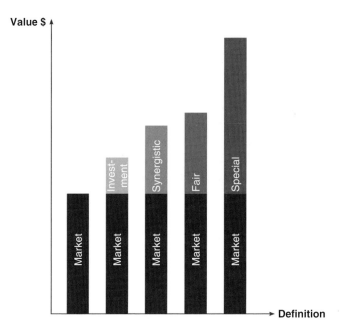

Figure 2.14   Relative contribution to value.

Effectively, the different definitions of value may be distinguished by their relative participants and relative market together with the existence or absence of exchange either on or off market. As considered in detail, above, each of the definitions of value may be reconciled with the conceptual framework for valuation developed in section 2.1 above through the relative roles of participant, market, exchange and on/off market as may be summarised in Figure 2.15.

Accordingly, therefore, the various definitions of value within IVSs may be reconciled with a conceptual framework for valuation that is consistent with economic, finance and capital market theory.

Having developed a conceptual framework for valuation based on economic theory, aligned this framework with finance and capital market theory and examined the definition of the market, this section sought to distinguish definitions of cost and price from defined concepts of value before reconciling these to the conceptual framework for valuation.

2.5 Summary and conclusions

Chapter 1 outlined the emergence of globalisation, the role of IFRS and the evolution of valuation standard setting, the role of IVSC and IVSs and an analysis of *market value*, being the central concept of IVSs, with an

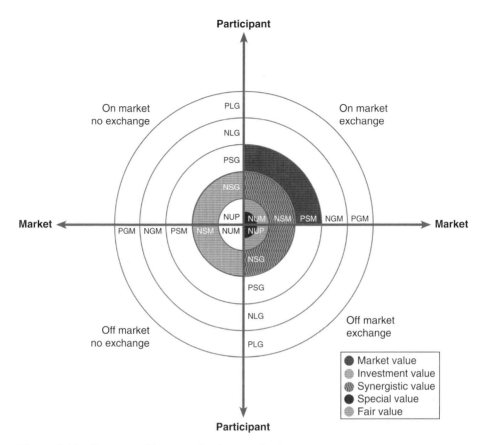

Figure 2.15 Conceptual framework – bases of value.

overview of other IVSs relevant to the valuation of businesses and business interests, intangible assets and financial instruments.

This chapter sought to develop a conceptual framework for valuation based on economic theory, align this framework with finance and capital market theory, examine the definition of the market and distinguish definitions of cost and price from defined concepts of value before reconciling these to the conceptual framework for valuation.

From the starting point of long-established economic theory, the concepts of supply, demand, price, market and participants were considered to develop a conceptual framework for valuation that is consistent with economic theory. Incorporating both actual markets with nominated participants and hypothetical markets with postulated participants as well as concepts of on/off market and exchange/no exchange, it may be contended that such a conceptual framework is consistent with IVSs and places the concepts of *market value, investment value, synergistic value, fair value* and *special value* within a theoretically based market/participant framework.

Having developed a conceptual framework for valuation that is consistent with economic theory, it may be contended that it is also generally consistent with the concepts of risk-return and aligned, in principle, with the concepts of systematic, unsystematic and idiosyncratic influences within finance and capital market theory. Accordingly, the *bases of value* within IVSs may be placed within a conceptual framework for valuation that is consistent with not only economic theory but also capable of alignment with finance theory and capital market theory.

While the IVSs general conceptual definition of a market is broadly consistent with economic theory, the particular definition of a property market focuses on the sub-market and small group participants. Significantly, for IVSs, the market is conceptualised as that which actually exists with a resulting level of market activity at the valuation date rather than that which the user may consider normal and the small group participants conceptualised as typical rather than as individual with care therefore required in application concerning possible incursion into *investment value, fair value* and *special value*.

Distinguishing between concepts of value, cost and price is fundamental to an understanding and application of IVSs. With price and cost conceptually being matters of fact as the outcome of a contemplated or actual transaction and an observable outcome, respectively, they are fundamentally distinguishable from value which is a matter of opinion.

Further, different definitions of value may be distinguished by their relative participants and market together with the existence or absence of exchange either on or off market. While the considered and rigorous definition of *market value* clearly places it within the participant/market space of the conceptual framework for valuation, the still evolving nature of the definitions of *investment value, synergistic value, fair value* and *special value* render classification somewhat more challenging.

The next chapter will consider various aspects of valuation standard definitions within IVSs, discuss the definitions of other relevant contextual terms and identify the principal approaches to valuation within IVSs including a focus on the market approach to valuation.

Chapter 4 will then describe and analyse those elements of IVSs that are of relevance to the three principal stages of the real property valuation process, being the instruction of the valuer, undertaking the valuation and reporting the valuation.

Chapter 5 will consider IVSs in the context of the valuation of investment property, with particular reference to IAS 40 *Investment Property* and the income approach to valuation, including an examination of IVSC TIP 1 *Discounted Cash Flow*.

Finally, Chapter 6 will focus on IVSs in the context of the valuation of owner occupied property held by operating businesses, with particular reference to IAS 16 *Property, Plant and Equipment* and the cost approach to valuation, including an examination of IVSC TIP 2 *The Cost Approach to Tangible Assets*.

References

Banfield, A. (2014) *A Valuer's Guide to the RICS Red Book 2014*, RICS, London.

Bonbright, J. (1937) *Valuation of Property*, McGraw-Hill, New York.

Gilbertson, B. (2002) Valuation or Appraisal: An Art or a Science?, *Australian Property Journal*, February.

International Financial Reporting Council (2012) *A Briefing for Chief Executives, Audit Committees and Boards of Directors*, IFRC, London.

International Financial Reporting Standards (2013) *International Financial Reporting Standards 2013*, International Accounting Standards Board, London.

International Valuation Standards Council (2013) *International Valuation Standards 2013*, IVSC, London.

Royal Institution of Chartered Surveyors (2013) *RICS Professional Standards, Global and UK 2014*, RICS, London.

3

Definitions

3.0 Introduction

In the context of the valuation of real property assets, this book provides an analysis of the International Valuation Standards (IVS), International Accounting Standards (IAS) and International Financial Reporting Standards (IFRS) which, being dynamic, are regularly updated and/or replaced. Accordingly, readers should not rely upon this book as a current statement of an IVS, IAS or IFRS publication and should visit www.ifrs.org and/or www.ivsc.org to find the most recent version.

Chapter 1 outlined the emergence of globalisation, the role of IFRS and the evolution of valuation standard setting, the role of IVSC and IVSs and an analysis of *market value*, being the central concept of IVSs, with an overview of other IVSs relevant to the valuation of businesses and business interests, intangible assets and financial instruments.

Chapter 2 sought to develop a conceptual framework for valuation based on economic theory, aligned this framework with finance and capital market theory, examined the definition of the market and distinguished definitions of cost and price from defined concepts of value before reconciling these to the conceptual framework for valuation.

This chapter considers various aspects of valuation standard definitions within IVSs, discusses the definitions of other relevant contextual terms and identifies the principal approaches to valuation within IVSs including a focus on the market approach to valuation.

Chapter 4 will then describe and analyse those elements of IVSs that are of relevance to the three principal stages of the real property valuation

International Valuation Standards: A Guide to the Valuation of Real Property Assets,
First Edition. David Parker.
© 2016 John Wiley & Sons, Ltd. Published 2016 by John Wiley & Sons, Ltd.

process, being the instruction of the valuer, undertaking the valuation and reporting the valuation.

Chapter 5 will consider IVSs in the context of the valuation of investment property, with particular reference to IAS 40 *Investment Property* and the income approach to valuation, including an examination of IVSC TIP 1 *Discounted Cash Flow*.

Finally, Chapter 6 will focus on IVSs in the context of the valuation of owner occupied property held by operating businesses, with particular reference to IAS 16 *Property, Plant and Equipment* and the cost approach to valuation, including an examination of IVSC TIP 2 *The Cost Approach to Tangible Assets*.

In many countries around the world, national and local valuation professional bodies adopt IVSs and supplement them with national or local valuation practice guidance which may expand upon IVSs in a national or local context for the benefit of their membership. However, only the Royal Institution of Chartered Surveyors (RICS) produces global valuation practice guidance that adopts and expands upon IVSs but is not country specific, comprising mandatory professional standards and valuation practice statements and non-mandatory practice guidance applications and practice guidance notes for use by members globally – generally referred to as the RICS Red Book Global (RICS 2013). Accordingly, this book refers to the RICS Red Book Global for the purposes of considering how a professional body interprets IVSs for application by its members worldwide but without a country specific application.

This book is based upon International Valuation Standards 2013 (IVSC, 2013) and International Financial Reporting Standards 2013 (IFRS, 2013). Given their nature, IVSs, IAS's and IFRSs are dynamic, being regularly updated and with the most recently published versions replacing previously published versions. Accordingly, readers should not rely upon this book as a current statement of an IVS, IAS or IFRS publication and should visit www. ifrs.org and/or www.ivsc.org to find the most recent version.

3.1 Definition of valuation

This section will consider various aspects of valuation standard definitions within IVSs, with the following section discussing the definitions of other relevant contextual terms and the final section identifying the principal approaches to valuation within IVSs including a focus on the market approach to valuation.

Aspects of valuation standard definitions within IVSs to be considered in this section include the definition of such terms as *valuation, valuation review, value, basis of value, basis of valuation, valuation input, assumption* and *special assumption* which are of fundamental importance to IVSs.

3.1.1 What is valuation?

Within the IVSs, valuation may be an outcome or a process, depending on the context:

> The word 'valuation' can be used to refer to the estimated value (the valuation conclusion) or to refer to the preparation of the estimated value (the act of valuing). In these standards it should generally be clear from the context which meaning is intended. Where there is potential for confusion or a need to make a clear distinction between the alternative meanings, additional words are used. (IVSC, 2013, para 9, page 13)

Valuer care is required as the description of valuation does not provide guidance regarding the minimum components of the process or the minimum level of support for the conclusion, with the determination of same being jurisdiction specific depending on relevant professional body requirements and negligence law.

Valuation is, however, temporal and time specific requiring statement as at a particular date for a property or a particular time for assets such as gold whose value changes materially during a day:

> **Valuation date** – the date on which the opinion of value applies. The valuation date shall also include the time at which it applies if the value of the type of asset can change materially in the course of a single day. (IVSC, 2013, page 9; RICS, 2013, page 10 and *date of valuation*, page 6)

While the valuation date is the date upon which the opinion of value or valuation outcome applies, the various valuation process steps such as inspection, analysis, application, reporting and so forth should be contemporaneous but may be later or earlier. Recognising this issue, the RICS Red Book (RICS, 2013) distinguishes *valuation date* from *date of the report*, being 'The date on which the valuer signs the report' (RICS, 2013, page 6), such that valuer care is required if the two dates are a significant period apart.

IVSs distinguish a valuation review as a distinct service from valuation:

> **Valuation Review** – The act or process of considering and reporting on a valuation undertaken by another party, which may or may not require the reviewer to provide their own valuation opinion. (IVSC, 2013, page 9)

Accordingly, provision of 'their own valuation opinion' as part of a valuation review should be undertaken as an independent process, rather than relying on the valuation being reviewed, unless the instructions clearly require otherwise and the report transparently records this.

3 Definitions

3.1.2 What is value?

Fundamental to IVSs is the concept of value being a judgement that may, implicitly, vary between practitioners and is not necessarily provable, which distinguishes value from cost and price (considered in Chapter 2):

> Value is not a fact but an opinion of either:
>
> (a) the most probable price to be paid for an asset in an exchange, or
> (b) the economic benefits of owning an asset. (IVSC, 2013, para 8, page 13)

Further, value can only be a judgement of one of two things, being either the most probable price in exchange or the economic benefits of ownership. The IVSs provide further clarification of each which broadly accord with concepts of *market value* and concepts of *investment value*, respectively, but also include a third opinion (though problematic as discussed in Chapter 2), being *fair value*:

> A value in exchange is a hypothetical price and the hypothesis on which the value is estimated is determined by the purpose of the valuation. A value to the owner is an estimate of the benefits that would accrue to a particular party from ownership. (IVSC, 2013, para 8, page 13)

The references to 'asset' require treatment with care by valuers having regard to the discussion in section 3.2.2, below, with the IVS premis that it is an interest in a real property rather than real property itself that is relevant.

3.1.3 What is a basis of value?

A basis of value is not a valuation approach or valuation method adopted but is a statement of the assumptions underlying the assessment of value or valuation:

> **Basis of value** – a statement of the fundamental measurement assumptions of a valuation. (IVSC, 2013, page 7; IVSC, 2013, para 25, page 17; RICS, 2013, page 6)

> (A *basis of value*) describes the fundamental assumptions on which the reported value will be based, eg the nature of the hypothetical transaction, the relationship and motivation of the parties and the extent to which the asset is exposed to the market. The appropriate basis will vary depending on the purpose of the valuation. A *basis of value* should be clearly distinguished from:
>
> (a) the approach or method used to provide an indication of value,
> (b) the type of asset being valued,

(c) the actual or assumed state of an asset at the point of valuation,

(d) any additional assumptions or *special assumptions* that modify the fundamental assumptions in specific circumstances. (IVSC, 2013, paras 25 and 25, page 17)

Examples of assumptions that may underlie a valuation include the form of the transaction, the participants to the transaction and market exposure, being determined by the purpose of the valuation. Accordingly, each should be specifically identified and logically consistent within the valuation process and discussed within the valuation report with the latter being clearly stated in the valuation instruction.

For the purposes of IVSs, assumptions for *basis of value* differ from additional assumptions and *special assumptions* which are considered further in sections 3.1.5 and 3.1.6, below. Valuers should note that the RICS Red Book Global (RICS, 2013) adopts the same definition of *basis of value* but also defines 'assumption', which is also considered further in section 3.1.5, below. Valuers should, therefore, exercise great care when using such terms to ensure consistency with their description and definition within IVSs and the RICS Red Book Global, respectively.

As noted in section 3.1.2, above, value can only be a judgement of one of two things, being either the most probable price in exchange or the economic benefits of ownership, broadly according with concepts of *market value* and concepts of *investment value*, respectively. Consistently, this principle is extended in the IVSs to basis of valuation:

A *basis of valuation* can fall into one of three principal categories:

(a) The first is to indicate the most probable price that would be achieved in a hypothetical exchange in a free and open market. *Market value* as defined in these standards falls into this category.

(b) The second is to indicate the benefits that a person or an entity enjoys from ownership of an asset. The value is specific to that person or entity, and may have no relevance to market participants in general. *Investment value* and *special value* as defined in these standards fall into this category.

(c) The third is to indicate the price that would be reasonably agreed between two specific parties for the exchange of an asset. Although the parties may be unconnected and negotiating at arm's length, the asset is not necessarily exposed in the market and the price agreed may be one that reflects the specific advantages or disadvantages of ownership to the parties involved rather than the market at large. *Fair value* as defined in these standards falls into this category. (IVSC, 2013, para 27, page 17)

3 Definitions

It should be noted that a *basis of valuation* 'can' rather than will fall into one of the three nominated categories, leaving open the possibility that there may be other categories of basis of valuation:

> Valuations may require the use of different *bases of value* that are defined by statute, regulation, private contract or other document. Although such bases may appear similar to the *bases of value* defined in these standards, unless unequivocal reference is made to IVS in the relevant document, their application may require a different approach from that described in IVS. Such bases have to be interpreted and applied in accordance with the provisions of the source document. Examples of *bases of value* that are defined in other regulations are the various valuation measurement bases found in International Financial Reporting Standards (IFRS) and other accounting standards. (IVSC, 2013, para 28, pages 17–18)

While not 'principal categories' within the *basis of valuation*, such other categories of *basis of value* may be particular to a specific purpose of valuation, such as statutory, regulatory (including IFRS) or by some form of documented agreement, lying outside the IVSs and so not necessarily subject to the requirements of the IVSs unless unequivocally stated otherwise. In this regard, valuers should take particular care concerning *fair value* for the purposes of IFRS (as distinct from IVS) which is considered at length in Chapter 5.

The RICS Red Book Global (RICS, 2013) notes that a valuer may be instructed to provide valuation advice based on other criteria, so other *bases of value* may be appropriate. However, in such cases, the definition adopted must be set out in full and explained together with a brief comment indicating the difference, if any, from *market value* (RICS VPS4, para 1.2.6, page 54).

Further, the RICS Red Book Global (RICS VPS4, para 1.1.4, page 53) notes that bases of value are not necessarily mutually exclusive, with the *worth* (*investment value*) of a property to a specific party or *fair value* (using the IVS definition) of a property in exchange between two specific parties potentially matching *market value* even though different assessment criteria are used.

Significantly, forced sale is not a *basis of value* but considered, by IVSs, to be a description of a situation under which an exchange takes place:

> The term 'forced sale' is often used in circumstances where a seller is under compulsion to sell and that, as (a) consequence, a proper marketing period is not possible. The price that could be obtained in these circumstances will depend upon the nature of the pressure on the seller and the reasons why proper marketing cannot be undertaken. It may also reflect the consequences for the seller of failing to sell within the period available. Unless the nature of

and the reason for the constraints on the seller are known, the price obtainable in a forced sale cannot be realistically estimated. The price that a seller will accept in a forced sale will reflect its particular circumstances rather than those of the hypothetical willing seller in the *market value* definition. The price obtainable in a forced sale has only a coincidental relationship to *market value* or any of the other bases defined in this standard. A 'forced sale' is a description of the situation under which the exchange takes place, not a distinct *basis of value*. (IVSC, 2013, para 52, page 23)

Central to the distinction of forced sale as a description of a situation under which an exchange takes place and not a *basis of value* is the constraint on marketing. Accordingly, evidence of transactions comprising forced sales in the valuation process should be treated with great caution by valuers.

However, not all transactions in falling markets are necessarily forced sales with the inclusion of compulsion or involuntary participation being the principal determining feature, given that the marketing may be designed to match the period available (excepting extremely short periods such as a matter of days which may be likely to occur very infrequently):

> Sales in an inactive or falling market are not automatically 'forced sales' simply because a seller might hope for a better price if conditions improved. Unless the seller is compelled to sell by a deadline that prevents proper marketing, the seller will be a willing seller within the definition of *market value*. (IVSC, 2013, para 54, page 23)

Accordingly, sales in a falling market may be valid evidence of that market provided they can be clearly established not to be forced sales.

An assessment of value to a vendor for a property under forced sale conditions may be contended to be an assessment of *investment value* to the vendor, having regard to the constraint on marketing in the transaction process:

> If an indication of the price obtainable under forced sale circumstances is required, it will be necessary to clearly identify the reasons for the constraint on the seller including the consequences of failing to sell in the specified period by setting out appropriate assumptions. If these circumstances do not exist at the *valuation date*, these must be clearly identified as *special assumptions*. (IVSC, 2013, para 53, page 23)

Therefore, within the valuation process to assess value under forced sale conditions and within the valuation report, the valuer should clearly follow and describe the situation under which an exchange is assumed to have taken place.

3 Definitions

3.1.4 What is a valuation input?

The information adopted and included in the valuation process may have a significant impact on the valuation conclusion, with a substantial body of practice having developed within the valuation profession concerning the relevance and suitability of differing forms of information which has more recently been influenced by the requirements of IFRS.

For the purposes of IVSs, information is considered to be valuation inputs which may comprise data or other information and may be either actual or assumed:

> Valuation inputs refer to the data and other information that are used in any of the valuation approaches described in this standard. These inputs may be actual or assumed. (IVSC, 2013, para 65, page 25)

Examples of actual inputs include:

- prices achieved for identical or similar assets,
- actual cash flows generated by the asset,
- the actual cost of identical or similar assets. (IVSC, 2013, para 66, page 25)

Examples of assumed inputs include:

- estimated or projected cash flows,
- the estimated cost of a hypothetical asset,
- market participants' perceived attitude to risk. (IVSC, 2013, para 67, page 25)

The examples provided are neither an exclusive nor exhaustive list, so further data and other information may be relevant, with cited data including transaction price evidence, cash flows and cost data that may be actual or assumed (estimated) and the only other information cited being market participant perception of risk (being undefined), which may be contended to be particularly challenging qualitative information to both source and interpret.

Significantly, IVSs do not constrain or limit the information considered in the valuation process provided it is actual or assumed data or other information, though the ability to prove actual information from source documents is implied by the examples of actual information given. This provides valuers with scope to consider a very wide range of information in the valuation process but that which is actual and that which is assumed should be clearly stated in the report.

However, IVSs do provide a hierarchy of information with actual information taking precedence over assumed information, provided it is current and relevant:

Greater reliance will normally be placed on actual inputs; however, where these are less relevant, eg where the evidence of actual transactions is dated, historic cash flows are not indicative of future cash flows or the actual cost information is historic, assumed inputs will be more relevant. (IVSC, 2013, para 68, page 25)

Therefore, valuers adopting assumed information when current and relevant actual information is available should explain why in the valuation report. Similarly, where only limited information is available, valuers should take great care and should confirm the veracity of the information and discuss the reliability of the valuation conclusion (given the small sample relied upon) in the valuation report:

A valuation will normally be more certain where multiple inputs are available. Where only limited inputs are available particular caution is required in investigating and verifying the data. (IVSC, 2013, para 69, page 26)

Consistency between information inputs and the *basis of value* and purpose of a valuation is essential to ensure a like-with-like comparison and the onus is upon the valuer to undertake a process of verification and to record this on the valuation file.

Where the input involves evidence of a transaction, care should be taken to verify whether the terms of that transaction were in accord with those of the required *basis of value*. (IVSC, 2013, para 70, page 26)

The nature and source of the valuation inputs should reflect the *basis of value*, which in turn depends on the valuation purpose. For example, various approaches and methods may be used to indicate *market value* providing they use market derived data. The *market approach* will by definition use market derived inputs. To indicate *market value* the *income approach* should be applied using inputs and assumptions that would be adopted by market participants. To indicate *market value* using the *cost approach*, the cost of an asset of equal utility and the appropriate depreciation should be determined by analysis of market-based costs and depreciation. The data available and the circumstances relating to the market for the asset being valued will determine which valuation method or methods are most relevant and appropriate. If based on appropriately analysed market derived data each approach or method used should provide an indication of *market value*. (IVSC, 2013, para 71, page 26)

Valuation approaches and methods are generally common to many types of valuation. However, valuation of different types of assets involves different sources of data that must reflect the market in which the assets are to be valued. For example, the underlying investment of *real estate* owned by a company will be valued in the context of the relevant *real estate* market in which the *real estate* trades, whereas the shares of the company itself will be valued in the context of the market in which the shares trade. (IVSC, 2013, para 72, page 26)

With a clear focus on the relevant market, market participants and market-based inputs, it should be noted that it is the nature of the valuation inputs that determines the most appropriate valuation method(s) for use, rather than selecting the method(s) and then attempting to find relevant inputs. Significantly, if the valuation inputs have been carefully selected, properly analysed and appropriately applied, the use of different valuation methods should result in a common assessment of value.

However, the challenge of compliance should not be underestimated, with an explicit need to identify the market participants and market-based inputs, assumptions, costs and depreciation implying a requirement for some form of recorded data collection rather than simple assertion by the valuer in the valuation process.

As noted above, the provisions of IVSs concerning valuation inputs have more recently been influenced by the requirements of IFRS, with IFRS 13 *Fair Value Measurement* classifying valuations according to the nature of the inputs and adopting a three-level hierarchy:

Level 1 inputs are 'quoted prices (unadjusted) in active markets for identical assets or liabilities that the entity can access on the measurement date'

Level 2 inputs are 'inputs other than quoted prices included within Level 1 that are observable for the asset or liability, either directly or indirectly'

Level 3 inputs are 'unobservable inputs for the asset or liability' (IFRS 13, paras 76–90, pages A503–6; IVS 300, para G4, page 95)

The requirements of Level 1 for quoted prices, active markets and identical assets align with the equity market and the debt market more than with the direct property market, though indirect property market products such as REITs and some unlisted property funds may qualify. Accordingly, valuation inputs for the direct property valuation process may be expected to be more likely to comprise Level 3 inputs, being unobservable, rather than Level 2 which is observable and so requires a very high level of comparable similarity, as considered further in Chapter 5.

As IFRS 13 requires the input level in the hierarchy of any asset or liability measured at fair value to be disclosed in the financial statements, a valuation report prepared for financial reporting should include sufficient information on valuation inputs to enable the reporting entity to correctly categorise assets within this hierarchy (IVS 300, para G5, pages 95–96).

3.1.5 What is an assumption?

IVSs definition of *basis of value* requires clear identification of assumptions and *special assumptions* (IVSC, 2013, para 36, page 17). Valuers should note that, for the purposes of IVSs, there is no such concept as 'standard' assumptions that may be assumed and do not need to be stated (RICS VPS4, para 2.5, page 57).

Significantly, IVSs provide a description, but not a definition, of assumption that concerns either the state of an asset (presumably, in a property context, state of repair or physical condition) or the circumstances of exchange (such as vacancy assumption for owner occupied property), placing much greater emphasis on the definition and role of *special assumptions*. Therefore, valuers should take great care as this description of permissible assumptions can have an effect on the valuation outcome:

> In addition to stating the *basis of value*, it is often necessary to make an assumption or multiple assumptions to clarify either the state of the asset in the hypothetical exchange or the circumstances under which the asset is assumed to be exchanged. Such assumptions can have a significant impact on value. (IVSC, 2013, para 48, page 22)

> Examples of additional assumptions in common use include, without limitation:

> - an assumption that a business is transferred as a complete operational entity,
> - an assumption that assets employed in a business are transferred without the business, either individually or as a group,
> - an assumption that an individually valued asset is transferred together with other complementary assets,
> - an assumption that a holding of shares is transferred either as a block or individually,
> - an assumption that a property that is owner-occupied is vacant in the hypothetical transfer. (IVSC, 2013, para 49, page 25)

In contrast to IVS, the RICS Red Book Global (RICS, 2013) seeks to define assumptions, without limiting its application to only the state of an asset or the circumstances of exchange:

> A supposition taken to be true. It involves facts, conditions or situations affecting the subject of, or approach to, a valuation that, by agreement, do not

need to be verified by the valuer as part of the valuation process. Typically, an assumption is made where specific investigation by the valuer is not required in order to prove that something is true. (RICS, 2013, page 6)

Further, the RICS Red Book Global (RICS 2013) distinguishes an assumption from a valuation input as not requiring investigation by the valuer to prove its accuracy:

> ... is made where it is reasonable for the valuer to accept that something is true without the need for specific investigation or verification. (RICS VPS4, para 2.1, page 56)

The RICS Red Book (RICS 2013) also provides guidance on usual assumptions for property, based on its definition of assumption, to include:

- title;
- condition of buildings;
- services;
- planning (zoning);
- contamination and hazardous substances;
- environmental matters; and
- sustainability,

though noting that this list is not exclusive and care should be taken to identify any assumptions that may have to be made in order to fulfil a particular instruction (RICS VPS4, para 2.5, page 57).

Where adopting a basis other than *market value* requiring the adoption of assumptions or *special assumptions*, the RICS Red Book Global (RICS, 2013) requires that, because bases other than *market value* may produce a value that could not be obtained in an actual sale, whether or not in the general market, the valuer must clearly distinguish the assumptions or *special assumptions* that are different from or additional to those that would be appropriate in an estimate of *market value* (RICS VPS4, para 1.1.5, page 53).

3.1.6 What is a special assumption?

Having described assumptions, *special assumptions* are defined in IVSs as two alternatives, either to comprise matters of fact that are assumed to be different for the purposes of valuation from actuality as at the date of valuation and which have a direct impact on the assessment of value or to reflect an assumption that would not be made by a typical market participant.

Special assumption – an assumption that either assumes facts that differ from the actual facts existing at the *valuation date* or that would not be made by a typical market participant in a transaction on the *valuation date* (IVSC, 2013, page 8; RICS, 2013, page 9)

Where an assumption is made that assumes facts that differ from those existing at the *date of valuation*, it becomes a *special assumption* (see IVS 101 Scope of Work). *Special assumptions* are often used to illustrate the effect of possible changes on the value of an asset. They are designated as 'special' so as to highlight to a valuation user that the valuation conclusion is contingent upon a change in the current circumstances or that it reflects a view that would not be taken by market participants generally on the *valuation date*. (IVSC, 2013, para 50, page 23)

Assumptions and *special assumptions* must be reasonable and relevant having regard to the purpose for which the valuation is required. (IVSC, 2013, para 51, page 23)

Therefore, both assumption and *special assumption* are qualified by a requirement for reasonableness and relevance, both being required rather than as alternatives, having regard to the purpose of the valuation.

Consistently, Banfield (2014) succinctly describes a *special assumption* as:

... an assumption that either:
1. requires a valuation to be based on facts that differ materially from those that exist at the date of valuation; or
2. is one that a prospective purchaser (excluding a purchaser with a special interest) could not reasonably be expected to make at the date of valuation having regard to prevailing market conditions. (Banfield, 2014, page 113)

giving 'typical examples' as that:

- planning consent has been granted;
- a physical change has taken place (such as refurbishment or redevelopment);
- new lettings have taken place;
- a special purchaser exists;
- a constraint on marketing exists;
- there is an anticipation of new economic or environmental designation; and
- anything else, provided it is reasonable in the opinion of the valuer. (Banfield, 2014, page 114)

3 Definitions

The RICS Red Book Global (RICS, 2013) provides a useful example of a *special assumption* as concerning the way a property has been altered, such as *market value* on the *special assumption* that works have been completed (RICS VPS4, para 2.1, page 56). Further examples provided include that planning consent has been or will be granted, that a building will be completed in accordance with a defined plan, that the property is vacant/let, that a special interest creates synergistic value or, where a property is damaged, assumed reinstatement, site clearance or redevelopment for a different use (RICS VPS4, para 3.7, pages 60–61).

However, both the RICS Red Book Global (RICS, 2013) and IVSs provide limitation to special assumptions, stating they can only be made if they can reasonably be regarded as realistic, relevant and valid for the particular circumstances of the valuation (RICS VPS4, para 3.3, page 60), noting that a special assumption may qualify the application of *market value* if it has the effect of changing an underlying principle of *market value* such as a constraint on marketing (RICS VPS4, para 3.6, page 60) or assumed future market conditions (RICS VPS4, para 3.9, page 60).

3.1.7 Definition of valuation – summary

As valuation standards, the conceptual meaning of terms such as *value*, *valuation*, *basis of value*, *basis of valuation* and *valuation input* are of fundamental importance to IVSs. *Valuation* is a time-specific outcome or process with *value* being a judgement of either the most probable price in exchange or the economic benefits of ownership, each of which is specifically defined and for which valuers should exercise caution in application.

Similarly, *basis of value* is carefully defined and interdependent with the description of assumption and the definition of *special assumption*, to which the valuer should have careful regard.

The range of *valuation inputs* is relatively wide but qualified by the hierarchical requirement to comprise data or other information which may be actual or assumed and requirements for assessment of veracity and consistency.

The impact of constrained marketing renders forced sale a basis of exchange in IVSs rather than a *basis of value*, though valuer care is required to distinguish forced sales from sales in a falling market.

This section sought to consider various aspects of valuation standard definitions within IVSs with the next section discussing the definitions of other relevant contextual terms and the following section then identifying the principal approaches to valuation within IVSs including a focus on the market approach to valuation.

3.2 Definition of contextual terms

Consideration of the definition of the following relevant contextual terms within IVSs serves to facilitate the consistent use of and a clear understanding of each term, in order to provide a basis for the effective application of IVSs:

3.2.1 Real estate;
3.2.2 Real property;
3.2.3 Investment property;
3.2.4 Trade related property;
3.2.5 Intangible asset;
3.2.6 Goodwill; and
3.2.7 Market rent.

3.2.1 Real estate

Real estate and *real property* are different in IVSs, with *real estate* being 'land' and 'things' whereas *real property* is a right, interest or benefit related to *real estate*:

> **Real estate** – land and all things that are a natural part of the land, eg trees, minerals and things that have been attached to the land, eg buildings and site improvements and all permanent building attachments, eg mechanical and electrical plant providing services to a building, that are both below and above the ground (IVSC, 2013, page 8; RICS, 2013, page 9)

Under the IVSs definition, *real estate* may comprise up to four components:

- *land* – recognising jurisdictional differences such as high water and low water marks;
- *all things that are a natural part of the land, eg trees, minerals* – being those 'things' that are organically attached to the land rather than being man-made, though recognising jurisdictional differences such as right to crops;
- *things that have been attached to the land, eg buildings and site improvements* – being those 'things' that are man-made, though recognising jurisdictional differences of the nature of attachment with common ambiguities such as buildings capable of removal;
- *all permanent building attachments, eg mechanical and electrical plant providing services to a building* – recognising jurisdictional differences for attachments not providing a service with common ambiguities including in-situ artworks and sculpture attached to the building.

3 Definitions

The inclusion of the four components 'both below and above the ground' mirrors the ancient western land law concept of ownership from the core of the earth to the outermost part of the heavens (*usque ad caelum et ad infernos*), but without the traditional exclusions such as precious metals below ground, swans at ground level and air space for flight paths above ground. In the event of national or local jurisdictions providing exclusions, valuers should state these in the valuation report with particular attention paid to the status of water.

While investment property may accord closely with the definition of *real estate*, valuer vigilance is required in the consideration of owner occupied property, such as major operating facilities (such as car manufacturing plants, airports and so forth), where careful interpretation may be required. Valuers should exercise care when 'things' that may not be within the definition of *real estate* are identified and clear instruction sought together with a clear statement of treatment in the valuation report.

While *real estate* is required to exist to provide the physical framework within which a right, interest or benefit may exist, it is that right, interest or benefit (*real property*) that is effectively the source of value:

> The immovability of land and buildings means that it is the right that a party holds that is transferred in exchange, not the physical land and buildings. The value, therefore, attaches to the property interest rather than to the physical land and buildings. (IVS 230, para C3, page 63)

3.2.2   *Real property*

As noted above, *real estate* and *real property* are different in IVSs, with *real property* being distinguished from *real estate*. The essential difference is that *real estate* is 'land' and 'things' whereas *real property* is a right, interest or benefit related to *real estate*. While *real estate* is required to exist to provide the physical framework within which a right, interest or benefit may exist, it is that right, interest or benefit (*real property*) that is effectively the source of value:

> **Real property** – all rights, interests and benefits related to the ownership of *real estate* (IVSC, 2013, page 8)

With value attaching to the property interest held rather than to the physical land and buildings, the threshold issue for the valuer to address is 'ownership' of *real estate* as the form of ownership (freehold, leasehold, licence and so forth) will determine the nature of property interest and the extent of the 'rights, interests and benefits' arising, because, without ownership, there is no property interest to value.

The concept of 'all rights, interests and benefits' is relatively wide, focusing on the positive but without clear definition and silent concerning the negative such as obligations, encumbrances and liabilities. However, such 'rights, interests and benefits' must relate to the ownership and valuer care is required in the event of any 'rights, interests and benefits' arising from a third party such as a government issued licence to extract water.

Interestingly, the RICS Red Book Global (RICS, 2013) definition of real property interprets 'all' to include both the positive and the negative:

> All rights, interests and benefits related to the ownership of *real estate*, including any negative rights, interests or benefits (i.e. obligations, encumbrances or liabilities) relating to the interest being valued. (RICS, 2013, page 9)

Accordingly, when applying IVSs, valuers should take care to clearly state the approach adopted to negative 'rights, interests and benefits' such as obligations, encumbrances and liabilities.

Within IVS 230, the concepts of 'rights' and 'interests' are considered alongside and 'ownership' appears to exist in three potential forms, being control, use and occupation comprising, effectively, freehold, leasehold and licence interests:

> A *real property* interest is a right of ownership, control, use or occupation of land and buildings. There are three basic types of interest:
>
> (a) the superior interest in any defined area of land. The owner of this interest has an absolute right of possession and control of the land and any buildings upon it in perpetuity subject only to any subordinate interests and any statutory constraints;
> (b) a subordinate interest that gives the holder rights of exclusive possession and control of a defined area of land or buildings for a defined period, eg under the terms of a lease contract;
> (c) a right to use land or buildings but without a right of exclusive possession or control, eg a right to pass over land or to use it only for a specified activity. (IVS 230, para C1, page 63)

which 'may be held jointly, where a number of parties have the right to the share the whole interest, or severally, where each party has a defined proportion of the whole interest' (IVS 230, para C2, page 63), with superior and subordinate interests being hierarchical and not mutually exclusive (IVS 230, para C3, page 63).

Accordingly, IVS 230 illustrates the definition of *real property* and valuer care is required to identify and specify the exact nature of the 'rights, interests and benefits' which are the subject of the valuation and to identify the potential impact of any other parallel interests:

> When valuing a *real property* interest it is therefore necessary to identify the nature of the rights accruing to the holder of that interest and reflect any constraints or encumbrances imposed by the existence of other interests in the same property. (IVS 230, para C6, page 64)

being 'normally defined by state law and often regulated by national or local legislation' (IVS 230, para C7, page 64) rendering a knowledge of the relevant jurisdictional legal framework essential.

Significantly, *real property* applies generically to all forms including subsets such as *investment property* and *trade related property*, which are considered further below.

3.2.3 Investment property

Echoing IAS 40 *Investment Property*, which will be considered in detail in Chapter 5, the definition of *investment property* in IVSs emphasises the income and capital return characteristics while distinguishing from owner occupied property used by a business (considered in Chapter 6) and from property identified for sale under IFRS 5 *Non-Current Assets Held for Sale*:

> **Investment property** – property that is land or a building, or part of a building, or both, held by the owner to earn rentals or for capital appreciation, or both, rather than for:
>
> (a) use in the production or supply of goods or services or for administrative purposes, or
> (b) sale in the ordinary course of business (IAS 40, para 5, page A1146; IVSC, 2013, page 7; RICS, 2013, page 8)

Concerning the physical composition of *investment property*, the definition is wide and includes land, and/or part or whole buildings which include strata title, community title and other shared title property. Similarly, income generation and/or capital appreciation as the basis for ownership is relatively wide and may include other bases such as tax minimisation but possibly not prestige or security.

Concerning the characteristics of *investment property*, 'rather than' suggests a primary use for earning rentals or capital appreciation but that this may not be the exclusive or sole use, such that an entity may occupy accommodation within an investment property that its owns without this then being deemed to be a property used by the business. However, the extent of such occupation is unclear and it may be contended that occupation of a small area or minority of the total building accommodation may remain within the definition of investment property but occupation of a large area or majority of total building accommodation may be outside the definition of investment property, as considered in Chapter 5. Therefore, given the potential for ambiguity, it would be prudent for a valuer to obtain clear client instructions if a property that is partially owner occupied is to be classified as an *investment property*.

3.2.4 Trade related property

The definition of trade related property includes two key elements, being design and a value/trading link:

> **Trade related property** – any type of *real property* designed for a specific type of business where the property value reflects the trading potential for that business. (IVSC, 2013, page 8; RICS, 2013, page 10)

While *trade related property* may be any type of real property, it must be designed for a 'specific' business type and the value of the property must be linked to the trading potential of that business. The traditional example usually cited is a petrol filling station, where the property was designed specifically to be a petrol filling station and the value of the property is inextricably linked to the trading potential of the petrol filling station. Similarly, crematoria and purpose built cinemas and multistorey car parks may fall within the classification of *trade related property*.

Valuers should take care in classification as *trade related property* if a property was not designed for the current purpose of use but comprises an adaptive re-use or where property value may not be entirely linked to the trading potential of that specific business. For example, high street or suburban heritage bank buildings converted for use as a restaurant may not fall within the classification of *trade related property*.

Similarly, valuers should take care when considering the value of a *trade related property* and the value of the business conducted therein and/or the value of licenses or permits to trade, as conceptual and practical overlap between each may occur and double or triple counting should be avoided.

3 Definitions

3.2.5 Intangible asset

While this book considers issues associated with the valuation of tangible assets, IVSs address the valuation of all assets including tangible and intangible as well as all liabilities:

> **Intangible asset** – a non-monetary asset that manifests itself by its economic properties. It does not have physical substance but grants rights and economic benefits to its owner. (IVSC, 2013, page 7; RICS, 2013, page 8)

In the context of property valuation, the issue of an *intangible asset* may arise in association with the valuation of a tangible asset, such as consideration of the value of the name 'Waldorf Astoria', 'The Dorchester' or 'Peace Hotel' in association with the valuation of the *real property*.

3.2.6 Goodwill

Traditionally considered as a component of the value of a business, *goodwill* as defined by IVS may be applicable to the valuation of a group of properties as a portfolio:

> **Goodwill** – any future economic benefit arising from a business, an interest in a business or from the use of a group of assets which is not separable. (IVSC, 2013, page 7; RICS, 2013, page 7 *'that is not'*)

Accordingly, valuers should take care when instructed to value a 'group of assets' which may comprise a portfolio of properties as a portfolio and where there is market support for a premium or discount to apply at the portfolio level, as such a premium or discount may be capable of classification as *goodwill*.

3.2.7 Market rent

While included here for completeness, *market rent* will be considered in greater detail in the context of owner occupied property in Chapter 6.

> **Market rent** – the estimated amount for which an interest in real property should be leased on the *valuation date* between a willing lessor and a willing lessee on appropriate lease terms in an arm's length transaction, after proper marketing and where the parties had each acted knowledgably, prudently and without compulsion. (IVSC, 2013, page 8; RICS, 2013, page 8)

The definition of *market rent* in IVSs shares much in common with the definition of *market value* but with the addition of 'on appropriate lease terms'. As a plural, it suggests the conditions of lease rather than a period of time and that there should be more than one condition of lease. Valuers should take care to identify relevant conditions in a hypothetical lease of the subject property as these may vary by sector (such as between a department store or a small office suite), by geography (such as longer leases in the UK and parts of Europe or shorter leases in Asia) and by market conventions and local legislation (such as rent review clauses, alienation clauses or make good clauses).

3.2.8 *Definition of contextual terms – summary*

The definition of other relevant contextual terms in IVSs serves to facilitate the consistent use of and a clear understanding of that term as the basis for the effective application of IVSs. Such contextual terms may be considered as four groups, being:

- those that are critical to precisely establishing that which is to be valued, such as *real estate* and *real property*;
- those that assist in the classification of assets, such as *investment property* and *trade related property*;
- those that comprise an additional element of value that may require consideration in the context of the valuation of *real property*, such as *goodwill* and *intangible assets*; and
- that which forms a key input into the valuation process, such as *market rent* in the valuation of owner occupied property.

The previous section sought to consider various aspects of valuation standard definitions within IVSs with this section discussing the definitions of other relevant contextual terms and the next section seeking to identify the principal approaches to valuation within IVSs, including a focus on the market approach to valuation.

3.3 Principal approaches to valuation

The principal approaches to valuation within IVSs comprise the cost, income and market approach, with a focus on the market approach to valuation considered through the four steps of accumulation, analysis, adjustment and application.

In a refreshing contrast to various textbooks in the UK, USA and Australia over the last five decades, IVSs recognise only three principal approaches to valuation, being the cost, income and market approach that:

> can all be applicable for the valuation of a *real property* interest (IVS 230, para C12, page 65)

Significantly, the three approaches are founded in economic theory, being 'based on the economic principles of price equilibrium, anticipation of benefits or substitution' and are not mutually exclusive, with the use of more than one approach for cross-verification encouraged, particularly where *valuation inputs* are limited:

> One or more valuation approaches may be used in order to arrive at the valuation defined by the appropriate *basis of value*. The three approaches described and defined in this Framework are the main approaches used in valuation. They all are based on the economic principles of price equilibrium, anticipation of benefits or substitution. Using more than one valuation approach or method is especially recommended where there are insufficient factual or observable inputs for a single method to produce a reliable conclusion. (IVSC, 2013, para 55, pages 23–24)

While only three approaches are recognised in IVSs, these are described as 'main approaches' allowing the valuer to adopt an alternative approach, if necessary, though the rationale for doing so should be robust and clearly explained in the valuation report.

While each of the three principal approaches is considered below, the focus in this chapter is upon the market approach with the income approach to valuation considered in greater detail in Chapter 5 and the cost approach to valuation considered in greater detail in Chapter 6.

3.3.1 Cost approach

The cost approach is one of the three principal valuation approaches recognised by IVSs and is grounded in economic theory, being based on the economic principle of 'substitution':

> The *cost approach* provides an indication of value using the economic principle that a buyer will pay no more for an asset than the cost to obtain an asset of equal utility, whether by purchase or by construction. (IVSC, para 62, page 25; RICS, 2013, page 6)

While the economic principle of substitution is relatively simple to understand as a principle, its application in practice in the context of property is much more challenging, exacerbated by the type of property for which the approach is considered most relevant within the IVSs:

> It is normally used when there is either no evidence of transaction prices for similar property or no identifiable actual or notional income stream that would accrue to the owner of the relevant interest. It is principally used for the valuation of specialised property, which is property that is rarely if ever

sold in the market, except by way of sale of the business or entity of which it is part. (IVS 230, para C22, page 67)

With the *cost approach* most applicable to 'specialised property', such as public buildings (town halls, museums and so forth) or major operating facilities (car manufacturing plants, airports and so forth), a range of complex issues arise in assessing 'the cost to obtain an asset of equal utility', 'by purchase' and 'by construction' which will be considered in greater detail in Chapter 6:

> This approach is based on the principle that the price that a buyer in the market would pay for the asset being valued would, unless undue time, inconvenience, risk or other factors are involved, be not more than the cost to purchase or construct an equivalent asset. Often the asset being valued will be less attractive than the alternative that could be purchased or constructed because of age or obsolescence. Where this is the case, adjustments may need to be made to the cost of the alternative asset depending on the required *basis of value*. (IVSC 2013, para 63, page 25)

> The first step requires a replacement cost to be calculated. This is normally the cost of replacing the property with a modern equivalent at the relevant *valuation date*. An exception is where an equivalent property would need to be a replica of the subject property in order to provide a market participant with the same utility, in which case the replacement cost would be that of reproducing or replicating the subject building rather than replacing it with a modern equivalent. The replacement cost needs to reflect all incidental costs such as the value of the land, infrastructure, design fees and finance costs that would be incurred by a market participant in creating an equivalent asset. (IVS 230, para C23, page 67)

> The cost of the modern equivalent is then subject to adjustment for obsolescence. The objective of the adjustment for obsolescence is to estimate how much less valuable the subject property would be to a potential buyer than the modern equivalent. Obsolescence considers the physical condition, functionality and economic utility of the subject property compared to the modern equivalent. (IVS 230, para C24, page 68)

Included within the myriad range of complex issues for consideration are 'undue time, inconvenience, risk or other factors', 'an equivalent asset', 'less attractive', 'age', 'obsolescence', 'adjustments', 'replacement cost', 'modern equivalent', 'replica', 'utility', 'incidental costs', 'physical condition', 'functionality', 'economic utility' and so forth which will also be considered in greater detail in Chapter 6.

With valuation being a matter of opinion rather than a matter of fact, the diversity of variables within and complexity of the *cost approach* may be expected to result in a potentially wide range of opinions of value.

3 **Definitions**

3.3.2 Income approach

The income approach is one of the three principal valuation approaches recognised by IVSs and is grounded in economic theory, being based on the economic principle of 'anticipation of benefits':

> The *income approach* provides an indication of value by converting future cash flows to a single current capital value. (IVSC, 2013, page 7; IVSC, 2013, para 58, page 24; RICS, 2013, page 7)

Consistent with the forward looking nature of the underlying economic principle, the *income approach* conceptualises value as a single expression of future cash flows, masking within its simplicity a range of complex measurement issues and other related issues including valuation accuracy, behavioural influences and so forth.

> Various methods are used to indicate value under the general heading of the *income approach*, all of which share the common characteristic that the value is based upon an actual or estimated income that either is or could be generated by an owner of the interest. (IVS 230, para C16, page 66)

Methods that fall under the *income approach* include:

- income capitalisation, where an all-risks or overall capitalisation rate is applied to a representative single period income,
- discounted cash flow where a discount rate is applied to a series of cash flows for future periods to discount them to a present value,
- various option pricing models. (IVSC, 2013, para 60, page 24)

Accordingly, within the *income approach*, actual income or estimated income arising from an interest may be capitalised, discounted or incorporated within an option pricing model to assess a 'single current capital value'.

While only three methods for the *income approach* are cited in IVSs, the reference to 'include' allows the valuer to adopt an alternative method for the *income approach*, if necessary, though the rationale for doing so should be robust and clearly explained in the valuation report.

3.3.2.1 Income capitalisation

IVSs cite income capitalisation as one of three methods falling under the *income approach*, being:

> where an all-risks or overall capitalisation rate is applied to a representative single period income (IVSC, 2013, para 60, page 24)

as:

> An income stream that is likely to remain constant can be capitalised using a single multiplier, often known as the capitalisation rate. (IVS 230, para C17, page 66)

where the capitalisation rate is:

> based on the time cost of money and the risks and rewards attaching to the income stream in question (IVS 230, para C18, page 66)

and:

> This approach considers the income that an asset will generate over its useful life and indicates value through a capitalisation process. Capitalisation involves the conversion of income into a capital sum through the application of an appropriate discount (sic) rate. The income stream may be derived under a contract or contracts, or be non-contractual, eg the anticipated profit generated from either the use of or holding of the asset. (IVSC, 2013, para 59, page 24)

though while quick and simple, the method:

> cannot be reliably used where the income is expected to change in future periods to an extent greater than that generally expected in the market or where a more sophisticated analysis of risk is required (IVS 230, para C17, page 66)

This identifies the two key variables within the capitalisation method as the multiplier or capitalisation rate (known as 'all risks' in the UK and 'overall' in the US) and a 'representative single period income'. The concept of multiplying a single income figure by a single rate to assess value is deceptively simple with each variable masking a myriad of complex issues that are considered in greater detail in Chapter 5.

The income capitalisation method may be used to assess *market value* or *investment value:*

- with an assessment of *market value* adopting a yield derived from observations of returns implicit in the price paid for real property interests traded in a market between market participants (IVS 230, para C19, page 67); and
- with an assessment of *investment value* to an owner/potential owner based on their investment criteria adopting a yield that may reflect their required rate of return or the weighted average cost of capital (IVS 230, para C19, page 67).

The capitalisation method may, therefore, be most appropriate for adoption where there is a stable property in a stable property market with stable comparable sales transactions where each has a relatively simple risk profile.

This effectively limits the use of the capitalisation method to simpler, smaller properties for which there is a substantial pool of comparable sales evidence in a deep market and valuers should take great care in attempting to apply the capitalisation method to complex, larger properties and/or markets of limited depth.

3.3.2.2 Discounted cash flow

IVSs cite discounted cash flow as one of three methods falling under the *income approach*, being:

> where a discount rate is applied to a series of cash flows for future periods to discount them to a present value (IVSC, 2013, para 60, page 24)

> These vary significantly in detail but share the basic characteristic that the net income for a defined future period is adjusted to a present day value using a discount rate. The sum of the present day values for the individual periods represents the capital value. (IVS 230, para C18, page 66)

This identifies the two key variables within the discounted cash flow method as the 'net income for a defined future period' and the discount rate. The concept of discounting periodic cash flows over a given future period by a single rate to assess value is deceptively simple with each variable masking a myriad of complex issues that are considered in greater detail in Chapter 5.

While the discount rate is:

> based on the time cost of money and the risks and rewards attaching to the income stream in question (IVS 230, para C18, page 66)

unlike the capitalisation rate, it may either be identified through analysis of comparable sale transactions or constructed from a typical risk-free rate adjusted for additional risks and opportunities specific to a particular real property interest and having regard to whether income inputs or cash flows are based on current levels or projections (IVS 230, paras C20 and C21, page 67), being considered in greater detail in Chapter 5.

As with the income capitalisation method, the discounted cash flow method may be used to assess *market value* or *investment value:*

- with an assessment of *market value* adopting a discount rate derived from observations of returns implicit in the price paid for real property interests traded in a market between market participants (IVS 230, para C19, page 67); and

- with an assessment of *investment value* to an owner/potential owner based on their investment criteria adopting a discount rate that may reflect their required rate of return or the weighted average cost of capital (IVS 230, para C19, page 67).

Reflecting the limitations of the capitalisation of income method, the discounted cash flow method may be appropriate for adoption for complex or larger properties and/or markets of limited depth or instability.

3.3.2.3 *Option pricing models*

IVSs cite option pricing models as one of three methods falling under the *income approach*. However, for property, research into the theory and practice of option pricing models as a valuation approach is nascent. Generally, with new methods of valuation and as was observed with the development and adoption of discounted cash flow as a valuation method, there is a period of approximately 20 years between development of a method by academia and adoption of a method by practitioners.

Having briefly considered the *cost approach* and the *income approach*, comprising the *income capitalisation method*, *discounted cash flow method* and option pricing models, the third principal valuation approach recognised by IVSs is the *market approach*.

3.3.3 *Market approach*

The market approach is one of the three principal valuation approaches recognised by IVSs and is grounded in economic theory, being based on the economic principle of 'price equilibrium':

> The *market approach* provides an indication of value by comparing the subject asset with identical or similar assets for which price information is available. (IVSC, 2013, page 8; IVSC, 2013, para 56, page 24; RICS, 2013, page 8)

The *market approach* is dependent upon there being 'identical or similar assets for which price information is available', with the absence of such sales evidence rendering the approach inapplicable. When using the *market approach* for the assessment of *market value*, consistency with underlying assumptions is essential such that, for example, sales evidence arising from forced sales or special purchasers would not be considered relevant.

As the *market approach* is grounded in comparison, the level of similarity between the subject asset and those assets recently transacted is of fundamental importance, as 'property interests are not homogenous' (IVS 230, para C13, page 65) and even if physically identical, location will always differ albeit marginally (IVS 230, para C13, page 65). Decreasing levels of similarity may be likely to result in increasing levels of required

3 Definitions

adjustment to a point where the recently transacted asset cannot reasonably be claimed to be comparable.

Consistent with recent case law in specialist Australian courts (see, for example, *Adams v Valuer General* [2014] NSWLEC 1005), the market approach may be contended to comprise four sequential steps, being:

- the accumulation step;
- the analysis step;
- the adjustment step; and
- the application step

which may be considered in greater detail as follows.

3.3.3.1 Accumulation step

The accumulation step seeks to identify a pool of recently transacted assets which comprise potentially genuinely comparable sales to the subject property from which information may be deduced concerning the value of the subject property:

> Under this approach the first step is to consider the prices for transactions of identical or similar assets that have occurred recently in the market. If few recent transactions have occurred, it may also be appropriate to consider the prices of identical or similar assets that are listed or offered for sale provided the relevance of this information is clearly established and critically analysed. (IVSC, 2013, para 57, page 24)

The hierarchical preference is to first consider recent completed transactions of identical assets, then recent completed transactions of similar assets and then to consider identical assets currently offered for sale and finally similar assets currently offered for sale, rather than then considering historic (or non-recent) completed transactions of identical or similar assets. However, in the event of considering assets offered for sale, valuers should take care to clearly explain and so establish the relevance of same in the valuation report.

Consistent with the conceptual framework for valuation developed in Chapter 2, the 'market' in this context comprises the relevant sub-market for the subject property such that relevant comparable sales for super-regional shopping centres are other super-regional shopping centres rather than convenience shopping centres. Further, 'few' is a relative measure, clearly indicating greater than one but how much greater being dependent on the sub-market. For example, within the super-regional shopping centre market 'few' may be interpreted as a sample of four to six comparable sales, whereas within the convenience shopping centre market 'few' may be interpreted as a sample of eight to ten comparable sales.

At the first step in the application of the *market approach*, the identified pool may comprise a large number of potentially genuinely comparable sales which, while sharing some elements of similarity with the subject property, may be likely to be of differing degrees of comparability. Reflecting the heterogeneity of property, it is prudent in this step for the valuer to include as many similar sales as possible and exclude as few as possible with the sample size likely to be diminished during the course of undertaking the following steps.

3.3.3.2 Analysis step

Having accumulated a pool of potentially genuinely comparable sales, the analysis step provides a common basis of measurement by seeking to convert all potentially genuinely comparable sales to a common basis of expression such as a unitary rate (rate per square metre, rate per hectare, etc.), improved or unimproved (through allowance for the absence or existence of improvements, etc.) and so forth.

The IVSs caution that such unitary rate should be that commonly used in the market and must be consistently applied:

> To the extent possible any unit of comparison used should be one commonly used by participants in the relevant market. (IVS 230, para C14, page 65)

> A unit of comparison is only useful when it is consistently selected and applied to the subject property and the comparable properties in each analysis. (IVS 230, para C14, page 65)

with the key issue being homogeneity or commonality of the unitary rate across the sample (IVS 230, para C14, page 65).

3.3.3.3 Adjustment step

Having accumulated a pool of potentially genuinely comparable sales and analysed each to a common unitary rate basis, the adjustment step acknowledges the fact that no two properties are ever identical and seeks to convert the unitary rate for each potentially genuinely comparable sale to a hypothetical expression of value as a unitary rate in the context of the subject property through the reflection of differences between the respective potentially genuinely comparable sales and the subject property:

> It may be necessary to adjust the price information from other transactions to reflect any differences in the terms of the actual transaction and the *basis of value* and any assumptions to be adopted in the valuation being undertaken.

3 Definitions

There may also be differences in the legal, economic or physical characteristics of the assets in other transactions and the asset being valued. (IVSC, 2013, para 57, page 24)

IVSs contemplate three types of differences for which adjustment may be required, being:

- differences between the terms of the transaction and the *basis of value*, such as any constraint on marketing;
- differences between the terms of the transaction and any assumptions to be adopted in the valuation, such as a transaction of occupied property and a valuation assumption of vacant property; and
- differences between legal, economic or physical characteristics between the transaction and the subject property, such as easements, use, location and so forth.

Accordingly, following common valuation practice, a five-line adjustment matrix would appear to be the minimum required by the valuer, with further rows for sub-sets of legal, economic and physical characteristics, if necessary. Valuers should take care if making adjustment for any other differences and explain the rationale for the requirement for such adjustment in the valuation report.

Such adjustment should be consistently made and may be explicitly made (for example, say +5% for superior location) or implicitly made (for example, say +10% for size and location) with fewer adjustments preferred to more adjustments and smaller adjustments preferred to larger adjustments.

Accepted valuation practice permits both explicit and implicit adjustment for differences to enable valuers to have evidentiary comparable values which, following adjustment, account for the various differences with the subject property. Such adjustment is generally based on a reasoning process drawing on the skill and experience of the valuer and undertaken to derive an opinion of value through a deductive process.

3.3.3.4 Application step

Having accumulated a pool of potentially genuinely comparable sales, analysed each to a common unitary rate basis and then adjusted each unitary rate for respective differences to the subject property in order to derive a hypothetical expression of value as a unitary rate in the context of the subject property, the potentially genuinely comparable sales are then applied to the subject property to determine the value of the subject property through a consideration of the relevance (such as being limited, indirect or direct) of each potentially genuinely comparable sale.

The application step may be expected to result in greater attention being given to consideration of potentially genuinely comparable sales considered of direct relevance to the subject property than to those considered of indirect or limited relevance to the subject property. While all comparable sales evidence may be considered relevant and so cannot be disregarded, the level of relevance of different comparable sales to the subject property may vary leading to the valuer attributing differing weight to each comparable sale.

The IVSs suggest that the weight to be attributed to each comparable sale may be determined by the following characteristics of the subject property relative to the potentially genuinely comparable sale:

- the interest providing the price evidence and the interest being valued;
- the respective locations;
- the respective quality of the land or the age and specification of the buildings;
- the permitted use or zoning at each property;
- the circumstances under which the price was determined and the *basis of value* required; and
- the effective date of the price evidence and the required *valuation date*. (IVS 230, para C15, pages 65–66)

3.3.3.5 *Market approach – summary*

While the principle of the *market approach* may appear relatively straight-forward, the practice is somewhat more challenging:

> The *market approach* provides an indication of value by comparing the subject asset with identical or similar assets for which price information is available. (IVSC, 2013, page 8; IVSC, 2013, para 56, page 24; RICS, 2013, page 8)

The process of identification and accumulation of 'identical or similar assets' and then analysing, adjusting and applying same to the subject property requires significant input of valuer judgement on a consistent basis. However, when such valuer judgement is applied consistently, the *market approach* may be both logical and rational, leading to an assessment of value that is transparently supported.

3.3.4 *Principal approaches to valuation – summary*

Three principal approaches to valuation are recognised by IVSs and founded in economic theory, being the *cost approach*, the *income approach* and the *market approach*, with other approaches not being excluded and so capable of adoption by valuers with appropriate justification in the valuation report.

While the *cost approach* is based on the economic principle of 'substitution' and appears deceptively simple, the application of concepts such as utility, equivalency, obsolescence and replication to property, particularly specialised property, is very challenging in practice.

Similarly, the *income approach* is based on the economic principle of 'anticipation of benefits' and the application of capitalisation of income and discounted cash flow also appear deceptively simple. However, the measurement of the appropriate income stream(s) and the determination of the appropriate rate involve complex judgements in the assessment of an opinion of value.

The *market approach* is based on the economic principle of 'price equilibrium', also appearing deceptively simple but requiring the logical and rational application of four principal steps, each of which require a significant input of valuer judgement on a consistent basis, to derive an assessment of value that is transparently supported.

With the previous sections seeking to consider various aspects of valuation standard definitions within IVSs and to discuss the definitions of other relevant contextual terms, this section has identified the principal approaches to valuation within IVSs including a focus on the market approach to valuation.

3.4 Summary and conclusions

Chapter 1 outlined the emergence of globalisation, the role of IFRS and the evolution of valuation standard setting, the role of IVSC and IVSs and an analysis of *market value*, being the central concept of IVSs, with an overview of other IVSs relevant to the valuation of businesses and business interests, intangible assets and financial instruments.

Chapter 2 developed a conceptual framework for valuation based on economic theory, aligned this framework with finance and capital market theory, examined the definition of the market and distinguished definitions of cost and price from defined concepts of value before reconciling these to the conceptual framework for valuation.

This chapter sought to consider various aspects of valuation within IVSs, discuss the definitions of other relevant contextual terms and identify the principal approaches to valuation within IVSs including a focus on the market approach to valuation.

As valuation standards, the conceptual meaning of terms such as *valuation*, *value*, *basis of value*, *valuation basis* and *valuation input* are of fundamental importance to IVSs. *Valuation* is a time-specific outcome or process with *value* being a judgement of either the most probable price in exchange or the economic benefits of ownership, being interdependent with and overlapping the definitions of *basis of value*, *valuation input* and *special assumption* and so requiring the valuer to exercise caution to ensure consistency in application with the stated definitions of each and description of assumption in order to avoid undermining the validity of the assessment of value and confidence in the valuation process.

The definition of other relevant contextual terms, being *real estate, real property, investment property, trade related property, goodwill, intangible assets* and *market rent*, in IVSs serves to facilitate the consistent use of and a clear understanding of each term which provides the basis for the effective application of IVSs. Mis-interpretation of the specific meaning of such contextual terms may lead to ambiguity, confusion and inconsistency which may undermine the validity of the assessment of value and confidence in the valuation process.

Three principal approaches to valuation are recognised by IVSs, being the *cost approach*, the *income approach* and the *market approach*, based in the economic principles of 'substitution', 'anticipation of benefits' and 'price equilibrium', respectively, so aligning with economic theory. Though each appears deceptively simple, the application of each in practice requires consideration of myriad issues which, if undertaken in a cautious and considered manner, will result in a defensible assessment of value.

The next chapter will describe and analyse those elements of IVSs that are of relevance to the three principal stages of the real property valuation process, being the instruction of the valuer, undertaking the valuation and reporting the valuation.

Chapter 5 will consider IVSs in the context of the valuation of investment property, with particular reference to IAS 40 *Investment Property* and the income approach to valuation, including an examination of IVSC TIP 1 *Discounted Cash Flow*.

Finally, Chapter 6 will focus on IVSs in the context of the valuation of owner occupied property held by operating businesses, with particular reference to IAS 16 *Property, Plant and Equipment* and the cost approach to valuation, including an examination of IVSC TIP 2 *The Cost Approach to Tangible Assets*.

References

Banfield, A. (2014) *A Valuer's Guide to the RICS Red Book 2014*, RICS, London.

International Financial Reporting Council (2012) *A Briefing for Chief Executives, Audit Committees and Boards of Directors*, IFRS Foundation, London.

International Financial Reporting Standards (2013) *International Financial Reporting Standards 2013*, International Accounting Standards Board, London.

International Valuation Standards Council (2013) *International Valuation Standards 2013*, IVSC, London.

Royal Institution of Chartered Surveyors (2013) *RICS Professional Standards, Global and UK 2014*, RICS, London.

4

Valuation Process

4.0 Introduction

In the context of the valuation of real property assets, this book provides an analysis of the International Valuation Standards (IVS), International Accounting Standards (IAS) and International Financial Reporting Standards (IFRS) which, being dynamic, are regularly updated and/or replaced. Accordingly, readers should not rely upon this book as a current statement of an IVS, IAS or IFRS publication and should visit www.ifrs.org and/or www.ivsc.org to find the most recent version.Chapter 1 outlined the emergence of globalisation, the role of IFRS and the evolution of valuation standard setting, the role of IVSC and IVSs and an analysis of *market value*, being the central concept of IVSs, with an overview of other IVSs relevant to the valuation of businesses and business interests, intangible assets and financial instruments.

Chapter 2 sought to develop a conceptual framework for valuation based on economic theory, aligned this framework with finance and capital market theory, examined the definition of the market and distinguished definitions of cost and price from defined concepts of value before reconciling these to the conceptual framework for valuation.

Chapter 3 considered various aspects of valuation within IVSs, discussed the definitions of other relevant contextual terms and identified the principal approaches to valuation within IVSs including a focus on the *market approach* to valuation.

This chapter describes and analyses those elements of IVSs that are of relevance to the three principal stages of the real property valuation process, being instructing the valuer, undertaking the valuation and reporting the valuation.

Chapter 5 will then consider IVSs in the context of the valuation of investment property, with particular reference to IAS 40 *Investment Property* and the income approach to valuation, including an examination of IVSC TIP 1 *Discounted Cash Flow*.

Finally, Chapter 6 will focus on IVSs in the context of the valuation of owner occupied property held by operating businesses, with particular reference to IAS 16 *Property, Plant and Equipment* and the cost approach to valuation, including an examination of IVSC TIP 2 *The Cost Approach to Tangible Assets*.

In many countries around the world, national and local valuation professional bodies adopt IVSs and supplement them with national or local valuation practice guidance which may expand upon IVSs in a national or local context for the benefit of their membership. However, only the Royal Institution of Chartered Surveyors (RICS) produces global valuation practice guidance that adopts and expands upon IVSs but is not country specific, comprising mandatory professional standards and valuation practice statements and non-mandatory practice guidance applications and practice guidance notes for use by members globally – generally referred to as the RICS Red Book Global (RICS 2013). Accordingly, this book refers to the RICS Red Book Global for the purposes of considering how a professional body interprets IVSs for application by its members worldwide but without a country specific application.

This book is based upon International Valuation Standards 2013 (IVSC, 2013a) and International Financial Reporting Standards 2013 (IFRS, 2013). Given their nature, IVSs, IAS's and IFRSs are dynamic, being regularly updated and with the most recently published versions replacing previously published versions. Accordingly, readers should not rely upon this book as a current statement of an IVS, IAS or IFRS publication and should visit www.ifrs.org and/or www.ivsc.org to find the most recent version.

4.1 Preliminary questions

This section seeks to identify preliminary questions to be considered prior to instruction, with the following sections seeking to describe and analyse those elements of IVSs that are of relevance to the three principal stages of the real property valuation process, being instructing the valuer, undertaking the valuation and reporting the valuation, respectively.

Banfield (2014) suggests a fourth or initial stage in the valuation process, being preliminary questions prior to instruction, suggesting the valuer ask the following seven basic questions relevant to compliance with IVSs:

- what is the purpose of the valuation?
- is the request to provide a written valuation?
- is the valuer suitably qualified?
- are there any conflicts of interest?
- are there any specific national or other overriding requirements for the purpose?
- is the valuation one in which third parties or the public have an interest?; and
- is the purpose of the valuation one that falls within an exception under national valuation standards? (Banfield, 2014, pages 11, 12)

While these questions are more in the nature of practice issues which may be addressed by national standards and guidance that differ between countries, three are specifically addressed within IVSs being:

- what is the purpose of the valuation? – considered further in sections 4.2.2.3 and 4.4.2.3, below;
- is the valuer suitably qualified? – considered within the IVS Framework and providing a high standard for qualification, stating there to be 'a fundamental expectation that valuations are prepared by an individual or firm having the appropriate technical skills, experience and knowledge of the subject of the valuation, the market in which it trades and the purpose of the valuation' (IVSC, 2013a, para 4, page 12); and
- are there any conflicts of interest? – considered within the IVS Framework and the IVSC *Code of Ethical Principles for Professional Valuers*, focusing on controls and procedures to achieve objectivity and the maintenance of an environment that promotes transparency and minimises the influence of any subjective factors on the valuation process in order to provide credibility and freedom from bias (IVSC, 2013a, para 2 and 3, page 12).

Further, the IVS Framework states:

> Matters relating to the conduct and ethical behaviour are for Valuation Professional Organisations or other bodies that have a role in regulating or licensing individual valuers. (IVSC, 2013a, para 3, page 12)

By way of example of operation, the RICS Red Book Global includes PS2 *Ethics, competency, objectivity and disclosures* which seeks to address the seven questions above and to articulate the phrase 'appropriate technical skills, experience and knowledge of the subject of the valuation, the market in which it trades and the purpose of the valuation' from the IVS Framework through requirements concerning:

- responsibility for the valuation;
- professional and ethical standards;
- member qualification;
- independence, objectivity and conflict of interest;
- maintaining strict separation between advisers,
- duty of care to third parties;
- terms of engagement;
- disclosures where the public has an interest or upon which third parties may rely; and
- reviewing another valuer's valuation (RICS, 2013, PS2, Implementation, page 17).

Given the fundamental importance of competence, objectivity, disclosure and general ethical conduct to the credibility of the valuation process and the valuation profession, it is strongly recommended that valuers ensure they are fully aware of the requirements of relevant regional and national valuation professional organisations and government regulatory bodies within their jurisdiction.

4.2 Instructing the valuer

The previous section sought to identify preliminary questions to be considered prior to instruction, with this section seeking to describe and analyse those elements of IVSs that are of relevance to the first principal stage of the real property valuation process, being instructing the valuer, with the following sections seeking to describe and analyse the second and third principal stages, being undertaking the valuation and reporting the valuation, respectively.

4.2.1 Transparency

IVS 101 *Scope of Work* addresses the issue of valuer instruction and acknowledges that there are many different types and levels of valuation advice that may be provided and to which IVS 101 applies, including *Valuation Review* where an opinion of value may not be required (IVS 101, para 1, page 27). There are, however, two key caveats being:

- all valuation advice and the work undertaken in its preparation must be appropriate for the intended purpose; and
- that the intended recipient of the valuation advice understands what is to be provided and any limitations on its use before it is finalised and reported. (IVS 101, para 1, page 27)

There is, therefore, a fundamental requirement for transparency. That which is to be provided and that which is not to be provided need to be commonly understood by both the provider and the recipient, with the provider then providing a product that is appropriate for purpose. In practice, this may be achieved by a dialogue between provider and recipient to ensure that a common understanding of the scope of work is achieved.

Having achieved such a common understanding verbally, IVS 101 requires this to be committed to writing by one party and confirmed by the other, including at least 12 nominated issues plus others as may be required for certain asset classes or applications (IVS 101, para 2, page 27). Of the 12 nominated issues, 11 are later required to be addressed in the valuation report, so completing the loop between instruction and reporting and facilitating the fundamental requirement for transparency.

IVS 101 recognises that changes to the scope of work envisaged in the written instructions may either not be capable of determination until the valuation assignment is in progress or may change during the course of the assignment such as due to additional information becoming available or a matter emerging that requires investigation. Accordingly, IVS 101 contemplates the scope of work being either contained in a single document issued at the outset or in a series of documents prepared throughout the course of the assignment, provided all matters are recorded before the assignment is completed and the valuation report issued (IVS 101, para 3, pages 30–31).

4.2.2 Nominated issues to be addressed in written instructions

The 12 nominated issues to be addressed in written instructions effectively comprise a basic due diligence list for the valuation process, building upon those pre-instruction practical issues considered in section 4.1, above, comprising:

- identification and status of valuer;
- identification of the client and any other intended users;
- purpose of the valuation;
- identification of the asset or liability to be valued;

4 Valuation Process

- basis of value;
- valuation date;
- extent of investigation;
- nature and source of the information to be relied upon;
- assumptions and special assumptions;
- restriction on use, distribution or publication;
- confirmation that the valuation will be undertaken in accordance with the IVS; and
- description of report,

each of which will be considered sequentially below. By working through this checklist in the instruction stage, the by whom, for whom, why, what, how, when and with what of the valuation process may be clearly established.

4.2.2.1 Identification and status of valuer

IVS 101 requires that the 'by whom' of the valuation process be stated, with written instructions including a statement confirming:

(i) the identity of the valuer, who may be an individual or firm;

(ii) that the valuer is in a position to provide an objective and unbiased valuation;

(iii) whether the valuer has any material connection or involvement with the subject of the valuation assignment or the party commissioning the assignment; and

(iv) that the valuer is competent to undertake the valuation assignment. If the valuer needs to seek material assistance from others in relation to any aspect of the assignment, the nature of such assistance and the extent of reliance shall be agreed and recorded (IVS 101, para 2(a), page 28).

Effectively, this nominated issue is simply basic good practice requiring the valuer to consciously consider if he is capable of undertaking the assignment independently and solely, or whether there may be issues of conflict of interest or the need for assistance from others.

When stating the person who will undertake the valuation, care is required to ensure that the stated person undertakes a significantly large proportion of the valuation to satisfy the statement, rather than delegating an excessive proportion to an assistant and so invalidating the statement.

The required statement of independence and conflict of interest necessitates a focus on 'material connection or involvement' in the event of prior contact with the property or the client. That which may be considered 'material' has evolved to different degrees in different jurisdictions around the world, with common membership of Rotary (or similar organisation) or an inspection of the property a decade ago on behalf of a potential purchaser being possibly considered 'material' in some parts of the world. Accordingly, therefore, declaration of any perceived conflict of interest may be a safer course than omission. The RICS Red Book Global goes further to require that, where there has not been any previous material involvement, a statement to that effect be made in the valuation report (VPS3, para 7(a)4, page 43).

The required statement of competence makes explicit that which is generally required and enunciated by the practice standards, guidance notes and codes of regional and national valuation professional organisations, with care required in the event of 'material assistance' being required. That which may be material is a particularly vexed issue given that, on the one hand, the valuation is the independent opinion of the valuer while, on the other hand, the formation of such an opinion often requires interaction with a range of others who may each provide information of differing levels of significance. As with the statement of independence or conflict of interest, declaration of any assistance relied upon may be a safer course than omission.

When operationalising the IVSs for application by members, the RICS Red Book Global expands on the requirements of IVS 101 through requiring the valuation to be the responsibility of an individual valuer 'for and on behalf of a firm but not by a firm' (RICS, 2013, para 9a1, page 30), addressing the role of internal and external valuers in the context of independence, objectivity and conflict of interest (RICS, 2013, para 9a2, page 31) and suggesting the valuer confirm competence through having sufficient current local, national and international (as appropriate) knowledge of the particular market and the skills and understanding to undertake the valuation competently. (RICS, 2013, para 9a4, page 31)

4.2.2.2 Identification of the client and any other intended users

IVS 101 requires that the 'for whom' of the valuation process be stated with written instructions including:

- confirmation of those for whom the valuation assignment is being produced; and
- any restriction on those who may rely upon the valuation assignment (IVS 101, para 2(b), page 28).

The confirmation of those for whom the valuation assignment is being produced is stated in the IVSs as being required to determine the form and content of the report in order to ensure that it contains information relevant to their needs. Not only does this address the key caveats referred to in section 4.2.1, above, but it also provides a risk management benefit for

4 Valuation Process

the valuer in excluding those for whom and that for which the valuation is not intended.

Further, as the RICS VPS1 notes, requests for a valuation may be made by the directors of a company while the instructing party will be the company itself which has a separate legal standing to that of the directors (RICS, 2013, para 9b1, page 31). Commonly, as noted in the RICS Red Book Global, a valuation required for loan purposes may be commissioned by the borrower but be for the lender, the effective client (RICS, 2013, para 9b1, page 31).

Specifying the restrictions on those who may rely upon the valuation assignment is particularly important where there is a risk that the valuation report may be provided to a common interest group, such as potential debt providers or potential equity providers. By specifying a restriction, a valuation report prepared for High Street Bank A contemplating secured lending against Property X may not be relied upon by High Street Bank B contemplating secured lending against the same property. Similarly, a valuation report prepared for Investment Bank C contemplating an equity investment in Business Y may not be relied upon by Investment Bank D contemplating an equity investment in the same business.

4.2.2.3 Purpose of the valuation

IVS 101 requires that the 'why?' of the valuation process be clearly stated, being the purpose for which the valuation assignment is being prepared, such as loan security or to support a share issue, with the purpose of the valuation determining the *basis of value* (IVS 101, para 2(c), page 28).

As IVS 101 states:

> It is important that valuation advice is not used out of context or for purposes for which it is not intended. (IVS 101, para 2(c), page 28)

further addressing one of the key caveats referred to in section 4.2.1, above, that all valuation advice and the work undertaken in its preparation must be appropriate for the intended purpose.

Inconsistently, the RICS VPS1 addresses the scenario where a client declines to reveal the purpose of the valuation but the valuer is willing to proceed and requires the omission to be referred to in the valuation report (RICS VPS1, para 9(c)1, page 31). It is challenging to contemplate how a valuer could prepare a valuation without having agreed the purpose of the valuation through written instructions, other than by treating the purpose as an assumption or *special assumption*.

4.2.2.4 Identification of the asset or liability to be valued

IVS 101 requires that the 'what' of the valuation process be stated with written instructions including a clear statement of that which is to be valued, being either an asset or an interest in an asset or a right of use of an asset (IVS 101, para 2(d), page 28).

For example, a self-storage warehouse leased for 99 years and then occupied by users on monthly licenses may be valued, depending on the requirements of the instructing party, as either an asset being the freehold title subject to the 99-year lease, an interest in an asset being the 99-year leasehold interest or a right of use of the asset being the monthly license.

Further, IVS 101 addresses assets used in conjunction with other assets, requiring clarification as to whether those assets:

- are included in the valuation assignment;
- are excluded but assumed to be available; or
- are excluded and assumed not to be available (IVS 101, para 2(d), page 28)

being linked to the issues concerning *aggregation* considered in Chapter 6.

For example, a freestanding multi-storey car park adjacent to a hospital but in separate ownership may not be valued as part of the hospital but, when valued alone, requires an explicit statement as to whether the adjacent hospital is assumed to exist and so provide demand for the car park or is not assumed to exist and so not to provide demand for the car park.

RICS VPS1 usefully adds that, when valuing a real property interest subject to a tenancy, it may be necessary to identify any improvements undertaken by the tenant and to clarify their status at rent review, lease renewal or lease termination (RICS VPS1, para 9(d), page 32).

4.2.2.5 Basis of value

IVS 101 requires that the 'how' of the valuation process be stated with written instructions including the *basis of value* (IVS 101, para 2(e), page 29). As considered in Chapter 3, the *basis of value* may fall into one of three principal categories, being:

- most probable price in hypothetical exchange (such as *market value*);
- the benefits that a particular entity enjoys from ownership (such as *investment value* or *special value*); or
- the price in exchange that may be agreed between two specific parties (such as *fair value*). (IVSC 2013a, para 27, page 17)

This requirement goes to the fundamental issue of transparency and the key caveats of the valuation being appropriate for its intended purpose and the intended recipient of the valuation advice understanding what is to be provided and any limitations on its use.

Consistently, IVS 101 requires that the *basis of value* be appropriate for purpose and the basis either cited or explained, recognising that a *basis of value* other than those referred to above may be adopted (IVS 101, para 2(e), page 29).

Further, the currency in which the valuation will be reported should be agreed and stated in the instructions, being particularly relevant when a portfolio of assets in different countries with different currencies are being valued simultaneously and where minor differences in the exchange rate could result in a significant difference in the valuation.

RICS VPS1 suggests that reproducing the definition of the *basis of value* may be helpful and that, in the absence of regulatory requirement, the selection of the *basis of value* is a matter for the valuer's professional judgement with particular care required where fair value is selected in the light of the specific purpose or context of the valuation (RICS VPS1 para 9(e)1, page 32).

4.2.2.6 Valuation date

IVS 101 requires that the 'when' of the valuation process be stated within written instructions, being that date upon which the valuation applies. This may differ from the date upon which investigations were undertaken or completed or the date on which the valuation report is issued (IVS 101, para 2(f), page 29).

For example, a large portfolio valuation for financial reporting purposes as at 30th June may be undertaken in the months leading up to 30th June with the report finally settled and dated sometime in July. While the valuation date may be 30th June, increasing levels of care are required as the preparation period prior to the valuation date increases with specific attention required to ensure transactions close to 30th June and prevailing market conditions as at 30th June are fully reflected in the valuation.

Explicit statement of the valuation date is required by the RICS VPS1, extending IVS 101 to state that an assumption that the valuation date is the date of the report is unacceptable (RICS 2013, para 9(f)1, page 33).

4.2.2.7 Extent of investigation

IVS 101 requires that the first of the 'with what' of the valuation process be stated with written instructions including a summary of any limitations or restrictions on the inspection, inquiry and analysis for the purposes of the valuation assignment. Depending on the nature of the limitation or restriction, an assumption or a *special assumption* may be required as part of the instructions for the valuation assignment (IVS 101, para 2(g), page 29).

Consistent with the fundamental requirement for transparency, if the ability of the valuer to inspect the entire asset is to be in any way fettered, this should be stated clearly in the instructions such that it can be mirrored in the valuation report. Such limitations or restrictions are not uncommon in high security or high risk buildings, such that the instructions should state that which may be inspected and that which may not.

Similarly, if the valuer anticipates facing any constraint on the open inquiry and analysis of information for and during the valuation assignment, this should be included in the instructions. Such a situation may arise with the provision by a client of commercially sensitive financial information in aggregate form rather than in granular form and this should be acknowledged in the instructions.

Limitations arising from instructions for the provision of automated valuation models, 'drive by', 'desk top' and 'pavement valuations' and issues arising are considered in RICS VPS1 with particular reference to the requirement for the statement of assumptions (RICS 2013, para 9(g)1, page 33).

4.2.2.8 Nature and source of the information to be relied upon

IVS 101 requires that the second of the 'with what' of the valuation process be stated with written instructions including the nature and source of any relevant information that is to be relied upon and the extent of any verification that is to be undertaken during the valuation process (IVS 101, para 2(h), page 29).

A common issue in investment property, for example, concerns the nature and source of lease information to be relied upon by the valuer. This may range from provision of a tenancy schedule summarising the leases or provision of a précis of each of the leases to be adopted by the valuer through to the provision of photocopies of leases or provision of original leases from which the valuer is required to extract the requisite information. These are two very different scenarios in the context of reliance upon and verification of relevant information, so requiring clarity in instructions in order to maintain transparency and common understanding.

While IVSs describe, but do not define, assumptions, RICS VPS1 requires that client provided information which is accepted as reliable by the valuer should be referred to as an *assumption* (RICS, 2013, para 9(h)2, page 34).

4.2.2.9 Assumptions and special assumptions

IVS 101 requires that the third of the 'with what' of the valuation process be stated with written instructions comprising the assumptions and *special assumptions* that are to be made in the conduct and reporting of the valuation assignment (IVS 101, para 2(i), page 29).

As noted in Chapter 3, an assumption may be a matter that is reasonable to accept as fact in the context of the valuation assignment without specific investigation or verification whereas a *special assumption* is that which either assumes facts that differ from actual facts existing at the *valuation date* or that would not be made by a typical market participant in a transaction on the *valuation date* (such as a *special assumption* that a proposed building had actually been completed on the *valuation date*).

Significantly, IVS 101 requires that only assumptions and *special assumptions* that are reasonable and relevant having regard to the purpose for which the valuation assignment is required shall be made and so should be included in the instructions (IVS 101, para 2(i), page 30).

Given the importance of assumptions and the critical importance of *special assumptions* in the valuation process and their possible impact on the valuation outcome, transparency is vital and very careful recording of either or both in the valuation instructions is essential.

4.2.2.10 Restriction on use, distribution or publication

IVS 101 requires that the fourth of the 'with what' of the valuation process be stated with written instructions specifying any restriction on the use of the valuation advice or those relying upon it and recording any matters likely to cause the valuation advice to be qualified (IVS 101, para 2(j), page 30).

Restrictions on the use of or reliance upon the valuation advice echoes IVS 101 paragraph 2(b) in the context of restricting those who may rely upon the valuation advice and IVS 101 paragraph 2(c) in the context of restricting the use of the valuation advice. Accordingly, while those who may and may not rely on the valuation advice and the purpose of the valuation advice may be repeated in the written instructions, restrictions on use may be originally stated.

Consistent with the key caveats referred to in section 4.2.1, above, that all valuation advice and the work undertaken in its preparation must be appropriate for the intended purpose, any permitted use of the valuation advice other than for the intended purpose should be clearly stated in the written instructions or generically restricted through the use of a general exclusion such as 'this valuation advice may not be used for any purpose other than *xyz*'.

The specification of identified matters that may cause the valuation advice to be qualified requires careful consideration within the written instructions. Such qualification may arise from matters addressed elsewhere in the written instructions, such as identification of the asset or liability to be valued as considered in section 4.2.2.4, above, or extent of investigations as considered in section 4.2.2.7, above.

Alternatively, qualification may arise from incomplete information such as an uncompleted report on contamination where the valuer is made aware an issue exists, is provided with some information as to its extent or nature but is not provided with complete information with which to fully quantify the possible impact such that qualification of the valuation advice is required and so should be recognised in the written instructions.

RICS VPS1 extends the IVSs by requiring the written instructions for an 'unusually qualified valuation' (such term not being defined) to state that it is not to be used for any other purpose than that originally agreed with the client (RICS, 2013, para 9(c)2, page 32).

Further, RICS VPS1 notes that limitations are only effective if notified to the client in advance, may have implications for professional indemnity insurance, may be precluded in certain cases (such as where exclusion of third party liability is contrary to law) and may require careful wording if the client is a syndicate lender (RICS, 2013, para 9(j), page 35).

4.2.2.11 Confirmation that the valuation will be undertaken in accordance with the IVS

IVS 101 requires that the fifth of the 'with what' of the valuation process be stated within written instructions comprising a statement of conformance with or departure from IVS (IVS 101, para 2(k), page 30). A similar statement of conformance with professional body standards may be required by members of such bodies, such as a statement of conformance with the RICS Red Book Global. (RICS VPS3, para 7(k)1, page 49). While conformance with IVS is likely to be required in most written instructions, great care is required in the event that the written instructions require departure from IVS for the purpose of the valuation assignment.

Reflecting the unusual nature of a requirement to depart from IVS, written instructions should not only identify the departure but also the justification for the departure, with a departure not being justifiable if it results in a valuation that is misleading. Consistent with the fundamental requirement of IVSs for transparency, a required departure that results in a misleading valuation would be inappropriate as a matter of principle.

Therefore, in the event that a departure is required, its justification should be both logical and compelling in order to permit the provision of valuation advice that affords clarity and is of relevance and use.

4.2.2.12 Description of report

IVS 101 requires that the sixth and final of the 'with what' of the valuation process be stated within written instructions comprising confirmation of the agreed format of the report that is to be provided (IVS 101, para 2(l), page 30).

As noted in section 4.2.2.11, above, unless a departure from IVSs has been required and justified, conformance with IVS 103 *Reporting* (considered further in section 4.4, below) should be required within the written instructions.

Reference is required in the written instructions to any of the report contents specified in IVS 103 *Reporting* that are to be excluded, such exclusion requiring justification consistent with IVS 101 paragraph 2(k) considered in section 4.2.2.11, above, lest such exclusion result in diminished transparency.

Further, RICS VPS1 helpfully cautions against the use of the terms 'certificate of value', 'valuation certificate' and 'statement of value' which have specific meanings in certain jurisdictions (RICS 2013, para 9(l)3, page 36).

4.2.3 IVS 101 in practice

Within the RICS Red Book Global, RICS PS2 sets out the minimum terms of engagement which provide a guide to the drafting of terms to suit a specific case (RICS, 2013, PS2, para 7.3, page 23). Further, RICS VPS1 *Minimum terms of engagement* includes the requirements of IVS 101 and adds the requirement for written instructions to also include:

- the basis upon which the fee will be calculated;
- where the firm is registered for regulation by RICS, reference to the firm's complaints handling procedure; and
- a statement that compliance with RICS standards may be subject to monitoring under RICS conduct and disciplinary regulations (RICS 2013, PS1, para 3, page 29)

each being both useful for practitioners and consistent with the IVSs fundamental requirement of transparency.

Further, RICS PS2 notes that any matters material to the report and arising during the valuation assignment are to be fully brought to the client's attention and appropriately documented, effectively comprising a revision of the original written instructions of which both the valuer and client are aware (RICS, 2013, PS2, para 7.1, page 23).

In the context of the RICS Red Book Global, Banfield (2014, page 9) identifies 'terms of engagement' as the second of four stages to consider when carrying out a valuation before helpfully setting out flowcharts for the valuation instruction process (Banfield, 2014, pages 13–15) with the inclusion of the role of standard terms (where adopted by a valuation firm) and the distinction between instructions for new clients and for existing clients, where previously agreed valuation instructions may be helpful.

4.3 Undertaking the valuation

The previous sections sought to identify preliminary questions to be considered prior to instruction and to describe and analyse those elements of IVSs that are of relevance to the first principal stage of the real property valuation process, being instructing the valuer, with this section seeking to describe and analyse those elements of IVSs that are of relevance to the second principal stage, being undertaking the valuation, and the following, final section seeking to describe and analyse those elements of IVSs that are of relevance to the third principal stage, being reporting the valuation.

IVS 102 addresses the implementation stage of the real property valuation process, being applicable to the undertaking of each valuation or *Valuation Review* (IVS 102, para 1, page 32). As previously noted, IVS 101 addresses the issue of valuer instruction and acknowledges that there are many different types and levels of valuation advice that may be provided and to which the IVSs apply, including *Valuation Review* where an opinion of value may not be required (IVS 101, para 1, page 27).

As an overarching requirement, valuations are required to be undertaken in accordance with the principles set out in the IVS Framework appropriate for the intended purpose for which the valuation is required and within the terms and conditions set out in the instructions (IVS 102, para 1, page 32). Accordingly, a holistic approach is adopted which wraps numerous elements from various IVSs together inextricably, requiring comprehensive and consistent compliance by the valuer unless specifically stated otherwise in the valuation instructions and report.

IVS 102 addresses three components of the implementation stage of the real property valuation process, being:

- the extent and nature of investigation and information required;
- selection of the most appropriate valuation approach or method; and
- keeping records of the work done.

4.3.1 Extent and nature of investigation

Concerning the extent of investigation to be made by the valuer when undertaking the valuation, the IVSs leave considerable scope for and invite professional judgement (IVS 102, para 3, page 32), requiring only that investigations must be 'adequate having regard to the purpose for which the valuation is required and the *basis of value* to be reported' (IVS 102, para 2, page 32). Accordingly, there are no prescriptive requirements for the minimum investigation based on the size or type of the asset being valued, but instead a requirement of adequacy based on the purpose of the valuation and the *basis of value* with an anticipation that 'practical expediency' may provide a limit to investigation which should be recorded in the instructions (IVS 102, para 3, page 32).

The nature of investigation suggested when undertaking a valuation may include the four elements of 'inspection, inquiry, computation and analysis' (though these are neither essential nor exclusive – being 'such as') in order to collate 'sufficient evidence' to 'properly' support the valuation (IVS 102, para 3, page 32). Accordingly, great care is required in the event of the absence of any of 'inspection, inquiry, computation and analysis'.

4 Valuation Process

The IVSs acknowledge that information may be supplied to a valuer when undertaking a valuation and address the credibility and reliability of that information as part of the valuation process. In determining the credibility and reliability of that information supplied, as recorded in the written valuation instructions, there is considerable scope for valuer judgement with the IVSs requiring consideration of:

- the purpose of the valuation, per the written valuation instructions;
- the materiality of the information to the valuation conclusion;
- the expertise of the source of the information in relation to the subject matter;
- the expertise of the valuer in relation to the subject matter;
- whether the source of the information is independent of either the subject or the recipient of the valuation;
- the extent to which the information is in the public domain; and
- the limits on the duty to investigate included in the instructions (IVS 102, para 4 and 5, pages 32 and 33).

Therefore, the valuer has considerable discretion, within the criteria provided, to consider the credibility and reliability of the information provided and to form an opinion as to its usefulness in undertaking the valuation. If the valuer does not consider the information supplied to be credible and/or reliable, it should either not be used or 'the valuer's concerns made known to the commissioning party' (IVS 102, para 4, page 32). It is suggested that, if the valuer has sufficient concern over the credibility and reliability of the information supplied to advise the commissioning party, then specific reference should be made to same in the valuation report and consideration given to classifying the information supplied as a *special assumption*.

Further, the IVSs acknowledge that, if the investigations included in the original instructions may be found to be unlikely to result in a credible valuation or third party information is found to be unavailable or inadequate, then appropriate revision to the instructions shall be made (IVS 102, para 5, page 33).

4.3.2 Selection of approach or method

Concerning selection of the most appropriate valuation approach or method, IVS 102 simply requires 'consideration' to be given to 'the relevant and appropriate valuation approaches', leaving considerable scope for professional judgement in selection by the valuer, provided that which is selected is both 'relevant' and 'appropriate' (IVS 102, para 6, page 33), with appropriateness dependent on consideration of:

- the adopted *basis of value* as determined by the purpose of the valuation; and
- the availability of valuation inputs and data; and
- the approaches and methods used by participants in the relevant market (IVS 102, para 7, page 33)

with the latter appearing to provide the criteria for relevance and supported by both *Commentary* in various IVSs and by TIPs. IVS 102 acknowledges that more than one valuation approach or method may be used, such as in the case where there is insufficient information to produce a reliable conclusion, advocating analysis and reconciliation of the resulting indications of value to reach a valuation conclusion (IVS 102, para 8, page 33).

For transparency, valuers should consider including commentary on the appropriateness and relevance of the valuation approach(es) and method(s) selected in the valuation report.

4.3.3 Record keeping

Concerning keeping records of the work done, subject to jurisdiction specific legal or regulatory requirements, IVS 102 requires a record to be kept for a 'reasonable' period of 'key inputs, all calculations, investigations and analyses relevant to the final conclusion, and a copy of any draft or final report provided to the client' (IVS 102, para 9, pages 33–34).

Accordingly, it may be prudent for valuers to retain a file comprising the IVS required information and such other information as may be relevant in sufficient detail for another valuer to be able to follow the valuation process adopted and for such a period of time as meets both legal and regulatory requirements and professional indemnity insurance requirements.

4.3.4 IVS 102 in practice

At an overarching level, RICS VPS2 extends IVS 102 by:

- making inspections and investigations mandatory 'to the extent necessary to produce a valuation that is professionally adequate for its purpose';
- requiring the valuer to take reasonable steps to verify the information relied on in the preparation of the valuation (RICS VPS2, para 1, page 38);
- requiring an *assumption* to be changed to a *special assumption* if, following inspection, the valuer considers such an *assumption* would not realistically be made by a prospective purchaser and it is still to be adopted (RICS VPS2, para 5, page 38); and

- requiring legible notes of the findings and limits of the inspection and circumstances in which it was carried out be made, for record keeping (RICS VPS2, para 10, page 40); and
- in addition to assessing the credibility and reliability of information supplied, the valuer taking reasonable care to verify both information supplied and obtained, with any limitations on this clearly stated (RICS VPS2, para 9, page 39).

Further, the RICS Red Book Global includes a list of suggested matters which may impact the market's perception of value (including character-istics of the property and of the surrounding area, repair and condition, natural hazards, hazardous materials, etc.) (RICS VPS2, para 7, page 38) and information relevant to valuing an interest in real property (improvements, planning, taxes, outgoings, etc.) (RICS VPS2, para 8, page 38).

Significantly, the RICS Red Book Global addresses revaluations (as dis-tinct from original valuations) without reinspection (therefore assuming an inspection has been previously undertaken) which should only be provided where the valuer is satisfied that there have been no material changes to the physical attributes of the property or the nature of its location since the last inspection (RICS VPS2, para 11, page 40). This may be achieved, in the case of regular update valuations, by advice from the client treated as an assump-tion (RICS VPS2, paras 12, 13, 14). In the event that the valuer considers reinspection appropriate, the valuation may be undertaken without rein-spection provided the client confirms in writing that the valuation is solely for internal management purposes, will not be disclosed to third parties and accepts responsibility for the associated risk (RICS VPS2, para 15, page 40).

In the context of the RICS Red Book Global, Banfield identifies 'valuation preparation' as the third of four stages to consider when carrying out a valu-ation (Banfield, 2014, page 9) before helpfully setting out a flowchart for the valuation preparation process (Banfield, 2014, page 16) with the inclusion of resolution of any reservations in the initial instructions prior to preparation of the valuation.

4.4 Reporting the valuation

The previous sections sought to identify preliminary questions to be consid-ered prior to instruction and to describe and analyse those elements of IVSs that are of relevance to the first and second principal stages of the real prop-erty valuation process, being instructing the valuer and undertaking the valuation, respectively, with this section seeking to describe and analyse those elements of IVSs that are of relevance to the third principal stage, being reporting the valuation.

4.4.1 Transparency

IVS 103 acknowledges the final step in the valuation process to be the communication of the results to the commissioning party and any other end users (IVS 103, para 1, page 35), emphasising the need for transparency in the valuation report:

- through communicating the information necessary for proper understanding of the valuation (IVS 103, para 1, page 35);
- by not being ambiguous or misleading and providing a clear understanding of the valuation or other advice provided (IVS 103, para 1, page 35); and
- by providing comparability, relevance and credibility (IVS 103, para 2, page 35).

Consistent with IVS 101 and IVS 102, IVS 103 also applies to valuations and *Valuation Reviews*. (IVS 103, paras 3 and 5, page 35). Further, IVS 103 applies to valuation reports and reports on the outcome of a *Valuation Review* either printed on paper or transmitted electronically (IVS 103, para 3, page 35).

4.4.2 Nominated issues to be addressed in the valuation report

Of the 12 nominated issues to be addressed within written instructions considered in section 4.2.2, above, 11 are later required to be addressed in the valuation report, so completing the loop between instructing and reporting and facilitating the fundamental requirement for transparency.

The 11 nominated issues to be addressed in the valuation report comprise:

- identification and status of valuer;
- identification of the client and any other intended users;
- purpose of the valuation;
- identification of the asset or liability to be valued;
- basis of value;
- valuation date;
- extent of investigation;
- nature and source of the information to be relied upon;
- assumptions and special assumptions;
- restriction on use, distribution or publication; and
- confirmation that the valuation will be undertaken in accordance with the IVS,

with a description of the report being the omitted twelfth nominated issue addressed in written instructions (IVS 103, para 5, page 35).

IVS 103 specifies the following for inclusion in the valuation report:

- a clear and accurate description of the scope of the assignment, its purpose and intended use and disclosure of any assumptions, *special assumptions*, material uncertainty or limiting conditions that directly affect the valuation, considered in 4.4.2.2 to 4.4.2.4 and 4.4.2.7 to 4.4.2.9, respectively, below (IVS 103, para 2, page 35);
- a recommendation that the instructions (scope of work) be referred to in the report, considered in 4.4.2.2, below (IVS 103, para 5, page 35);
- valuation approach and reasoning, considered in 4.4.2.12, below (IVS 103, para 5(l), page 37);
- amount of the valuation or valuations, considered in 4.4.2.13, below and (IVS 103, para 5(m), page 38);
- date of the valuation report, considered in 4.4.2.14, below (IVS 103, para 5(n), page 38).

The format of the valuation report and any exclusion from the above specified content is required to have been agreed between the valuer and the client in the valuation instructions (IVS 103, para 4, page 35).

Concerning the level of detail within the valuation report, this should be 'appropriate' given the 'purpose of the valuation, the complexity of the asset being valued and the users' requirements' (IVS 103, para 4, page 35). Accordingly, this is a matter for the professional judgement of the valuer and affords the valuer considerable scope in interpretation with the minimum being that which provides a proper or clear understanding of the valuation.

Concerning the disclosure of 'material uncertainty' required by IVS 103 (IVS 103, para 2, page 35), TIP 4 *Valuation Uncertainty* (IVSC, 2013b) provides extensive guidance on the nature and identification of material *valuation uncertainty* for disclosure, with *valuation uncertainty* being defined as:

> The possibility that the estimated value may differ from the price that could be obtained in a transfer of the subject asset or liability taking place on the *valuation date* on the same terms and in the same market. (TIP 4, para 7, page 2)

TIP 4 focuses only on *valuation uncertainty* in the context of *market value* and fair value for IFRS (TIP 4, para 2, page 1), identifying categories of causes (TIP 4, para 17, page 4) with guidance for qualitative and quantitative disclosure (TIP 4, paras 38 and 39, page 8).

4.4.2.1 Identification and status of valuer

Being the 'by whom' section of the report, the valuation should include a statement confirming and detailing each of the matters referred to in the instructions considered in section 4.2.2.1, above together with the signature of the individual or firm responsible for the valuation assignment (IVS 103, para 5(a), page 36).

While IVS 103 does not require inclusion of a statement concerning whether the valuer has a material connection or involvement with the subject of the valuation assignment or the party commissioning the assignment, it may be prudent to include any disclosure provided in the instructions within the valuation report.

4.4.2.2 Identification of the client and any other intended users

Being the 'for whom' section of the report, the valuation should include a statement confirming and detailing each of the matters referred to in the instructions considered in section 4.2.2.2, above, with careful focus, from a risk management viewpoint, on those parties whom it is intended may rely on the valuation which should be consistent with the restrictions on use, distribution or publication referred to in 4.4.2.10, below (IVS 103, para 5(b), page 36).

4.4.2.3 Purpose of the valuation

Being the 'why' section of the report, the valuation should include a statement confirming and detailing each of the matters referred to in the instructions considered in section 4.2.2.3, above, with a clear statement of the purpose of the valuation to ensure that the valuation advice is not used out of context of for a purpose for which it is not intended (IVS 103, para 5(c), page 36).

Concerning the importance of clarity regarding purpose, the RICS Red Book Global goes further with reference to the statement of the purpose of the valuation assignment requiring that 'The report must be unambiguous' (RICS VPS3, para 7(c)1, page 43).

4.4.2.4 Identification of the asset or liability to be valued

Being the 'what' section of the report, the valuation should include a statement confirming and detailing each of the matters referred to in the instructions considered in section 4.2.2.4, above, clearly distinguishing between an asset and an interest in or right of use of that asset (IVS 103, para 5(d), page 36).

Further, where the asset being valued is used in conjunction with other assets, the valuation report should clearly state whether those assets:

- are included in the valuation assignment;
- are excluded but assumed to be available; or
- are excluded and assumed not to be available (IVS 103, para 5(d), page 36).

4.4.2.5 Basis of value

Being the 'how' section of the report, the valuation should include a statement confirming and detailing each of the matters referred to in the instructions considered in section 4.2.2.5, above, including either:

- citation of the source of the definition of any *basis of value* used; or
- an explanation (not simply a statement) of the 'basis' where this is not among the 'common valuation bases defined and discussed in the IVS Framework' (IVS 103, para 5(e), page 36).

However, this is not applicable when reporting a *valuation review* where no opinion of value is provided or no comment required on the basis used (IVS 103, para 5(e), page 36).

4.4.2.6 Valuation date

Being the 'when' section of the report, the valuation should include a statement confirming and detailing each of the matters referred to in the instructions considered in section 4.2.2.6, above, with specific statement, where appropriate, of different dates for the *valuation date*, the date of the report, the date investigations were undertaken and/or the date investigations were completed (IVS 103, para 5(f), pages 36–37).

Again, this is not applicable when reporting a *valuation review* unless the reviewer is required to comment on the *valuation date* used in the valuation under review (IVS 103, para 5(f), page 37).

4.4.2.7 Extent of investigation

Being the first of the 'with what' sections of the report, the valuation should include a statement confirming and detailing each of the matters referred to in the instructions considered in section 4.2.2.7, above, with careful focus on disclosing the extent of and limitations on investigations undertaken as set out in the valuation instructions (IVS 103, para 5(g), page 37).

Having regard to the extent of professional judgement required in the valuation process and permitted within the IVSs, detailed disclosure of the extent of and limitations or restrictions on inspection, inquiry and analysis undertaken and, in particular, any *special assumptions*, is recommended to provide a clear record of what was and what was not considered, so forming a key element in professional practice risk management.

4.4.2.8 Nature and source of the information to be relied upon

Being the second of the 'with what' sections of the report, the valuation should include a statement confirming and detailing each of the matters referred to in the instructions considered in section 4.2.2.8, above, disclosing not only the nature and source of 'any relevant information relied upon' but also the extent of any steps taken to verify that information (IVS 103, para 5(h), page 37).

It may be contended that 'any relevant information relied upon' is significant from the viewpoint of professional practice risk management. While 'any' is potentially very wide, 'relevant' may be more limiting but the requirement for reliance pivotal. When undertaking the valuation of a shopping centre, the valuer may have in mind a wide range of information that provides context (such as economic indicators, major retailer strategies, consumer trends and so forth) and information specific to the property (such as construction, leases, operating costs and so forth) but only a portion of this information may be relevant and only a fraction of the portion may be relied upon and therefore require verification and disclosure – however, such a fraction of the portion must be sufficient to form the basis of a reasoned professional judgement.

While IVS 103 is not prescriptive concerning the level of verification required, the extent of steps taken to verify relevant information relied upon shall be disclosed. It is, therefore, a matter of professional judgement for the valuer as to the extent of verification appropriate and the process by which such verification may be undertaken. While some verification may be cursory and other invasive, for that extent comprising the fraction of the portion of information relied upon it would be prudent, from a risk management viewpoint, for the verification process to be very thorough.

In the event that disclosed information has been provided by either the commissioning party or another party but has not been verified by the valuer, this should be clearly stated in the report with particular reference to any representation from that party (IVS 103, para 5(h), page 37). As suggested in the RICS Red Book Global (RICS VPS1, para 9(h)2, page 34), classification of such information as a stated *assumption* would be prudent and contribute to professional practice risk management.

4.4.2.9 *Assumptions and special assumptions*

Being the third of the 'with what' sections of the report, the valuation should include a statement confirming and detailing each of the matters referred to in the instructions considered in section 4.2.2.9, above, including the clear statement of any assumptions and of any *special assumptions* (IVS 103, para 5(i), page 37) that are reasonable and relevant having regard to the purpose for which the valuation assignment is required.

While an assumption was noted in Chapter 3 to be a matter that is reasonable to accept as fact in the context of the valuation assignment without specific investigation or verification, a *special assumption* is an assumption that either assumes facts that differ from actual facts existing at the *valuation date* or that would not be made by a typical market participant in a transaction on the *valuation date*. It would, therefore, be prudent from a professional practice risk management viewpoint to carefully consider each assumption and reclassify as a *special assumption* in the valuation instructions, prior to valuation reporting, if there is any possibility that the matter thereof may not be reasonable to accept as fact in the context of the valuation assignment without specific investigation or verification.

4.4.2.10 Restriction on use, distribution or publication

Being the fourth of the 'with what' sections of the report, the valuation should include a statement confirming and detailing each of the matters referred to in the instructions considered in section 4.2.2.10, above, including any restriction on the use of the valuation advice or those relying upon it (IVS 103, para 5(j), page 37) and any matters causing the valuation advice to be qualified.

Particular attention is required where issues arise during the valuation process that impact upon the possible use of the valuation advice or those relying upon it. Subsequent unilateral change of restriction on the use of the valuation advice or those relying upon it by the valuer in the valuation report may be inappropriate and it may be preferable to discuss such issues with the commissioning party and amend the valuation instructions as necessary prior to completion of the valuation report.

4.4.2.11 Confirmation that the valuation will be undertaken in accordance with the IVS

Being the fifth of the 'with what' sections of the report, the valuation should include a statement confirming and detailing each of the matters referred to in the instructions considered in section 4.2.2.11, above, including an IVS conformity confirmation statement and the following where the purpose of the valuation assignment required departure from the IVSs:

- identification of such departure; and
- justification for such departure, having regard to departure being unjustified if it results in a valuation that is misleading (IVS 103, para 5(k), page 37).

Given the role of IVSs as standards for valuation that are applicable internationally, any identified departure would be unusual and its justification should be both logical and compelling. Consistent with the IVSs fundamental requirement of transparency, a required departure that results in a misleading valuation would be inappropriate as a matter of principle.

As noted in section 4.4.2, above, the preceding 11 nominated issues to be addressed in the valuation report arise from and are consistent with the valuation instructions, with IVS 103 nominating a further three issues to also be addressed in the valuation report as follows.

4.4.2.12 *Valuation approach and reasoning*

IVS 103 requires that the valuation report 'make reference' to the approach or approaches adopted, the key inputs used and principal reasons for the conclusions reached in order to 'understand the valuation figure in context' (IVS 103, para 5(l), page 37).

Effectively, this provides the valuer with an opportunity to explain how the valuation amount was derived, with the extent of the explanation being a matter of professional judgement provided that it is sufficient to facilitate an understanding of the valuation figure in the context of the given valuation assignment.

Reference to the valuation approach or approaches may range from simply nominating an approach to describing how an approach functions to a comparative discussion where more than one approach is adopted. For the purposes of IVS 103, key inputs may be fewer where a capitalisation of income method has been adopted and may be greater where a discounted cash flow method has been adopted. The number of key inputs for reference and the nature and depth of reference to each should be guided by the requirement to facilitate an understanding of the valuation figure in context.

Concerning the valuation rationale or process by which the outputs of the valuation approach or approaches were converted into a point estimate of value, IVS 103 requires the principal reasons for the conclusions reached to be stated in order to facilitate an understanding of the valuation figure in context. Accordingly, the reasons (plural) provided by the valuer should comprise the key elements in the valuer's thought process expressed with sufficient clarity for the reader of the valuation report to understand the determining issues considered by the valuer and the weight of attention given to each, while having regard to the needs, knowledge and technical familiarity of the intended user.

IVS 103 states that the above does not apply if the valuation instructions specifically record an agreement that a report shall be provided without reasons or other supporting information. IVS 103 further states that, where the report is of the results of a *valuation review*, it shall state the reviewer's conclusions about the work under review, including supporting reasons (IVS 103, para 5(l), page 38).

4.4.2.13 *Amount of the valuation or valuations*

IVS 103 requires that the amount of the valuation or valuations be stated in the valuation report and expressed in the applicable currency, as nominated in the valuation instructions (IVS 103, para 5(m), page 38). In the case of an international multi-asset portfolio valued in local currency and converted to the nominated currency as at the date of valuation, it would be prudent to specify the exchange rates used particularly in periods of high exchange rate volatility or where assets are located in countries with unstable currencies.

4 Valuation Process

However, this requirement does not apply to a *valuation review* if the valuer is not required to provide their own valuation opinion (IVS 103, para 5(m), page 38).

4.4.2.14 Date of the valuation report
Finally, IVS 103 requires the date on which the valuation report is issued to be stated in the report (IVS 103, para 5(n), page 38), noting that this may differ from the valuation date as considered in 4.4.2.6, above.

It is recommended that particular care be taken with reports that are frequently redrafted prior to being finalised, where the date of the initial draft may be a considerable period before the date of the final draft with the latter being the date of the valuation report.

4.4.2.15 Reporting the valuation
Preparation of a valuation report in conformance with IVS 103 is, effectively, an exercise in professional practice risk management. The approach required by IVS 103 requires the valuer to stand back from the valuation process and determine if all the elements in the process fit together logically and rationally.

Ensuring that the valuation undertaken and being reported is consistent with the valuation instructions, ensuring that all information relied upon is compliant with the standards and verified, ensuring that assumptions and *special assumptions* are enunciated and followed and so forth each contribute to high quality professional practice and mitigate risk in professional practice.

In the context of reporting, IVS 103 repeatedly requires clear statements, with clarity of expression in the reporting process reflecting clarity of thought and so being a significant contributor to increased transparency in the valuation process and user confidence therein.

4.4.3 IVS 103 in practice

At an overarching level, the RICS VPS3 extends IVS 103 by:

- requiring the valuer to draw attention to and comment on any issues affecting the degree of certainty or uncertainty of the valuation (RICS VPS3, para 2, page 41);
- requiring the report should be couched in terms that can be read and understood by someone with no prior knowledge of the subject asset (RICS VPS3, para 3, page 41);
- stating that a valuer may provide the client with a draft report in advance of the completion of the final report (RICS VPS3, para 5, page 41), though a faithful file record of any discussions with the client should be made,

particularly if this leads to a change in the valuation, in order to maintain transparency (Banfield, 2014, page 91);

- requiring that, irrespective of the location of the client, valuations are to be made in the currency of the country in which the property is located (RICS VPS3, para 7(d)3, page 44) with conversion to be at the closing 'spot rate' on the valuation date (RICS VPS3, para 7(d)4, page 44);
- requiring the valuer to draw attention to situations where there has been a material change in market conditions or in the circumstances of the property between the valuation date and a later date of report (RICS VPS3, para 7(f)2, page 45 and para 7(m)4, page 50);
- requiring the valuer to record the date and extent of any inspection in the valuation report, including reference to any part of the property which was inaccessible (RICS VPS3, para 7(g)1, page 46);
- requiring the valuer to only use *special assumptions* to reflect issues concerning the certainty of the valuation if they are realistic, relevant and valid in connection with the circumstances of the valuation (RICS VPS3, para 7(i)4, page 47);
- requiring the valuer to state the amount of the valuation or valuations in the main body of the report and in words as well as in figures (RICS VPS3, para 7(m)1, page 50); and
- requiring the valuer to state negative values separately (RICS VPS3, para 7(m)1, page 50), such as may arise for contaminated freehold land where the cost of remediation exceeds the value of the land after remediation (Banfield, 2014, page 90), rather than being offset against positive values.

In the context of the RICS Red Book Global, Banfield identifies 'reporting' as the last of four stages to consider when carrying out a valuation (Banfield, 2014, page 9) before helpfully setting out a flowchart for the valuation reporting process (Banfield 2014, pages 18–19) with the inclusion of suggested information for retention on file to evidence conformance.

4.5 Summary and conclusions

Chapter 1 outlined the emergence of globalisation, the role of IFRS and the evolution of valuation standard setting, the role of IVSC and IVSs and an analysis of *market value*, being the central concept of IVSs, with an overview of other IVSs relevant to the valuation of businesses and business interests, intangible assets and financial instruments.

Chapter 2 developed a conceptual framework for valuation based on economic theory, aligned this framework with finance and capital market theory, examined the definition of the market and distinguished definitions of cost and price from defined concepts of value before reconciling these to the conceptual framework for valuation.

Chapter 3 considered various aspects of valuation within IVSs, discussed the definitions of other relevant contextual terms and identified the principal approaches to valuation within IVS including a focus on the *market approach* to valuation.

This chapter sought to describe and analyse those elements of IVSs that are of relevance to the three principal stages of the real property valuation process, being the instruction of the valuer, undertaking the valuation and reporting the valuation.

IVS 101, IVS 102 and IVS 103 address issues associated with instructing the valuer, undertaking the valuation and valuation reporting, respectively. IVS 101, *Scope of Work*, articulates the requirements for instructing a valuer with 12 key elements premised on two fundamental caveats:

- all valuation advice and the work undertaken in its preparation must be appropriate for the intended purpose; and
- the intended recipient of the valuation advice understands what is to be provided and any limitations on its use before it is finalised and reported.

Accordingly, the valuation process starts from the overarching principle of transparency. That which is to be provided and that which is not to be provided need to be commonly understood by both the provider and the recipient, with the provider then providing a product that is appropriate for purpose. It may be trite to say, but if the valuation instructions are thoughtfully and carefully prepared at the outset, then the contract between client and valuer may be more effective and the valuation assignment may potentially progress much more smoothly.

Significantly, IVS 102, *Implementation*, is the briefest of the three reflecting the limited extent of principles to be expounded and greater role of valuation professional organisations in providing standards and guidance for what is, essentially, the practical component of valuation practice.

IVS 103, *Reporting*, provides the commissioning party and the valuer with a useful risk management process for professional practice. Thoughtfully and carefully preparing a report on the outcome of the valuation assignment requires adoption of and reflection on the *Scope of Work* or instructions and should focus the valuer on any disparities. Further, the use of assumptions and *special assumptions* afford the valuer a significant opportunity for effective risk management. If IVS 103 is followed, the valuation report should have a high level of clarity and provide transparency through the valuation process undertaken back to the original valuation instructions. Should any gaps or inconsistencies be identified, these may be addressed prior to completion of reporting with commensurate reduction in risk exposure for the valuer.

As Banfield notes:

> Although it is often suggested that a client never reads a report and only looks at the valuation figure, it is nonetheless absolutely essential that the report should be clear, unambiguous and comprehensible to someone with no knowledge of the subject. (Banfield, 2014, page 88)

This may be particularly poignant if the person with no knowledge of the subject happens to be the barrister opposing the valuer or the judge in a valuation negligence action.

The essence of IVS 101, IVS 102 and IVS 103 may be summed up as 'say what you are going to do, do it and say what you have done'. By carefully following the IVSs, the *Scope of Work* or instructions will be comprehensive and clear so that the valuer and client understand exactly what is required, the valuation process undertaken will be logical and explicable and the valuation report will be confirmatory and transparent.

Chapter 5 will consider IVSs in the context of the valuation of investment property, with particular reference to IAS 40 *Investment Property* and the income approach to valuation, including an examination of IVSC TIP 1 *Discounted Cash Flow*.

Finally, Chapter 6 will focus on IVSs in the context of the valuation of owner occupied property held by operating businesses, with particular reference to IAS 16 *Property, Plant and Equipment* and the cost approach to valuation, including an examination of IVSC TIP 2 *The Cost Approach to Tangible Assets*.

References

Banfield, A. (2014) *A Valuer's Guide to the RICS Red Book 2014*, RICS, London.

International Financial Reporting Council (2012) *A Briefing for Chief Executives, Audit Committees and Boards of Directors*, IFRS Foundation, London.

International Financial Reporting Standards (2013) *International Financial Reporting Standards 2013*, International Accounting Standards Board, London.

International Valuation Standards Council (2013a) *International Valuation Standards 2013*, IVSC, London.

International Valuation Standards Council (2013b) *TIP 4 – Valuation Uncertainty*, IVSC, London.

Royal Institution of Chartered Surveyors (2013) *RICS Professional Standards, Global and UK 2014*, RICS, London.

5

Valuation of Investment Property

5.0 Introduction

In the context of the valuation of real property assets, this book provides an analysis of the International Valuation Standards (IVS), International Accounting Standards (IAS) and International Financial Reporting Standards (IFRS) which, being dynamic, are regularly updated and/or replaced. Accordingly, readers should not rely upon this book as a current statement of an IVS, IAS or IFRS publication and should visit www.ifrs.org and/or www.ivsc.org to find the most recent version.

Chapter 1 outlined the emergence of globalisation, the role of IFRS and the evolution of valuation standard setting, the role of IVSC and IVSs and an analysis of market value, being the central concept of IVSs, with an overview of other IVSs relevant to the valuation of businesses and business interests, intangible assets and financial instruments.

Chapter 2 sought to develop a conceptual framework for valuation based on economic theory, aligned this framework with finance and capital market theory, examined the definition of the market and distinguished definitions of cost and price from defined concepts of value before reconciling these to the conceptual framework for valuation.

Chapter 3 considered various aspects of valuation within IVSs, discussed the definitions of other relevant contextual terms and identified the principal approaches to valuation within IVSs including a focus on the market approach to valuation.

International Valuation Standards: A Guide to the Valuation of Real Property Assets, First Edition. David Parker.
© 2016 John Wiley & Sons, Ltd. Published 2016 by John Wiley & Sons, Ltd.

Chapter 4 described and analysed those elements of IVSs that are of relevance to the three principal stages of the real property valuation process, being the instruction of the valuer, undertaking the valuation and reporting the valuation.

This Chapter considers IVSs in the context of the valuation of investment property, with particular reference to IAS 40 *Investment Property* and the income approach to valuation, including an examination of IVSC TIP 1 *Discounted Cash Flow*.

Finally, Chapter 6 will focus on IVSs in the context of the valuation of owner occupied property held by operating businesses, with particular reference to IAS 16 Property, Plant and Equipment and the cost approach to valuation, including an examination of IVSC TIP 2 The Cost Approach to Tangible Assets.

In many countries around the world, national and local valuation professional bodies adopt IVSs and supplement them with national or local valuation practice guidance which may expand upon IVSs in a national or local context for the benefit of their membership. However, only the Royal Institution of Chartered Surveyors (RICS) produces global valuation practice guidance that adopts and expands upon IVSs but is not country specific, comprising mandatory professional standards and valuation practice statements and non-mandatory practice guidance applications and practice guidance notes for use by members globally – generally referred to as the RICS Red Book Global (RICS 2013). Accordingly, this book refers to the RICS Red Book Global for the purposes of considering how a professional body interprets IVSs for application by its members worldwide but without a country specific application.

This book is based upon International Valuation Standards 2013 (IVSC, 2013) and International Financial Reporting Standards 2013 (IFRS, 2013). Given their nature, IVSs, IAS's and IFRSs are dynamic, being regularly updated and with the most recently published versions replacing previously published versions. Accordingly, readers should not rely upon this book as a current statement of an IVS, IAS or IFRS publication and should visit www.ifrs.org and/or www.ivsc.org to find the most recent version.

5.1 Valuation of investment property

This chapter focuses on the valuation of investment property, for the purposes of financial reporting or secured lending, with Chapter 6 focusing on the valuation of owner occupied property. It should be noted, however, that these are not mutually exclusive and considerable cross over will be observed between and within each chapter.

For the valuation of investment property, the IVSs of principal relevance are IVS 230 *Real Property Interests* and IVS 220 *Plant and Equipment* with TIP 1 *Discounted Cash Flow* and IVS 233 *Investment Property Under Construction* of particular relevance, each of which are considered further below.

Further, for investment property valuation for the purpose of financial reporting, the IVS of principal relevance is IVS 300 *Valuations for Financial Reporting*, with IAS 40 *Investment Property* and IFRS 13 *Fair Value Measurement* of particular relevance for investment property, each of which are then considered further below.

Concerning valuation for the purpose of secured lending for investment property, the IVS of principal relevance is IVS 310 *Valuations of Real Property Interests for Secured Lending* which is finally considered further below.

Further, IAS 36 *Impairment of Assets*, IFRS 5 *Non-Current Assets Held for Sale and Discontinued Operations* and IAS 17 *Leases* are also of relevance to the valuation of investment property and are also considered below.

Accordingly, the valuation of investment property for the purpose of financial reporting or secured lending requires the valuer to have regard to the interaction between several IVSs, TIP's, IAS's and IFRS's simultaneously with considerable care required to comply with the requirements of each at the same time.

This section seeks to consider IVSs, TIP's, IAS's and IFRS's in the context of the valuation of investment property, with the following sections considering the valuation of investment property in the context of financial reporting and secured lending, respectively.

5.1.1 IVS 230 Real Property Interests

For the valuation of investment property, the IVS of principal relevance is IVS 230 *Real Property Interests*, which comprises two sections, being *Requirements* (focusing on valuation instruction, implementation and reporting) and *Commentary* (focusing on issues that may arise in application of the Standard).

Concerning *Requirements*, IVS 230 includes modifications, additional requirements or specific examples of how the General Standards apply for the valuation of *real property* interests.

With application to investment property, IVS 230 expands IVS 101 with regard to valuation instructions requiring the inclusion of:

- a description of the *real property* interest to be valued;
- identification of any superior or subordinate interests that affect the interest to be valued (IVS 230, para 2, page 61);

- regard to the extent of investigation and the nature and source of the information to be relied upon concerning:
  - verification of the *real property* interest and any relevant related interests;
  - the extent of any inspection;
  - responsibility for information on the site area and any building floor areas;
  - responsibility for confirming the specification and condition of any building;
  - the nature, specification and adequacy of services;
  - the existence of any information on ground and foundation conditions;
  - responsibility for the identification of actual or potential environmental risks;
  - legal permissions or restrictions on the use of the property and any buildings (IVS 230, para 3, pages 61–62); and
- agreed and confirmed *special assumptions*, including:
  - that a defined physical change has occurred (such as a proposed building to be valued as if complete at the *valuation date*); and
  - that there had been a change in the status of the property (such as a vacant building had been leased or a leased building had become vacant at the *valuation date*) (IVS 230, para 4, page 62),

which, consistent with the requirements of IVS 101 and IVS 103 considered in Chapter 4, shall be referred to in the valuation report (IVS 230, para 6, page 62).

Concerning *Commentary*, in the context of investment property, IVS 230 addresses the following:

- types of property interests, such as superior and subordinate interests, rights of use and joint and several rights (IVS 230, para C1–3, page 63), as considered in section 3.2.2 of Chapter 3;
- the hierarchy of interests, including absolute interest, head lease interest, sub-lease interest and so forth (IVS 230, para C4–7, pages 63–64), as considered in section 3.2.2 of Chapter 3;
- rent (IVS 230, para C8–11, pages 64–65), as considered in section 6.1.1 of Chapter 6; and
- valuation approaches including the *market approach, income approach* and *cost approach* (IVS 230, para C12–24, pages 65–68), as considered in section 3.3 of Chapter 3.

5.1.1.1 IVS 230 Real Property Interests *in practice*

For the valuer in practice, the valuation of investment property may provide many challenges. At the outset, IVS 230 provides a framework for application to the property to be valued, allowing the valuer to develop a clear and logical approach to the valuation.

Unlike owner occupied property, where the challenges may concern issues of title and physical extent, for investment property the challenges are more likely to concern issues of establishing security and regularity of income and clarity of expenses.

While regularity of income may be established through a perusal of all relevant leases, licenses and other contractual documents, the valuer will need to establish with the client in the valuation instructions whether original documents, copies or summaries are to be provided for perusal together with any necessary assumptions arising (such as to the authenticity of copies) and reflect same in the valuation report.

Though security of income is a fundamental consideration in the valuation process, it may be challenging for the valuer to establish the security of the income stream for an investment property being valued. While government leases may generally be considered secure, leases to corporates are dependent on the ongoing viability of the corporate's business (with numerous unexpected collapses such as Enron and Arthur Andersen highlighting uncertainty in this regard) and leases to individuals are dependent on the financial capacity of the individual, each of which are difficult for the valuer to assess. Credit checks and bank references may assist, but use of appropriate disclaimers in the valuation report may be prudent for effective risk management.

Similarly, establishing clarity of expenses may be challenging with a review of past invoices being usual practice though it may be advisable to agree an assumption with the client in the valuation instructions that those past invoices provided are both legitimate and complete. Cross-checking outgoings for the subject property against other similar property recently valued may highlight any anomalies for further investigation.

5.1.2 *IVS 220* Plant and Equipment

While most items of plant and equipment may usually be attached to the building for the purposes of investment property valuation, occasions may arise where plant and equipment require separate valuation with the IVS of principal relevance being IVS 220 *Plant and Equipment*, comprising two sections, being *Requirements* (focusing on valuation instruction, implementation and reporting) and *Commentary* (focusing on issues that may arise in application of the Standard).

While the concepts and provisions of IVS 220 *Plant and Equipment* will be considered in detail in section 6.1.2 of Chapter 6 in the context of owner occupied property, the *Requirements* (focusing on valuation instruction, implementation and reporting) are commonly applicable to investment property with IVS 220 addressing:

- identification of the plant and equipment asset(s) for valuation with appropriate assumption*s* or *special assumptions* to address attachment to the building;
- assumptions in the valuation instructions to address the state and circumstances in which the plant and equipment asset(s) are valued, such as in whole, in place and as part of the business, considered as a going concern or other scenario;
- the care required not to omit or double count items when the *real property* interest is valued separately to the plant and equipment at the same location at the same time; and
- consistent with the requirements of IVS 103, the valuation report shall include appropriate references to any matters included in the valuation instructions, such as those as considered above.

Concerning *Commentary* (focusing on issues that may arise in application of the Standard), IVS 220 defines plant and equipment and addresses intangible assets, financing arrangements, forced sale and valuation approaches as will be considered in detail in section 6.1.2 of Chapter 6.

5.1.2.1 IVS 220 Plant and Equipment *in practice*

Of relevance for investment property, IVS 220 *Plant and Equipment* defines plant and equipment as:

> ... tangible assets that are held by an entity for use in the production or supply of goods or services, for rental by others or for administrative purposes and that are expected to be used over a period of time

but specifically excluding real property, stock and inventory and personal property such as artwork, jewellery and collectibles (IVS 220, para C1, page 58) and intangible assets (IVS 220, para C3, page 59).

In the context of investment property generally, IVS 220 notes that plant and equipment connected with the supply or provision of services to a building (such as plant with the primary function of supplying electricity, gas, heating, cooling or ventilation and equipment such as elevators) are often integrated within the building and once installed are not separable from it, with such items normally forming part of the *real property* interest and valued as such. If the purpose of the valuation requires plant and equipment to be valued separately, the valuation instructions should include a statement to the effect that such items would normally be included in the *real property* interest and may not be separately realisable.

This approach is consistent with IAS 40 which requires an entity measuring fair value in accordance with IFRS 13 to ensure that fair value reflects, among other things, rental income from current leases and other assumptions that market participants would use when pricing investment property under current market conditions (IAS 40, para 40, page A1151), including (rather than separately recognising) equipment such as lifts or air-conditioning which are an integral part of the building (IAS 40, para 50(a), page A1152).

Therefore, for example, when valuing a property investment such as a major shopping centre, the escalators, lifts, air-conditioning, electricity and water reticulation and so forth would generally be considered part of the *real property* interest (though some jurisdictions may permit separation for tax allowance purposes) whereas the customer courtesy buggies or shopper mini-buses may be valued separately for the purposes of financial statements.

5.1.3 *TIP 1* Discounted Cash Flow

As considered in section 3.3 of Chapter 3, IVSs recognise three 'main approaches' to valuation, being the *cost approach*, *income approach* and *market approach*, allowing the user to adopt an alternative approach, if necessary, though the rationale for doing so should be both robust and clearly explained in the valuation report. The valuation of investment property may be generally likely to require the adoption of the *income approach* for which TIP 1 *Discounted Cash Flow* is of particular relevance.

In the context of investment property valuation, the *cost approach* is unlikely to be adopted and is considered in greater detail in the context of owner occupied property valuation in section 6.1.3 of Chapter 6. Similarly, the *market approach* may be adopted for the valuation of smaller investment properties, assuming the existence of identical or similar assets for which price information is available as considered in section 3.3.3 of Chapter 3, but is unlikely to be adopted for the valuation of larger investment properties.

Investment property is generally likely to be valued using an *income approach* with IVSs recognising the following:

- income capitalisation, where an all risks or overall capitalisation rate is applied to a representative single period income, as considered in section 3.3.2.1 of Chapter 3;
- discounted cash flow, where a discount rate is applied to a series of cash flows for future periods to discount them to a present value, as considered in section 3.3.2.2 of Chapter 3; and
- various option pricing models, as considered in section 3.3.2.3 of Chapter 3.

In the context of investment property valuation, the income capitalisation method and the discounted cash flow method are considered further, below.

5.1.3.1 Income capitalisation approach

Section 3.3.2.1 of Chapter 3 considered the 'quick and simple' income capitalisation approach which was used almost exclusively in decades past for the valuation of investment property for financial statements and is still used today, though usually in association with the discounted cash flow approach reflecting the greater complexity of larger investment properties (such as super-regional shopping centres and super-prime office towers) and the challenges of forecasting variable cash flows into the future.

With the income capitalisation approach being:

> where an all-risks or overall capitalisation rate is applied to a representative single period income (IVSC 2013, para 60, page 24)

the two key variables within the capitalisation approach are the multiplier or capitalisation rate (known as 'all risks' in the UK and 'overall' in the US) and a 'representative single period income', each of which require assessment by the valuer.

Assessment of a 'representative single period income' requires the valuer to determine the hypothetical current market level of gross income, outgoings or expenses and net income with regard to transactions of comparable property in the relevant market and then apply a series of heuristics, including:

- assuming that the single period income will comprise the constant income;
- assuming that the single period income will comprise the income in perpetuity;
- assuming that the useful life of the property will be in perpetuity;
- making manually calculated income allowances for currently vacant space and/or space occupied at less than current market income levels;
- making percentage or similar adjustments for possible future vacancy and possible future incentives; and
- linking future tenant retention and leasing strategies to an assessment of possible capital costs for deduction

and so forth, each of which may have no firm grounding in transactions of comparable property in the relevant market but accumulate to comprise one of two key multipliers in the *income approach*. Accordingly, a small variation in any or all of the market derived and heuristic inputs may result in a significant variation in the assessment of the 'representative single period income' and so in the assessment of value.

In practice, such risks and uncertainties may be alleged to have been considered and recognised in the assessment of the multiplier for the 'representative single period income' or capitalisation rate. The valuer is required to determine the capitalisation rate with regard to transactions of comparable property in the relevant market (being 'derived from observations of the returns implicit in the price paid for *real property* interests traded in the market between market participants' (IVS 230, para C19, page 67)), deducing the capitalisation rates exhibited by such transactions and then applying professional judgement to reflect differences between such transactions and the subject property in order to assess an applicable capitalisation rate:

> ... based on the time cost of money and the risks and rewards attaching to the income stream in question (IVS 230, para C18, page 66)

Reflecting the significant role of professional judgement in the assessment of the capitalisation rate, two equally experienced valuers may assess two different capitalisation rates for the same property. While neither are necessarily wrong, even a small variation in capitalisation rate may result in a significant variation in the assessment of value, potentially compounded by the potential for variation in the 'representative single period income'.

Therefore, with the assessment of 'representative single period income' dependent on heuristics and the assessment of the capitalisation rate dependent on judgement, the reliability of the income capitalisation approach is inverse to the complexity of the investment property being valued and/or the stability of the market within which it is situated. As IVS 230 cautions, the income capitalisation approach:

> ... cannot be reliably used where the income is expected to change in future periods to an extent greater than that generally expected in the market or where a more sophisticated analysis of risk is required (IVS 230, para C17, page 66)

which potentially limits its future utility in an investment world of increasing complexity, objectivity and transparency.

Effectively, therefore, the income capitalisation approach is best suited to simpler, smaller, stable properties in stable markets, with complex, larger, less stable properties in less stable markets better suited to valuation by the discounted cash flow approach.

5.1.3.2 Discounted cash flow approach

Section 3.3.2.2 of Chapter 3 considered the discounted cash flow approach which, while used almost exclusively by the property funds management industry for the last three decades, has only slowly increased in use by the valuation profession over the last two decades for the valuation of complex, larger investment properties where forecasting variable cash flows into the future is challenging.

With the discounted cash flow approach being:

> where a discount rate is applied to a series of cash flows for future periods to discount them to a present value (IVSC, 2013, para 60, page 24)

the two key variables within the discounted cash flow approach are the discount rate and the future cash flows, each of which require assessment by the valuer.

The discounted cash flow approach is specifically addressed by IVSC in TIP 1 *Discounted Cash Flow* and by IFRS in IFRS 13 *Fair Value Measurement*, each of which are considered further, below.

5.1.3.3 *TIP 1* Discounted Cash Flow

The principal objective of a TIP is to reduce diversity of practice by identifying commonly accepted processes and procedures and discussing their use, being designed to be of assistance to professional valuers through the provision of information (TIP 1, page iii). While not intended to be mandatory and leaving the responsibility for the choice of appropriate valuation methods with the valuer (TIP 1, page iii), adherence to a TIP may be likely to be persuasive in the event of a dispute over or challenge to a valuation.

TIP 1 addresses the valuation of business interests and real property interests with illustrative examples (for real property valuation at TIP 1, pages 15–17), acknowledging that the discounted cash flow approach may be applied to a wide range of different assets for a range of differing bases of value including the assessment of the market value of investment property for financial reporting purposes (TIP 1, para 1 and 2, page 1; para 31, page 11).

Concerning inputs to the discounted cash flow approach, TIP 1 advocates the use of market derived data but, where insufficient:

> the inputs should reflect the thought processes, expectations, and perceptions of investors and other market participants as best as they can be understood (TIP 1, para 32, page 11)

with the test of reliability, significantly, being that:

> As a technique, the DCF method should not be judged on the basis of whether expected future income is proven to be correct or not after the event but rather on the degree of market support for the expectation at the valuation date. (TIP 1, para 32, page 11)

Concerning inputs, TIP 1 suggests that:

- if owner or prospective owner provided cash flows are to be used in estimating market value, these should be tested against market evidence and expectation (TIP 1, para 33, page 11);
- sufficient research should be undertaken to ensure that cash flow projections or expectations and the underlying assumptions for the discounted cash flow are appropriate, likely and reasonable for the subject market – being, significantly, a three-part, cumulative test (TIP 1, para 34, page 11);
- cash flows and discount rates should be internally consistent with the latter selected to consistently reflect cash flows that are either fixed or variable, before or after tax, before or after debt costs, real or nominal and so forth (TIP 1, para 37, page 12);
- the valuation report should identify the:
  - o assumptions made;
  - o valuation approach;
  - o key inputs used;
  - o principal reasons for the conclusion reached (TIP 1, para 41, page 12);
  - o nature and source of the information relied upon to construct the cash flows;
  - o explicit forecast period including the commencement date of the cash flow and the number, frequency and term of the periods employed;
  - o components of cash inflows and cash outflows grouped by category and the rationale behind their selection;
  - o derivation of, or rationale for, the discount rate;
  - o basis of the terminal value calculation (TIP 1, para 42, page 13);
  - o possible impact of changes in assumptions made about key inputs on the valuation result, with a sensitivity analysis (or similar) and commentary (TIP 1, para 43, page 13); and
  - o reconciliation between the result obtained using discounted cash flow and the result obtained using other valuation methods or a clear rationale for preferring one or other of the methods (TIP 1, para 44, page 13).

As referred to above, the two key variables requiring assessment by the valuer within the discounted cash flow approach are the future cash flows and the discount rate, each of which are considered further, below.

5.1.3.3.1 Future cash flows

TIP 1 notes that the key inputs required for the DCF model comprise an explicit period over which the cash flows will be forecast, the cash flow forecasts for that period, the terminal value of the asset and the appropriate discount rate (TIP 1, para 6, page 5).

Concerning the explicit forecast period, TIP 1 notes this is normally determined by one or more of the following:

- where cash flows are likely to fluctuate, the length of time for which changes in cash flows can be reasonably predicted; and/or
- the length of time to allow the asset to achieve a stabilised level of earnings; and/or
- the life of the asset; and/or
- the intended holding period of the asset; and/or (TIP 1, para 7, page 5);
- the incidence of scheduled future events such as lease expiries or rent reviews (TIP 1, para 9, page 6),

with selection dependent on the purpose of the valuation, the nature of the asset, the information available and the required *bases of value* (TIP 1, para 8, page 5). Reflecting such issues, the explicit forecast period adopted in the discounted cash flow approach for investment property in practice tends to be for the remaining lease period or for a fixed period such as 5, 10, 15 or 20 years.

Concerning cash flow forecasts for the explicit forecast period, TIP 1 notes that these are constructed with prospective financial information (PFI) for projected income (inflows) and expenditure (outflows) being either contracted or most likely (including probability weighted cash flows), with the periodic intervals (monthly, quarterly, annual and so forth) determined by the pattern of the cash flows, the data available and the length of the forecast period, for which the selection of the discount rate must be consistent (TIP 1, para 9 and 10, page 6). The assumptions underlying the cash flow forecast for assessments of market value should be appropriate and reflect those that would be anticipated by market participants (TIP 1, para 11, page 6).

Concerning the terminal value of the asset, TIP 1 requires regard to the potential for future growth of the asset beyond the explicit forecast period being, for the assessment of market value of real property, the market value of the asset at the end of the explicit forecast period which may be assessed by the income capitalisation approach based on the estimated net rent receivable in the year following the end of the explicit forecast period (TIP 1, para 15–17, page 7). TIP 1 acknowledges that, when the cash flow period is short, the discounted terminal value becomes a more significant portion of the present value such that particular care is required in the assumptions underlying the assessment of terminal value and assurance that there are no probable changes that may be better reflected by an extended forecast period (TIP 1, para 21, page 8).

5.1.3.3.2 Discount rate
In addition to an explicit period over which the cash flows will be forecast, the cash flow forecasts for that period and the terminal value of the asset, TIP 1 also notes that a key input required for the discounted cash flow model comprises the appropriate discount rate (TIP 1, para 6, page 5).

TIP 1 advocates that the discount rate should reflect not only the time value of money but also the risks associated with the future operations of the asset (TIP 1, para 22, page 8), being dependent on the basis of value required, the type of asset or the cash flows utilised (TIP 1, para 23, page 8). Where the valuation is to estimate *market value*, the discount rate should reflect the market participant's views of risk (TIP 1, para 23, page 8) and the nature of and risks embedded in forecasted cash flows, being commensurate with the risk inherent in the expected cash flows (TIP 1, para 24, page 8).

The discount rate may be determined from either:

- analysis of transactions in active markets or survey data allowing assessment of that discount rate which a market participant would require after taking into account such factors as:
  - o the quality of the building;
  - o the quality of the lessee(s); and
  - o the length and other terms of the lease(s); or (TIP 1, para 28, page 10)
- an estimate using a 'build-up' method, comprising the sum of an appropriate risk free rate (usually a long dated government bond rate) and an appropriate risk premium to reflect market risks (being risks associated with the real property market) and asset specific risks (such as the quality of the building, location, tenant, lease and so forth) (TIP 1, para 29, page 1) which, while a deceptively simple proposition, is exceptionally difficult to calculate in practice.

The discounted cash flow model may also be used to calculate the internal rate of return of an investment property, being that discount rate at which the net present value of all the cash flows including the acquisition cost equals zero (TIP 1, para 30, page 10) being more commonly used in an estimate of *investment value* than in an estimate of *market value*.

5.1.3.4 *IFRS 13* Fair Value Measurement

IFRS 13 addresses the use of present value techniques to measure fair value (as defined by IFRS), also focusing on the estimated cash flow and the discount rate. The use of a single specific present value technique is not prescribed with the technique used to measure fair value being dependent on facts and circumstances specific to the asset being measured (such as whether prices for comparable assets can be observed in the market) and the availability of sufficient data (IFRS 13, Appendix B, para B12, page A517).

Concerning an estimate of future cash flows for the asset being valued, IFRS 13 focuses on the perspective of market participants at the measurement date, seeking to capture expectations about possible variations in the amount and timing of cash flows representing the inherent uncertainty in the cash flows (IFRS 13, Appendix B, para B13, page A517).

Concerning the discount rate, IFRS 13 focuses on:

- the time value of money being represented by the rate on risk free monetary assets that have a maturity date or duration that coincides with the period covered by the cash flow, with neither uncertainty in timing nor risk of default to the holder and so being a relevant risk free rate; and
- the price for bearing the uncertainty inherent in the cash flow, being the relevant risk premium; and (IFRS 13, Appendix B, para B15–16, page A518)
- other factors that market participants would take into account in the circumstances (IFRS 13, Appendix B, para B13, page A517).

Concerning the discounted cash flow overall, IFRS 13 focuses on:

- cash flows and discount rates that reflect the assumptions that market participants would use when pricing the asset;
- cash flows and discount rates that take into account only the factors attributable to the asset being measured;
- avoiding double counting or omitting risk by adopting discount rates reflecting assumptions that are consistent with those inherent in the cash flows;
- assumptions about cash flows and discount rates being internally consistent, such as nominal cash flows being discounted at nominal discount rates and real cash flows being discounted at real discount rates; and
- discount rates being consistent with the underlying economic factors of the currency in which the cash flows are denominated (IFRS 13, Appendix B, para B14, page A518).

IFRS 13 considers two alternative present value techniques, being:

- adopt the contractual, promised or most likely cash flow and use a risk adjusted discount rate derived from observed rates of return for comparable assets that are traded in the market (the 'discount rate adjustment technique') (IFRS 13, Appendix B, para B17(a), B18, page A519), which is generally consistent with TIP 1;
- 'the expected present value technique' comprising:
  - o 'Method 1' using risk adjusted expected cash flows (defined as the probability-weighted average of possible future cash flows) (IFRS 13, Appendix A, page A511) and a risk free rate; and/or (IFRS 13, Appendix B, para B17(b) and B23–B25, pages A519–A521)
  - o 'Method 2' using expected cash flows that are not risk adjusted and a discount rate adjusted to include the risk premium that market participants require (IFRS 13, Appendix B, para B17(c) and B26-B30, pages A519 and A521–A522).

In the context of the 'discount rate adjustment technique', in the absence of a single comparable asset (being an asset with a similar nature of cash flows), IFRS 13 provides that the discount rate may be derived using data from several comparable assets in conjunction with the risk free yield curve, referred to as a 'build-up' approach with an example provided (IFRS 13, Appendix B, para B19–B22, pages A519–520). However, it should be noted that this differs from the 'build-up' approach described in TIP 1 such that, in the absence of sufficient comparable sales data, it would be prudent to refer in the valuation report to which 'build-up' approach was used to derive the discount rate adopted.

Accordingly, the 'discount rate adjustment technique' is generally consistent between TIP 1 and IFRS 13 with both advocating a clear focus on risk and uncertainty in the estimated cash flow, the discount rate and the interaction between each.

5.1.3.5 Summary – Valuation of investment property in IVSs

For the valuation of investment property, the IVS of principal relevance is IVS 230 *Real Property Interests* which comprises *Requirements* to be followed in valuation instructions, implementation and reporting and *Commentary* which includes issues of relevance in application.

While most items of plant and equipment may usually be attached to the building for the purposes of investment property valuation, IVS 220 *Plant and Equipment* is of principal relevance for the valuation of unattached plant and equipment with *Requirements* to be followed in valuation instructions, implementation and reporting and *Commentary* which includes issues of relevance in application.

As the valuation of investment property may generally be likely to require the adoption of the *income approach*, TIP 1 *Discounted Cash Flow* is of particular relevance with the focus on future cash flows and the discount rate seeking to address key risk management issues in the valuation of investment property.

However, the valuation of investment property is not only influenced by IVS 230, IVS 220 and TIP 1 but also by the provisions of IFRS, in those jurisdictions where such provisions apply for the purposes of financial reporting, which are considered in the following section.

5.1.4 Investment property in IFRS

Sections 5.1.1, 5.1.2 and 5.1.3, previously, considered those IVSs of principal relevance for the valuation of investment property, being IVS 230 *Real Property Interests* and IVS 220 *Plant and Equipment*, together with TIP 1 *Discounted Cash Flow*.

This section considers those IAS's and IFRS's of principal relevance for the valuation of investment property for financial reporting purposes where the reporting entity is using IFRS, being IAS 40 *Investment Property*, IAS 36 *Impairment of Assets*, IFRS 5 *Non-Current Assets Held for Sale and Discontinued Operations* and IAS 17 *Leases* in the context of investment property.

5.1.4.1 IAS 40 Investment Property

Reflecting the importance of the appropriate measurement of investment property in financial statements, accounting standards have recognised issues associated with investment property for around 30 years culminating in IAS 40 *Investment Property* which was originally adopted in 2001 (IAS 40, page A1139).

5.1.4.1.1 What is investment property?

Investment property is treated as a separate class of asset under IFRS's, being subject to specific accounting requirements under IAS 40.

IAS 40 defines investment property as:

> **Investment property** – property that is land or a building, or part of a building, or both, held by the owner to earn rentals or for capital appreciation, or both, rather than for:
>
> (a) use in the production or supply of goods or services or for administrative purposes, or
> (b) sale in the ordinary course of business (IAS 40, para 5, page A1146)

Accordingly, as land and/or a building or part of a building that is held to earn rentals and/or provide capital growth, the majority of office, retail and industrial investment property held by real estate investment trusts, property companies, superannuation funds and so forth around the world may be likely to fall within the definition of investment property for the purposes of financial reporting.

However, care is required where an entity provides ancillary services to the occupants of a property that it holds. If such services are insignificant to the arrangement as a whole, such as an owner provided security service in a multi-storey office tower, the property may be classified as an investment property (IAS 40, para 11, page A1147).

Where the situation is less clear, however, care in classification may be required when the level of services becomes significant such as, for example, in serviced apartment towers where the owner entity may be resident in an apartment in the property and a range of services may be provided to occupiers (having the characteristic of owner occupied property, being property used in the supply of goods and services) but rentals are earned and capital appreciation is anticipated from ownership of the balance of the apartments (having the characteristic of *investment property*). Generally, an entity will develop and disclose criteria for application in judging classification as investment property or owner occupied property (IAS 40, para 14, page A1147) and instructions to the valuer should clearly state the classification for the purposes of IFRS.

Where a property has been classified as investment property or owner occupied property, the bases upon which it may be reclassified are limited to change of use, change of occupation or commencement of development (IAS 40, para 57, pages A1153–A1154) with possible change from the fair value basis of measurement to the cost basis of measurement (IAS 40, para 60 and 61, page A1154).

Significantly, investment property is not:

- property held for sale in the ordinary course of business or property under construction or development for such sale (IAS 40, para 9(a), page A1147); nor
- owner occupied property used in the production or supply of goods or services or for administration (IAS 40, para 9(c), page A1147); nor
- property leased to another party under a finance lease (IAS 40, para 9(e), page A1147); nor
- biological assets related to agricultural activity (IAS 40, para 4(a), page A1145); nor
- mineral rights nor mineral reserves such as oil, natural gas or similar non-regenerative resources (IAS 40, para 4(b), page A1145).

If a property is partially owner occupied and partially an investment property, then each may be accounted for separately if capable of being sold separately or leased out separately under a finance lease. If incapable of separate sale, the property is only capable of classification as an investment property if an insignificant portion is owner occupied (IAS 40, para 10, page A1147).

While freehold investment property is clearly within IAS 40, investment property held under a lease requires careful consideration in the context of IAS 17 *Leases*, considered in section 5.1.4.4, below.

5.1.4.1.2 Investment property as independent assets

IAS 40 recognises that investment properties generate cash flows largely independently of each other and of other assets held by an entity and seeks to ensure financial statements provide existing and potential investors and other stakeholders with relevant information about income and expenses arising from each investment property (IFRS 2012, page 86). Significantly, for the purposes of IFRS, changes in capital value are conceptually viewed as either income (capital value increase) or expense (capital value decrease).

5.1.4.1.3 Investment property recognition in financial statements

IAS 40 requires that investment property be initially measured at cost, including related transaction costs provided they are directly attributable expenditure, in financial statements (IFRS 2012, page 86; IAS 40, para 20, page A1148). For the purposes of real estate investment trusts, property companies, superannuation funds and so forth who acquire an investment property, initial measurement at cost may include the acquisition price, stamp duty, registration fees, legal fees, consultants fees and so forth which may be likely to result in a cumulative cost that exceeds the value of the property acquired at the time of acquisition.

IFRS 13 addresses the acquisition of an asset in an exchange transaction where cost may or may not equal fair value (as defined by IFRS), requiring regard to factors specific to the transaction and to the asset in determination (IFRS 13, paras 57-60, page A500) such as related parties, duress or forced sale or the transaction market differing from the most advantageous market (IFRS 13, Appendix B, para B4, pages A515–516).

Subsequent to initial recognition, an entity must choose to adopt either the fair value model or the cost model for all investment properties (IFRS 2012, page 86). IAS 40 requires all entities to measure the fair value of investment property, for the purpose of either measurement (if the entity uses the fair value model) or disclosure (if it uses the cost model). An entity is encouraged, but not required, to measure the fair value of investment property on the basis of a valuation by an independent valuer who holds a recognised and relevant professional qualification and has recent experience in the location and category of the investment property being valued (IAS 40, para 32, page A1150).

In terms of geographic and sectoral experience, the requirements of IAS 40 mirror those of the IVS Framework and an entity is required to disclose in its financial statements the extent to which the fair value of investment property is based on independent valuation (IAS 40, para 75(e), page A1157).

The concept, definition and application of fair value is addressed in IFRS 13, being generally consistent with IVSs *market value* but differing significantly from the concept, definition and application of fair value in IVSs, as considered in section 5.2.2.2.

In the unlikely event that a real estate investment trust, property company, superannuation fund and so forth adopted the cost model, IAS 40 still requires the fair value of each property to be estimated and disclosed (IFRS 2012, p86). However, the IASB clearly anticipate fair value to be adopted for investment property:

> ... a voluntary change in accounting policy shall be made only if the change results in the financial statements providing reliable and more relevant information... It is highly unlikely that a change from the fair value model to the cost model will result in a more relevant presentation. (IAS 40, para 31, page A1150)

Whichever model is adopted, IAS 40 requires fair value to be measured or remeasured at the end of each reporting period in accordance with IFRS 13 *Fair Value Measurement* (see section 5.2.2, below) in order to reflect market conditions at the end of the reporting period. Changes in fair value are recognised in profit or loss in the period in which the change in fair value occurs (IAS 40, para 35, page A1151). Consistently, IAS 40 also requires that gains and losses on disposal of investment property be recognised in profit or loss (IFRS, 2012, page 86; IAS 40, para 69, page A1156).

This approach to recognition of fair value changes in financial statements has commonly led to real estate investment trusts, property companies, superannuation funds and so forth reporting two profit figures, the first being that profit figure in compliance with the requirements of IFRS and recognising fair value changes through profit/loss and the second being an 'underlying', 'operational' or similarly termed profit figure excluding changes in fair value, which is generally contended to provide a 'true' picture of the profitability or otherwise of the real estate investment trust, property company, superannuation fund and so forth.

5.1.4.2 *IAS 36* Impairment of Assets

IAS 36 *Impairment of Assets* is not applicable to *investment property* measured using the fair value model in IAS 40. Even where the cost model is adopted, the requirement to estimate and disclose fair value at the end of the reporting period should, in most circumstances, provide an indication of any impairment. Because of its limited application to *investment property*, IAS 36 is not considered in any detail in this chapter, but is discussed in Chapter 6.

5.1.4.3 *IFRS 5* Non-Current Assets Held for Sale and Discontinued Operations

IFRS 5 *Non-Current Assets Held for Sale and Discontinued Operations* may be more applicable to owner occupied property than to *investment property*, particularly where a valuer's assessment may soon be tested by a sale in the market.

5.1.4.4 *IAS 17* Leases

Most of the provisions of IAS 17 *Leases* have no relevance to *investment property*. However, the exception is where *investment property* is held by the lessor on terms that indicate that it might be classified as an operating lease under IAS 17. It is not uncommon for substantial *investment property* to be constructed on land that is leased. It could be argued that if the interest reverts to the owner of the land at the end of the term, however far in the future that may be, there has not been a transfer of substantially all the risks and rewards of ownership. Under IAS 17 that would normally indicate an operating lease.

However, providing the property held by the lessee meets the definition of *investment property* in IAS 40, IAS 40 overrides IAS 17 and the property is treated as a finance lease (IAS 40, para 25, page A1149). This means that the lessee can account for and measure the asset at fair value.

The accounting treatment of leases continues to be under review so readers should not rely upon this book as a current statement of IFRS and IVS positions and should visit www.ifrs.org and/or www.ivsc.org to find the most recent publicly stated position.

5.1.4.5 *IVS 233* Investment Property Under Construction

IAS 40 includes 'property that is being constructed or developed for future use as investment property' as an example of investment property (ISA40, para 8(e), page 1146).

Further, IAS 40 states that:

> If an entity determines that the fair value of an investment property under construction is not reliably measurable but expects the fair value of the property to be reliably measurable when construction is complete, it shall measure that investment property under construction at cost until either its fair value becomes reliably measureable or construction is completed (whichever is earlier). (IAS 40, para 53, page A1152)

IAS 40 considers such to be 'exceptional cases' with measurement to be on the basis of the cost model in accordance with IAS16 (see section 6.1.4.1, Chapter 6). (IAS 40, para 54, page A1153).

Similarly, IVS 233 is concerned with the situation where an *investment property* is in the course of construction as at the *valuation date* (IVS 233, para C2, page 71) with the purpose of valuation including:

- financial statements;
- loan security;
- litigation; or
- acquisitions, mergers and sales of businesses or parts of businesses (IVS 233, para C3, page 71).

Concerning valuation instructions, IVS 233 requires reference to be included to:

- the source of information on the proposed building, such as identifying the plans and specification which will be used to indicate the value of the competed project;
- the source of information on the construction and other costs required to complete the project (IVS 233, para 2, page 69) ; and

- any assumptions or *special assumptions* that may be required such as:
  - o that the building will be completed in accordance with the identified plans and specification; or
  - o that any preconditions required for agreed leases of the completed building would be met or complied with (IVS 233, para 3, pages 69–70).

Concerning valuation reporting, IVS 233 adds to the reporting requirements of IVS 230 to include appropriate references to matters addressed in the valuation instructions in addition to comments on the following, where relevant to the purpose of the valuation:

- a statement that the project is under construction;
- a description of the project;
- a description of the stage of development reached, the estimated cost to complete and the source of that estimate;
- identification of and, where possible, quantification of the remaining risks associated with the project, distinguishing between the risks in respect of generating rental income and construction risks;
- a description of how the risks have been reflected in the valuation;
- the key inputs to the valuation and the assumptions made in determining those inputs; and
- a summary of the status of any outstanding major contracts, if relevant (IVS 233, para 5, page 670).

Effectively, the above list provides a useful risk management tool for the valuer, requiring the valuer to carefully analyse the construction status of the project, identify those risks that remain on both the development and investment sides of the project and think through carefully how those risks have been incorporated into the valuation process.

However, IVS 233 acknowledges that few, if any, transactions occur of investment properties under construction and at the same stage in the construction process (IVS 233, para C5, page 71) and so requires value to be estimated using one or more market-based valuation approaches (IVS 233, para C6, pages 71–72).

While such approaches may use information from a variety of sources, such as:

- sales evidence of comparable properties in different locations or in a different condition with adjustments made to account for such differences;
- sales evidence of comparable properties transacted in different economic conditions with adjustments made to account for such differences; or

- discounted cash flow projections or income capitalisation supported by comparable market data on construction costs, lease terms, operating costs, growth assumptions, discount and capitalisation rates and other key inputs (IVS 233, para C6, pages 71–72),

the *market value* of a partially completed *investment property* will essentially comprise:

> value of property as complete deductions for costs required reflecting the expectations of less to complete the project and market participants adjustment for profit and risk. (IVS 233, para C7, page 72)

The principal valuation inputs are, therefore:

- value of property as complete, reflecting the expectations of market participants, which may be either:
  - value of the completed property based on current values and the *special assumption* that on the *valuation date* it had already been completed in accordance with the current specification (IVS 233, para C11(a), page 73), or
  - the projected or expected value of the property on the future date when it is anticipated to be completed,
    with allowance for the time and costs required to achieve stabilised occupancy through leasing (IVS 233, para C11(b), page 73);
- deduction for costs required to complete the project, usually being the sums remaining to be paid under any binding construction contract in existence at the *valuation date* or, if no contract, a reasonable expectation by market participants of costs remaining as at the *valuation date*, without regard to any previously paid amounts (IVS 233, para C11(c), page 73), together with finance costs using existing loan interest rates or appropriate market interest rates for a typical buyer as at the *valuation date* where the project is self-funded (IVS 233, para C11(d), page 74) and other costs (such as legal and professional costs, marketing costs and so forth) likely to be incurred by a typical buyer in completing the construction and letting of the *investment property* (IVS 233, para C11(e), page 74); and
- adjustment for profit and risk, reflecting the return required by a buyer of the partially completed *investment property* in the marketplace given the construction risk, finance risk, leasing risk and market risk anticipated on the *valuation date* and which may be expressed as a lump sum or a percentage return on cost or value or, if the discounted cash flow method is used, that discount rate reflecting the minimum rate of return that would be required by a typical buyer in the market (IVS 233, para C11(f) and (g), pages 74–75).

IVS 233 does not permit a valuation to be based on the percentage of project completed by reference to the project plans or initial feasibility study (IVS 233, para C8, page 72), advocates the use of discounted cash flow where the project extends over a period of time (IVS 233, para C9, page 72) and provides the choice between using a nominal or real cash flow model (IVS 233, para C10, page 72). Further, for financial statement purposes, the going concern assumption supports the assumption that the construction contract, contracts for letting and so forth would pass to the hypothetical purchaser in a hypothetical exchange, even though they might be non-assignable in an actual exchange (IVS 233, para C12, page 75).

5.1.4.6 Summary – Investment property in IFRS's

For the valuation of investment property, the IAS of principal relevance is IAS 40 *Investment Property* which focuses on property held to earn rentals and/or provide capital growth and so may be expected to include the majority of office, retail and industrial investment property held by real estate investment trusts, property companies, superannuation funds and so forth around the world.

5.2 Valuation of investment property for financial reporting

The previous section sought to consider IVSs, TIP's, IAS's and IFRS's in the context of the valuation of investment property generally, with this section considering the valuation of investment property in the context of financial reporting and the following section considering the valuation of investment property in the context of secured lending.

In the context of the valuation of *investment property* for the purpose of financial reporting, the IVS of principal relevance is IVS 300 *Valuations for Financial Reporting* with IFRS 13 *Fair Value Measurement* also of particular relevance. The following section then considers the valuation of *investment property* for the purpose of secured lending, with the IVS of principal relevance being IVS 310 *Valuations of Real Property Interests for Secured Lending*.

Major international investors such as Westfield Group owning significant property portfolios are required to record the value of their property portfolios in their financial statements on the basis of the combined requirements of IVSs, TIP's, IAS's and IFRS's. Therefore, the valuation of investment property for the purpose of financial reporting requires the valuer to have regard to the interaction between several IVSs, TIP's, IAS's and IFRS's simultaneously with considerable care required to comply with the requirements of each at the same time.

5 Valuation of Inv Prop

5.2.1 *IVS 300* Valuations for Financial Reporting

IVS 300 *Valuations for Financial Reporting* comprises four sections, being *Introduction, Definitions, Requirements* (focusing on valuation instruction, implementation and reporting) and *Application Guidance* (focusing on issues that may arise in application of the Standard).

Within the *Introduction*, IVS 300 addresses valuations for accounting purposes for the preparation of financial statements including:

- measurement of the value of an asset for inclusion on the statement of financial position;
- allocation of the purchase price of an acquired business;
- impairment testing;
- lease classification; and
- valuation inputs to the calculation of depreciation charges in the profit and loss account (IVS 300, Introduction, page 90).

While IVS 300 makes reference to various requirements of IFRS, this is noted to be subject to national accounting standards where relevant (IVS 300, Introduction, page 90).

Concerning *Requirements*, IVS 300 requires inclusion of the following:

- identification of the applicable Financial Reporting Standard;
- identification of the specific accounting purpose from the list, above, for which the valuation is required (IVS 300, para 2, page 91);
- identification of the asset to be valued;
- confirmation of how that asset is used or classified by the reporting entity, such as occupation, investment, surplus to requirement or stock in trade;
- where an asset is used in conjunction with other separately identifiable assets, the unit of account (being the level at which an asset to be valued is aggregated or disaggregated with other assets) shall be identified as an assumption (IVS 300, para 5, page 92);
- identification of the specific *basis of value* required by the relevant accounting standard, such as fair value, net realisable value or recoverable amount (IVS 300, para 3, pages 91, 92);
- statement of any assumptions to be made, such as the assumption that the entity is a going concern and that the asset(s) will continue to be used as part of the business of which they form part (unless management either intends to liquidate the entity or cease trading or has no realistic alternative but to do so), with *special assumptions* not normally appropriate for a valuation for inclusion in a financial statement (IVS 300, para 4 and 6, page 92); and

- any restrictions on reference to the valuation in the published financial statements and the extent of the valuer's duty to respond to valuation questions raised by the entity's auditor (IVS 300, para 7, page 92),

which, consistent with the requirements of IVS 101 and IVS 103 considered in Chapter 4, shall be referred to in the valuation report (IVS 300, para 9, page 93).

Further, the valuation report shall contain disclosures required by the relevant Financial Reporting Standard including:

- methods and significant assumptions used in the fair value measurement;
- whether the measurement was determined by reference to observable prices or recent market transactions;
- if required, information about the sensitivity of the measurement to changes in significant inputs (IVS 300, para 10, page 93);
- the effect on value of any assumption made, if material (IVS 300, para 11, page 93); and
- reference to any conditions on how the report may be reproduced or referred to in the published financial statements of the entity (IVS 300, para 12, page 93).

Concerning *Commentary*, in the context of investment property, IVS 300 addresses the following:

- fair value, as considered in section 2.4.3.4 of Chapter 2 (IVS 300, para G1-G2, pages 94–95);
- valuation inputs and the fair value hierarchy, as considered in section 5.2.2.4 of Chapter 5 (IVS 300, para G4–G5, pages 95–96);
- leased investment property, as considered in section 5.1.4.4 of Chapter 5 (IVS 300, para G29–G32, pages 101–102); and
- aggregation, as considered in section 6.2.1.1 of Chapter 6 (IVS 300, para G3, page 95).

Accordingly, IVS 300 provides a robust framework within which to undertake valuations for financial reporting, so contributing to effective risk management for the valuer.

5.2.1.1 *IVS 300* Valuations for Financial Reporting *in practice*

The RICS Red Book Global (2013) includes VPGA1 *Valuation for inclusion in financial statements* which comprises only one page and refers to strict compliance with IVS 300 and entity adopted applicable financial reporting standards (such as IFRS), cautioning:

> Valuers are strongly advised to clarify at the outset which standards their clients have adopted. (RICS 2013, VPGA1, para 1.2, page 66)

5 Valuation of Inv Prop

5.2.2 *IFRS 13* Fair Value Measurement

Fair value for the purposes of IFRS is defined in IFRS 13, with provision of a framework for the measurement of fair value and requirements for disclosure in financial statements (IFRS 13, para 1, page A490,) based on the fundamental premise that fair value is a market based measurement not an entity specific measurement (IFRS 13, para 2, page A490).

Accordingly, the IFRS concept of fair value is more closely allied with the IVS concept of *market value* than with that of *investment value*. As considered in section 2.4.3.4 Fair Value in Chapter 2, the IVSB considers the definition of fair value in IFRS is generally consistent with the definition of *market value* in IVSs:

> The definition of fair value in IFRS is different from the above. The IVSB considers that the definitions of fair value in IFRS are generally consistent with *market value*. The definition and application of fair value under IFRS are discussed in IVS 300 *Valuations for Financial Reporting*. (IVSC 2013, para 39, page 21)

> The commentary in IFRS 13 and, in particular, the reference to market participants, an orderly transaction, the transaction taking place in the principal or most advantageous market and to the highest and best use of an asset, make it clear that fair value under IFRSs is generally consistent with the concept of *market value* as defined and discussed in the IVS *Framework*. For most practical purposes, therefore, *market value* under IVS will meet the fair value measurement requirement under IFRS 13 subject to some specific assumptions required by the accounting standard such as stipulations as to the unit of account or ignoring restrictions on sale. (IVS 300, Para G2, Pages 94–95)

a view shared for most practical purposes by the RICS Red Book Global (2013).

IFRS 13 summarises the objective of a fair value measurement to be to estimate the price at which an orderly transaction to sell the asset would take place between market participants at the measurement date under current market conditions (IFRS 13, Appendix B, para B2, page A514).

The entity is required to determine all of the following:

- the identity of the asset;
- the highest and best use of the asset, whether the asset is used in combination with other assets (IFRS 13, para IN10, page A489) and the valuation premise that is appropriate for the measurement, consistent with the asset's highest and best use;
- the market in which an orderly transaction would take plac, (IFRS 13, para IN10, page A489), being the principal or most advantageous market for the asset; and
- the valuation technique(s) appropriate for the measurement, having regard to the availability of data and the fair value hierarchy of inputs (IFRS 13, Appendix B, para B2(a)-(d), page A514),

with highest and best use, definition of fair value, valuation techniques and hierarchy of inputs considered further, below.

5.2.2.1 *IFRS 13 highest and best use*

For the purposes of measuring fair value, IFRS 13 is premised on the assumption of highest and best use for the subject property:

> A fair value measurement of a non-financial asset takes into account a market participant's ability to generate economic benefits by using the asset in its highest and best use or by selling it to another market participant that would use the asset in its highest band best use. (IFRS 13, para 27, page A493)

Highest and best use is determined from the perspective of market participants not from that of the measuring entity (IFRS 13, para 29, page A494), even if the entity does not intend to use the asset for its highest and best use (IFRS 13, para 30, page A494).

Highest and best use is further defined as that use which would maximise the value of the asset or group of assets (IFRS 13, Appendix A, page A511) taking into account the use that is:

- physically possible – such as location or size, as may be taken into account by market participants when pricing the asset;
- legally permissible – such as any legal restrictions on the use of the asset, as may be taken into account by market participants when pricing the asset; and
- financially feasible – such as generating adequate income or cash flows, taking into account the costs of conversion, to produce an investment return that may be required by market participants when pricing the asset (IFRS 13, para 28, page A493–4).

Accordingly, for the purposes of measuring fair value, all three identified characteristics must be achievable if a higher and better use than the current use is to be considered.

5.2.2.2 *IFRS 13 definition of fair value*

For the purposes of financial statement preparation under IFRS, the definition of fair value in IFRS 13 is the relevant definition for adoption and the definition of fair value in the IVS Framework is of no relevance:

> The IFRS defines fair value as the price that would be received to sell an asset or paid to transfer a liability in an orderly transaction between market participants at the measurement date. (IFRS 13, para 9, page A491)

5 Valuation of Inv Prop

As the valuation of property for the purposes of financial statements will generally be concerned with the value of an asset rather than the value of a liability, the following focuses on the former without regard to the latter.

5.2.2.2.1 'the price'

Consistent with the concept of transaction underlying the definition of fair value in IFRS, the principal output of the assumed transaction is a transaction price which IFRS 13 refers to as an 'exit price' 'regardless of whether that price is directly observable or estimated using a valuation technique' (IFRS 13, para 24, page A493).

Fair value is, therefore, sale price requiring the measuring entity to determine, on the basis of the other assumptions, below, at what price would the subject property actually sell rather than at what price would the measuring entity prefer the subject property to sell.

Accordingly, IFRS 13 echoes the aspects of the 'estimated amount' within the definition of *market value* in the IVS Framework.

5.2.2.2.2 'that would be received'

IFRS 13 continues to require the sale price to be in the principal or most advantageous market (considered further, below) and to exclude transaction costs which are defined as costs directly attributable to or essential for the transaction (IFRS 13, Appendix A, page A513), being accounted for in accordance with other IFRS's.(IFRS 13, para 25, page A493).

The sale price has to be receivable so the assumed transaction must be capable of being undertaken and being concluded at the nominated sale price. Further, the assessment of fair value that appears in the financial statements is not the exit or sale price being that amount finally received after completion of the assumed transaction but the exit or sale price being an amount without allowance for agency costs, marketing, legal fees and so forth arising in the transaction.

Accordingly, IFRS 13 echoes the aspects of 'should exchange' within the definition of *market value* in the IVS Framework.

5.2.2.2.3 'to sell'

Fair value under IFRS 13 assumes an exchange or transaction to occur:

> ... that the asset... is exchanged in an orderly transaction between market participants to sell the asset... at the measurement date under current market conditions. (IFRS 13, para 15, page A492)

Further, the transaction is assumed to occur in the 'principal market for the asset' or, in its absence, 'the most advantageous market for the asset' (IFRS 13, para 16, page A492). Principal market is further defined as:

The market with the greatest volume and level of activity for the asset or liability. (IFRS 13, Appendix A, page A512)

In the context of property, the principal market may be considered to be that comprising the most likely purchasers of the property such that, for major investment property, the most likely purchasers are likely to be other major property investors. It is, therefore, only likely that a principal market may cease to exist when there is some form of market wide breakdown such as the collapse of the REIT market following the Global Financial Crisis as debt funding ceased to be available and the 'most advantageous market' for major investment properties became that comprising sovereign wealth funds. However, in the event that the principal market exists, IFRS 13 precludes adoption of value in a more advantageous market even if it is higher.

Therefore, a transaction is assumed to occur at the measurement date and in those market conditions prevailing at the measurement date such that the proposition that the owner of the asset (being the preparer of the financial statements) would not sell at that price is irrelevant. IFRS 13 specifically addresses measurement of fair value when the level of activity in an asset's market has significantly decreased, concluding that the measurement of fair value in such circumstances depends on the facts and circumstances at the measurement date and requires judgment, with an entity's intention to hold the asset not being relevant as fair value is a market based measurement not an entity-specific measurement (IFRS 13, Appendix B, para B37–42, pages A526–7).

This is, of course, of particular significance for real estate investment trusts, property companies, superannuation funds and so forth in a falling market or depressed market where the sale of an asset at a cyclically low price level would not be undertaken but the financial statements require the assumption that it could be undertaken. In the absence of reasons requiring sale, this may give rise to cross market consequences where the market capitalisation of a real estate investment trust and the fair value of the net assets in the financial statements may differ significantly as equity market participants price in a normalised market view of asset values.

Accordingly, IFRS 13 further echoes the aspects of 'should exchange' within the definition of *market value* in the IVS Framework.

5.2.2.2.4 'an asset'

Fair value under IFRS 13 refers to a specific asset or a group of assets (IFRS 13, para 13(b), page A491), requiring the valuer to take into account the characteristics of the asset if market participants would take those characteristics into account when pricing the asset at the measurement date, including:

- the condition and location of the asset; and
- restrictions, if any on the sale or use of the asset (IFRS 13, para 11, page A491).

While condition, location and use are commonly considered in the process of valuing property, IFRS 13 permits a wider consideration of those characteristics which a market participant would take into account. For example, this may include short lease terms and open market rent reviews in a booming market or long lease terms and fixed rent reviews in a collapsing market, with the characteristics considered potentially varying in different market conditions and/or when the profile of market participants varies.

Accordingly, IFRS 13 is premised on the 'asset', consistent with the definition of *market value* in the IVS Framework.

5.2.2.2.5 'in an orderly transaction'
IFRS 13 defines an orderly transaction as:

> A transaction that assumes exposure to the market for a period before the measurement date to allow for marketing activities that are usual and customary for transactions involving such assets or liabilities; it is not a forced transaction (eg a forced liquidation or distress sale). (IFRS 13, Appendix A, page A512)

Consistent with the discussion of 'to sell' in section 5.2.2.2.3, above, IFRS 13 requires the assumption of an 'orderly transaction' which infers a market exhibiting stability where transactions may be undertaken at a pace normal for that market and without the necessity for sale by an imminent deadline or in any other way unusual for that market.

IFRS 13 specifically considers transactions in a market where the volume of sales activity has significantly decreased and determination of whether a transaction was orderly or not orderly may be difficult, noting that it is not appropriate to conclude that all transactions in such a market were not orderly (ie forced liquidations or distressed sales) and providing a series of tests in order to determine whether, on the weight of the evidence available, the transaction was orderly. If found to be uncertain or not orderly, then little, if any, weight should be placed upon the transaction with appropriate weight being placed upon it if found to be orderly (IFRS 13, Appendix B, para B43–B44, pages A527–8).

Accordingly, IFRS 13 echoes the aspect of 'after proper marketing' within the definition of *market value* in the IVS Framework.

5.2.2.2.6 'between market participants'
Fair value under IFRS 13 requires the measuring entity to use the 'assumptions that market participants would use when pricing the asset… assuming that market participants act in their economic best interests' (IFRS 13, para 22, page A493). The measuring entity is not required to identify 'specific

market participants' but rather the 'characteristics that distinguish market participants generally' considering:

- the asset;
- the principal or most advantageous market for the asset; and
- market participants with whom the entity would enter into a transaction in that market (IFRS 13, para 23, page A493).

Accordingly, from the viewpoint of valuation of *investment property* for the purposes of financial statements, it is not necessary to identify that REIT A, REIT B or REIT C would be potential purchasers of the relevant asset, but rather than REITs generally would comprise the principal market. Similarly, it is not appropriate to exclude market participants from consideration simply because the entity would not enter into a transaction with such participants. Therefore, while the potential purchasers of the asset may be direct competitors of the measuring entity, they cannot be excluded from the consideration of principal or most advantageous market.

It is then relevant to use the assumptions that the identified group comprising the principal market or most advantageous market would use when pricing the asset assuming that market participants act rationally. Care is therefore required in the valuation of certain property assets for the purposes of financial statements, such as where supply is limited. For example, if REIT B was a shopping centre REIT and the acquisition of the subject property filled an asset allocation gap, REIT B may be prepared to pay more for the asset (consistent with definitions of *investment value* and/or *special purchaser* and *special value* in the IVS Framework). However, for the purposes of financial statements, the value to REITs generally (such as REIT A or REIT C) would reflect 'characteristics that distinguish market participants generally'.

Accordingly, IFRS 13 echoes the aspects of 'willing buyer', 'willing seller' and 'each acted knowledgably, prudently and without compulsion' within the definition of *market value* in the IVS Framework.

5.2.2.2.7 'at the measurement date'
IFRS 13 is temporally specific requiring the measuring entity to include an assessment of fair value current at the measurement or balance date (IFRS 13, para 9, page A491).

Therefore, if the balance date is 30 June then the measuring entity is required to include an assessment of fair value as at 30 June and should reflect this requirement in their valuation instructions (as considered in section 4.2.2.6 of Chapter 4).

In the context of *investment property*, particular care is required in periods of rapidly rising markets and rapidly falling markets where value levels may change within a month or less as the level of transactions increases or decreases. Similarly, changes in property taxes in a jurisdictional budget announcement or adoption of a new planning instrument may have a specific temporal effect on property values. From a risk management viewpoint in such markets, the valuer should pay careful attention to the agreed wording of the valuation instructions and follow such wording precisely.

Accordingly, IFRS 13 is consistent with 'on the valuation date' within the definition of *market value* in the IVS Framework.

5.2.2.3 IFRS 13 valuation techniques
IFRS 13 clearly states:

> An entity shall use valuation techniques that are appropriate in the circumstances and for which sufficient data are available to measure fair value, maximising the use of relevant observable inputs and minimising the use of unobservable inputs. (IFRS 13, para 61, page A500)

It may, therefore, be contended that IFRS 13 gives the measuring entity (and through that, potentially the valuer) considerable scope for judgement in determining which valuation techniques are appropriate in the particular circumstances of the subject property in the prevailing market, with the objective of the valuation technique being to 'estimate the price' within the definition of fair value (IFRS 13, para 62, page A501).

While IFRS 13 provides a choice of three valuation techniques for consideration, the principal criteria for selection of the valuation technique or techniques are:

- availability of sufficient data; and
- the priority of observable inputs that are relevant over unobservable inputs,

which is considered further in section 5.2.2.4, below.

Adopting the criteria of appropriateness, sufficiency of data and priority of observable inputs, IFRS 13 requires selection from 'three widely used valuation techniques', being:

- the market approach;
- the income approach; and
- the cost approach (IFRS 13, para 63, page A501)

advocating the use of more than one technique where the asset (such as property) does not have a quoted price in an active market for an identical asset (IFRS 13, para 63, page A501).

Consistent with the IVS Framework, IFRS 13 describes the market approach as using prices and other relevant information generated by market transactions involving identical or similar (comparable) assets (IFRS 13, Appendix B5, page A516).

Also, consistent with the IVS Framework, IFRS 13 describes the income approach as converting future amounts (e.g. cash flows or income and expenses) to a single current (i.e. discounted) amount with the fair value measurement reflecting current market expectations about those future amounts (IFRS 13, Appendix B10, page A517). Income approach valuation techniques are stated to include, for example:

- present value techniques (as considered in section 5.1.3);
- option pricing models (which are still in the early research stages for application to direct property investments); and
- multi-period excess earnings methods (being currently inapplicable to property valuation) (IFRS 13, Appendix B11, page A517).

Further, echoing the IVS Framework, IFRS 13 describes the cost approach as reflecting the amount that would be required currently to replace the service capacity of an asset (often referred to as current replacement cost) (IFRS 13, Appendix B9, page A516).

Reflecting that the assessment of fair value for inclusion in financial statements of an entity is a matter for the entity, IFRS 13 includes provision for 'calibration'. Where the transaction price is fair value at initial recognition and a valuation technique that uses unobservable inputs will be used to measure fair value in subsequent periods (as will be likely to be the case for *investment property*), the valuation technique shall be calibrated so that at initial recognition the result of the valuation technique equals the transaction price (IFRS 13, para 64, page A501).

Accordingly, if a REIT receives a valuation of an asset for acquisition at $95 million but decides to pay $100 million, the directors of the REIT have scope to 'calibrate' the assessment of fair value included in the financial statements. However, at the next valuation using unobservable inputs, the entity shall ensure that the valuation technique reflects observable market data (being the previous acquisition price of the subject property) at the measurement date (IFRS 13, para 64, page A501).

5.2.2.4 IFRS 13 fair value hierarchy of inputs

As noted in section 5.2.2.3, above, while IFRS 13 provides a choice of three valuation techniques for consideration, the principal criteria for selection of the valuation technique or techniques are:

- availability of sufficient data; and
- the priority of observable inputs that are relevant over unobservable inputs.

As an overarching requirement, inputs shall be consistent with the characteristics of the asset that market participants would take into account in a transaction for the asset (IFRS 13, para 69, page A502). Further, IFRS 13 requires that the use of relevant observable inputs be maximised and unobservable inputs minimised (IFRS 13, para 67, page A502), with observable inputs arising in markets such as exchange markets, dealer markets, brokered markets and principal-to-principal markets (IFRS 13, para 68, page A502).

To increase consistency and comparability in fair value measurements, IFRS 13 categorises inputs into three levels, being the fair value hierarchy of inputs, giving the highest priority to quoted prices (unadjusted) in active markets for identical assets (Level 1 inputs – for example, equity stocks traded on a stock market) and the lowest priority to unobservable inputs (Level 3 inputs – for example, heterogeneous investment property traded on a property market) (IFRS 13, para 72, pages A502–3).

If inputs are derived from different levels of the fair value hierarchy, the categorisation is deemed to be that of the lowest level input that is significant to the entire measurement (IFRS 13, para 73, page A503). Further, if an observable input is adjusted using an unobservable input resulting in a significantly higher or lower fair value measurement, the resulting measurement is categorised as Level 3. Interestingly, in the context of property, IFRS 13 gives the example of a market participant taking into account the effect of a restriction on the sale of an asset by adjusting the quoted price to reflect the effect of that restriction. If the quoted price is a Level 2 input and the adjustment is an unobservable input that is significant to the entire measurement, the measurement would be categorised as within Level 3 of the fair value hierarchy (IFRS 13, para 75, page A503).

The categorisation of inputs is important as the reporting entity is required to disclose, for the benefit of users of its financial statements, the valuation techniques and inputs used to develop the measurements of fair value used in its financial statements after initial recognition (IFRS 13, para 91(a), page A506). Further, where significant unobservable inputs (Level 3) are used for the measurement of fair value, the effects of the measurements on profit, loss or comprehensive income for the period are to be disclosed which may be a significant issue in the context of property valuation (IFRS 13, para 91(b), page A506).

While, the nature and extent of such disclosure is a matter for the reporting entity (IFRS 13, para 92, page A506), IFRS 13 requires disclosure of:

- the fair value measurement at the end of the reporting period;
- the level within the fair value hierarchy that the measurements are categorised within;
- the amount of any transfers between Level 1 and Level 2;

- the valuation techniques and inputs used within Level 2 and Level 3 categorisations;
- any changes in valuation technique;
- quantitative information about the significant unobservable inputs used within the Level 3 categorisation in tabular format unless another format is more appropriate (IFRS 13, para 99, page A510);
- a reconciliation between Level 3 opening and closing balances;
- a description of the valuation process used by the entity for Level 3 categorisations;
- a narrative description of the fair value measurement sensitivity to changes in unobservable inputs, if such change may result in a significantly higher or lower fair value measurement within the Level 3 categorisation, together with any inter-relationships and a focus on reasonably possible alternative assumptions where the change in fair value measurement may be significant; and
- where the highest and best use differs from the current use and why the asset is not being used for its highest and best use (IFRS 13, para 93(a)-(i), pages A506–9).

Given the extent to which property falls within the Level 3 classification, the disclosure requirements of IFRS 13 are potentially very extensive for reporting entities holding property measured at fair value.

It should also be noted that IVS 300 addresses valuation inputs and the fair value hierarchy, as considered in section 5.2.1 (IVS 300, para G4–G5, page 95).

5.2.2.4.1 Level 1 inputs – observable

IFRS 13 defines Level 1 inputs as:

> Level 1 inputs are quoted prices (unadjusted) in active markets for identical assets or liabilities that the entity can access at the measurement date. (IFRS 13, para 76, page A503)

Further, IFRS 13 defines an active market as:

> A market in which transactions for the asset or liability take place with sufficient frequency and volume to provide pricing information on an ongoing basis. (IFRS 13, Appendix A, page A511)

Concerning 'quoted prices (unadjusted) in active markets', IFRS 13 provides the examples of an exchange market where closing prices are both readily available and generally representative of fair value (such as a stock exchange) and a dealer market where the dealer quotes a price at which he is prepared to buy or sell (IFRS 13, Appendix B, para B34, page A523).

As the definition of Level 1 is reliant on identical assets and active markets and reflecting the heterogeneous nature and low volume, long selling period required for property, it is unlikely that property assets would meet the definition of a Level 1 input.

5.2.2.4.2 Level 2 inputs – observable but not quoted
IFRS 13 defines Level 2 inputs as:

> Level 2 inputs are inputs other than quoted prices included within Level 1 that are observable for the asset or liability, either directly or indirectly. (IFRS 13, para 81, page A504)

with Level 2 inputs including:

> quoted prices for identical or similar assets or liabilities in markets that are not active (IFRS 13, para 82(b), page A505)

and IFRS 13 recognising that adjustments to Level 2 inputs will vary depending on factors specific to the asset including the condition or location of the asset, the extent of comparability and the level of activity in the market (IFRS 13, para 83, page A505).

IFRS 13 provides examples of Level 2 inputs as including various interest rate swaps, options on exchange traded shares, licensing arrangements, finished goods inventory at a retail outlet and cash generating units (IFRS 13, Appendix B, para B35(a)–(h), pages A524–5).

In the context of *investment property*, the references to 'identical or similar' and 'markets that are not active' together with recognition of adjustment for asset specific factors suggests that some property transactions may fall within Level 2 of the fair value hierarchy. Potentially, transactions of other properties that are considered directly comparable to the subject property and require minimal adjustment for differences in location, building, tenant and so forth may fall within Level 2 of the fair value hierarchy. However, as adjustment is likely to be an unobservable input (unless there is ample directly comparable transaction evidence for each aspect of the adjustment, which is extremely unlikely), if it has a significant effect on the fair value measurement it may result in classification within Level 3 of the fair value hierarchy (IFRS 13, para 84, page A505).

5.2.2.4.3 Level 3 inputs – unobservable
IFRS 13 defines Level 3 inputs as:

> Level 3 inputs are unobservable inputs for the asset or liability (IFRS 13, para 86, page A505)

to be used where relevant observable inputs are not available such as where there is little, if any, market activity for the asset at the measurement date (IFRS 13, para 87, page A505).

IFRS 13 provides examples of Level 3 inputs as including currency swaps, options on exchange traded shares, interest rate swaps, decommissioning liabilities assumed in business combinations and cash generating units, but does not refer to property (IFRS 13, Appendix B, para B36(a)-(e), pages A525–6).

However, compared to an observable input such as equity stocks that trade on an electronic exchange effectively continuously where prices are immediately and constantly reported publically, property transactions being generally infrequent and usually private (public auction excepted) may be generally contended to be unobservable inputs and are recognised as such by several industry associations around the world.

Interestingly, in the context of property, IFRS 13 refers to assumptions about risk including the risk inherent in a particular valuation technique and the risk inherent in the inputs to the valuation technique, requiring adjustment for risk in the measurement of fair value if that is what market participants would do (IFRS 13, para 88, page A505). For example, in a property valuation using discounted cash flow, the valuation approach may include risk arising from the use of forecasting and there may also be risk inherent in such inputs as the assessment of income, outgoings, discount rate and so forth for which market participants would adjust.

5.2.2.5 *IFRS 13* Fair Value Measurement *in practice*
By way of example of IFRS 13 and IVSs in practice, the Westfield Group Annual Financial Report 2013 included a Balance Sheet for the year ended 31 December 2013 showing 'Non-current assets' comprising 'Investment properties' at A\$16,462 million, being the value of the interests in a global shopping centre portfolio spanning Australia, New Zealand, United States and the United Kingdom.

Note 12 to the Financial Report further broke this down to:

Shopping centre investments	\$15,405.7 million
Development projects and construction in progress	\$1,056.3 million

with the footnote:

> The fair value of investment properties at the end of the year of \$16,462.0 million… comprises investment properties at market value of \$16,418.3 million… and ground leases included as finance leases of \$43.7 million…

Note 13 to the Financial Report includes the statements:

> Investment properties are carried at the Director's determination of fair value which takes into account latest independent valuations, with updates at each balance date of independent valuations that were prepared previously. The carrying amount of investment properties comprises the original acquisition cost, subsequent capital expenditure, tenant allowances, deferred costs, ground leases, straight-line rent and revaluation increments and decrements.
>
> Independent valuations are conducted in accordance with International Valuations Standards Committee for Australian and New Zealand properties, RICS Appraisal and Valuation Standards which are mandatory for Chartered Surveyors for the United Kingdom properties and Uniform Standards of Professional Appraisal Practice for the United States properties. The independent valuations use the capitalisation of net income method and the discounting of future net cash flows to their present value method. The key assumptions in determining the valuation of the investment properties are the estimated weighted average yield and the net operating income. Significant movement in each of these assumptions in isolation would result in a higher/(lower) fair value of the properties.

with further disclosure including the names of the valuation firms used in Australia, New Zealand, United States and the United Kingdom and the 'estimated weighted average yield 31 Dec 13' for each property but not, interestingly, the fair value measurement for each property nor all of the required disclosures considered in section 5.2.2.4.

5.2.3 *Valuation of investment property for financial reporting*

For the purposes of financial reporting, the valuation of investment property is principally addressed by IVS 300 *Valuations for Financial Reporting* which considers various aspects of investment property valuation in common with owner occupied property but also focuses on disclosure concerning observability of inputs and sensitivity analysis.

Similarly, IFRS 13 *Fair Value Measurement* addresses various aspects of investment property valuation in common with owner occupied property but requires careful consideration in the context of investment property regarding such issues as highest and best use, the practical application of the definition of fair value and valuation techniques and the central role of Level 1, Level 2 and Level 3 inputs in the valuation process and resulting requirements for disclosure in financial reporting.

5.3 Valuation of investment property for secured lending

The previous sections sought to consider IVSs, TIP's, IAS's and IFRS's in the context of the valuation of investment property and in the context of financial reporting, with this section considering the valuation of investment property in the context of secured lending.

In the context of the valuation of investment property for the purpose of secured lending, the IVS of principal relevance is IVS 310 *Valuations of Real Property Interests for Secured Lending*.

5.3.1 *IVS 310* Valuations of Real Property Interests for Secured Lending

IVS 310 *Valuations of Real Property Interests for Secured Lending* comprises three sections, being *Introduction*, *Requirements* (focusing on valuation instruction, implementation and reporting) and *Application Guidance* (focusing on issues that may arise in application of the Standard).

Within the *Introduction*, IVS 310 notes that lending from banks and financial institutions is often secured by the collateral of the borrower's *real property* interests (IVS 310, Introduction, page 106), which may require the bank or financial institution to obtain a valuation of the *real property* interest.

5.3.1.1 *Valuation instructions and valuation reporting*
Concerning *Requirements* (focusing on valuation instruction, implementation and reporting), the provisions of IVS 310 apply commonly to both investment property and owner occupied property, being considered in detail in section 6.3.1 of Chapter 6 and may be summarised as follows:

- disclosure of any material involvement that the valuer has with either the property to be valued, the borrower or a prospective borrower (IVS 310, para 2, page 107);
- identification of the *real property* interest to be used as the collateral for securing the loan(s), together with the party in whom the interest is currently vested (IVS 310, para 3, page 107);
- the *basis of value* (IVS 310, para 4, page 107);
- a defined *special assumption* where a change in the state of the property is to be reflected (IVS 310, para 5, page 107); and
- various additional reporting requirements (IVS 310, para 7, page 108; para 8, page 108).

Such inclusions in the valuer instructions contribute to effective risk management for both the client/lender and the valuer, making explicit and transparent each of the important premises upon which the valuation is based and transparently explaining potential risks and the impact of the *special assumptions* stated in the valuer instructions.

5.3.1.2 Cautionary issues in valuations of real property for secured lending purposes
Concerning *Application Guidance* (focusing on issues that may arise in application of the Standard) and reflecting the importance of a valuation in the credit decision by a typically risk averse lender for real property, the provisions of IVS 310 apply commonly to both investment property and owner occupied property, with the following considered in detail in section 6.3.1.2 of Chapter 6:

- property interest;
- incentives; and
- valuation approaches for owner occupied property, trade related property and specialised property,

with valuation approaches for investment property and development property considered below.

5.3.1.2.1 Property types – investment and development property

IVS 310 cautions that different types of property have different characteristics as loan security which should be addressed in the valuation of the relevant interest to provide the lender with adequate information on the suitability of the property as security and to help the lender identify any risk factors associated with the property over the duration of the loan (IVS 310, para G5, page 109, 110).

In this context, IVS 310 addresses five property types with owner occupied property, specialised property and trade related property considered in section 6.3.1.2.2 of Chapter 6:

- **investment property:**
  For *investment property*, IVS 310 focuses on the risk of the income stream and the marketability of the *investment property*, requiring the impact of critical tenant dependencies to be considered in the valuation process (potentially with an assessment of value with vacant possession based on an alternative use) (IVS 310, para G9, page 110), regard to be given to publically available information concerning the tenants financial strength (IVS 310, para G8, page 110) and consideration to be given to the expected demand for the investment property over the life of the loan with advice on current market conditions and expectations (as distinct from predicting future events or values)

together with significant risks to future rent payments that impact value being included in the valuation report (IVS 310, para G7, page 110). Further, where the lending is to be secured against a portfolio of properties, the value of the property as part of the portfolio should be distinguished from the value of the property assuming it is sold individually (IVS 310, para G6, page 110); and

- **development property:**
  While the valuation of investment property where construction has yet to commence or is underway is addressed in IVS 233 (see section 5.1.4.5), IVS 310 addresses the valuation for secured lending purposes of properties held for development or sites intended for development. Such properties are to be valued having regard to existing and potential development entitlements and permissions, with any assumptions concerning zoning issues and other material factors required to be reasonable and reflect those that would be made by market participants (IVS 310, para G14, G17, page 111, 112). Further, regard should be had to the stage of the development process and the level of pre-sales or pre-leasing at the *valuation date*, the intended phasing of the development, the effect of any additional development requirements, anticipated market trends, risks associated with the development, the impact of any special relationships between the parties involved in the development and where comprising multiple individual units, a distinction between value if sold to a single buyer (who would on sell individual units) and if sold as individual units (IVS 310, para G15, G16, pages 111, 112).

  In the context of investment property under construction, IVS 233 notes that IVS 310 indicates the appropriate *basis of valuation* for secured lending is *market value*. However, in considering the value of such property as loan security, regard should be given to existing building contracts with any associated warranties and guarantees and to agreements to lease in the event of insolvency when the benefit of same may not pass to the buyer (IVS 233, para C13, page 75).

Accordingly, the provisions of IVS 310 concerning property types provide sensible and practical advice to the valuer which, if followed, will contribute to effective risk management.

5.3.1.3 IVS 310 Valuations of Real Property Interests for Secured Lending *in practice*
RICS VPGA2 *Valuations for Secured Lending* in the RICS Red Book Global provides additional commentary on the practical implementation of IVS 310 which is considered in detail in section 6.3.1.3 in Chapter 6. In the context of investment property, RICS VPGA2 extends IVS 310 by

5 Valuation of Inv Prop

indicating a range of useful matters that it may be appropriate to include in the valuation process:

- **investment property:**
  Additional valuation report contents, such as:
  - a summary of occupational leases, indicating whether the leases have been read or not, and the source of any information relied upon;
  - a statement of and commentary upon current rental income and comparison with current market rental value;
  - an *assumption* as to covenant strength where there is no information readily available, or comment on the market's view of the quality, suitability and strength of the tenant's covenant;
  - comment on the sustainability of the income over the life of the loan, with particular reference to lease breaks or determinations and anticipated market trends; and/or
  - comment on any potential for redevelopment or refurbishment at the end of the occupational leases(s) (RICS, 2013, para 6.2(b)(1), page 71, 72);
  Special assumptions such as that:
  - a different rent has been agreed or determined, for example, after a rent review;
  - any existing leases have been determined and the property is vacant and to let; and/or
  - a proposed lease on specified terms has been completed (RICS, 2013, para 6.2(b)(2), page 72); and
- **development property:**
  Additional valuation report contents, such as:
  - comment on costs and contract procurement;
  - comment on the viability of the proposed project;
  - if the valuation is based on a residual method, an illustration of the sensitivity of the valuation to any *assumptions* made;
  - the implications on value of any cost overruns or contract delays; and
  - comment on the anticipated length of time the development or refurbishment will take, as this may affect the current value due to inconvenience and/or temporary lack of utility (RICS, 2013, para 6.2(d)(1), page 72);
  Special assumptions such as that:
  - the works described have been completed in a good and workmanlike manner, in accordance with all appropriate statutory requirements (with regard to be given to current market conditions if the *special assumption* is that of completion at the *valuation date* with regard to be given to RICS VPS1, VPS3 and VPS4 for a *special assumption* and *valuation date* that is a future date) (RICS, 2013, para 6.2(d)(3), page 73);

o the completed development has been let, or sold, on defined terms; and/or

o a prior agreed sale or letting has failed to complete (RICS, 2013, para 6.2(d)(2), page 73).

with advice that it is good practice to attach the valuation instructions to the valuation report and to refer to these in the body of the report (RICS, 2013, para 6.3, page 73).

5.3.2 Summary – Valuation of investment property for secured lending

For the purposes of secured lending, the valuation of investment property is principally addressed by IVS 310 *Valuation of Real Property for Secured Lending* which considers various aspects of valuation in common with owner occupied property but also focuses on the importance of a *special assumption* where a change in the state of the property is to be reflected in the valuation and the particular aspects of investment property and development property that require careful attention, each of which contribute to effective risk management for both the client/lender and the valuer.

5.4 Summary and conclusions

Chapter 1 outlined the emergence of globalisation, the role of IFRS and the evolution of valuation standard setting, the role of IVSC and IVSs and an analysis of *market value*, being the central concept of IVSs, with an overview of other IVSs relevant to the valuation of businesses and business interests, intangible assets and financial instruments.

Chapter 2 developed a conceptual framework for valuation based on economic theory, aligned this framework with finance and capital market theory, examined the definition of the market and distinguished definitions of cost and price from defined concepts of value before reconciling these to the conceptual framework for valuation.

Chapter 3 considered various aspects of valuation within IVSs, discussed the definitions of other relevant contextual terms and identified the principal approaches to valuation within IVSs including a focus on the *market approach* to valuation.

Chapter 4 described and analysed those elements of IVSs that are of relevance to the three principal stages of the real property valuation process, being the instruction of the valuer, undertaking the valuation and reporting the valuation.

This chapter focused on IVSs in the context of the valuation of investment property, IAS 40 *Investment Property*, the *income approach* to valuation and TIP 1 *Discounted Cash Flow* for the purposes of secured lending or financial reporting, though acknowledging that certain aspects of these may also apply to owner occupied property.

IVS 230 *Real Property Interests* is of principal relevance for the valuation of investment property with IVS 220 *Plant and Equipment* of principal relevance for the valuation of that plant and equipment which may not be attached to the building, each Standard comprising *Requirements* to be followed in valuation instructions, implementation and reporting and *Commentary* which includes issues of relevance in application. With the valuation of *investment property* generally being likely to require the adoption of the *income approach*, TIP 1 *Discounted Cash Flow* is of particular relevance with the focus on future cash flows and the discount rate seeking to address key risk management issues in the valuation of *investment property*.

IVS 230, IVS 220 and TIP 1 complement IAS 40 *Investment Property* which defines *investment property* for the purposes of IFRS through a focus on rentals and/or capital growth that may be likely to include the majority of office, retail and industrial investment property held by real estate investment trusts, property companies, superannuation funds and so forth around the world for the purposes of valuation.

In the event of property requiring valuation during development, IVS 233 *Investment Property Under Construction* provides for assessment of value as complete less deduction for costs required to complete and adjustment for profit and risk.

For the purposes of financial reporting, the valuation of investment property is principally addressed by IVS 300 *Valuations for Financial Reporting* which focuses on disclosure concerning observability of inputs and sensitivity analysis in the context of *investment property*. This complements IFRS 13 *Fair Value Measurement* which addresses such issues as highest and best use, the practical application of the definition of fair value and valuation techniques in the context of *investment property*, the central role of Level 1, Level 2 and Level 3 inputs and resulting requirements for disclosure in financial reporting.

Concerning valuation for the purposes of secured lending for *investment property*, IVS 310 *Valuation of Real Property for Secured Lending* focuses on the importance of a *special assumption* where a change in the state of the property is to be reflected in the valuation and the particular aspects of *investment property* and development property that require careful attention, each of which contribute to effective risk management for both the client/lender and the valuer.

Accordingly, the valuation of *investment property* for the purpose of financial reporting or secured lending requires the valuer to have regard to the interaction between several IVSs, TIP's, IAS's and IFRS's simultaneously which is somewhat overwhelming, with considerable care required to comply with the requirements of each at the same time and careful discussion of valuation instructions with the client, their accountant and their auditor highly recommended as the first step.

The next and final chapter will focus on IVSs in the context of the valuation of owner occupied property held by operating businesses, with particular reference to IAS 16 *Property, Plant and Equipment* and the cost approach to valuation, including an examination of IVSC TIP 2 *The Cost Approach to Tangible Assets*.

References

Banfield, A. (2014) *A Valuer's Guide to the RICS Red Book 2014*, RICS, London.

International Financial Reporting Council (2012) *A Briefing for Chief Executives, Audit Committees and Boards of Directors*, IFRS Foundation, London.

International Financial Reporting Standards (2013) *International Financial Reporting Standards 2013*, International Accounting Standards Board, London.

International Valuation Standards Council (2012) *TIP 1 – Discounted Cash Flow*, IVSC, London.

International Valuation Standards Council (2013) *International Valuation Standards 2013*, IVSC, London.

Royal Institution of Chartered Surveyors (2013) *RICS Professional Standards, Global and UK 2014*, RICS, London.

Westfield Group (2013) *Westfield Group Annual Financial Report 2013*, Sydney.

6

Valuation of Owner Occupied Property

6.0 Introduction

In the context of the valuation of real property assets, this book provides an analysis of the International Valuation Standards (IVS), International Accounting Standards (IAS) and International Financial Reporting Standards (IFRS) which, being dynamic, are regularly updated and/or replaced. Accordingly, readers should not rely upon this book as a current statement of an IVS, IAS or IFRS publication and should visit www.ifrs.org and/or www.ivsc.org to find the most recent version.

Chapter 1 outlined the emergence of globalisation, the role of IFRS and the evolution of valuation standard setting, the role of IVSC and IVSs and an analysis of *market value*, being the central concept of IVSs, with an overview of other IVSs relevant to the valuation of businesses and business interests, intangible assets and financial instruments.

Chapter 2 sought to develop a conceptual framework for valuation based on economic theory, aligned this framework with finance and capital market theory, examined the definition of the market and distinguished definitions of cost and price from defined concepts of value before reconciling these to the conceptual framework for valuation.

Chapter 3 considered various aspects of valuation within IVSs, discussed the definitions of other relevant contextual terms and identified the principal approaches to valuation within IVSs including a focus on the *market approach* to valuation.

International Valuation Standards: A Guide to the Valuation of Real Property Assets,
First Edition. David Parker.
© 2016 John Wiley & Sons, Ltd. Published 2016 by John Wiley & Sons, Ltd.

6 Valuation of OOP

Chapter 4 described and analysed those elements of IVSs that are of relevance to the three principal stages of the real property valuation process, being the instruction of the valuer, undertaking the valuation and reporting the valuation.

Chapter 5 considered IVSs in the context of the valuation of investment property, with particular reference to IAS 40 *Investment Property* and the *income approach* to valuation, including an examination of IVSC TIP 1 *Discounted Cash Flow*.

This chapter focuses on IVSs in the context of the valuation of owner occupied property held by operating businesses, with particular reference to IAS 16 *Property, Plant and Equipment* and the cost approach to valuation, including an examination of IVSC TIP 2 *The Cost Approach to Tangible Assets*.

In many countries around the world, national and local valuation professional bodies adopt IVSs and supplement them with national or local valuation practice guidance which may expand upon IVSs in a national or local context for the benefit of their membership. However, only the Royal Institution of Chartered Surveyors (RICS) produces global valuation practice guidance that adopts and expands upon IVSs but is not country specific, comprising mandatory professional standards and valuation practice statements and non-mandatory practice guidance applications and practice guidance notes for use by members globally – generally referred to as the RICS Red Book Global (RICS 2013). Accordingly, this book refers to the RICS Red Book Global for the purposes of considering how a professional body interprets IVSs for application by its members worldwide but without a country specific application.

This book is based upon International Valuation Standards 2013 (IVSC, 2013) and International Financial Reporting Standards 2013 (IFRS, 2013). Given their nature, IVSs, IAS's and IFRSs are dynamic, being regularly updated and with the most recently published versions replacing previously published versions. Accordingly, readers should not rely upon this book as a current statement of an IVS, IAS or IFRS publication and should visit www.ifrs.org and/or www.ivsc.org to find the most recent version.

6.1 Valuation of owner occupied property

This chapter focuses on owner occupied property, being property held by operating businesses, for the purposes of financial reporting or secured lending, with Chapter 5 focusing on investment property. It should be noted, however, that these are not mutually exclusive and considerable cross-over will be observed between and within each chapter.

For the valuation of owner occupied property, the IVSs of principal relevance are IVS 230 *Real Property Interests* and IVS 220 *Plant and Equipment*, with TIP 2 *The Cost Approach to Tangible Assets* of particular relevance, each of which are considered further below.

Further, for owner occupied property valuation for the purpose of financial reporting, the IVS of principal relevance is IVS 300 *Valuations for Financial Reporting*, with IAS 16 *Property, Plant and Equipment* and IFRS 13 *Fair Value Measurement* also of relevance for owner occupied property, each of which are then considered further below.

Concerning valuation for the purpose of secured lending for owner occupied property, the IVS of principal relevance is IVS 310 *Valuations of Real Property for Secured Lending* which is finally considered further below.

Further, IAS 36 *Impairment of Assets*, IFRS 5 *Non-Current Assets Held for Sale and Discontinued Operations* and IAS 17 *Leases* are also of relevance to the valuation of owner occupied property and are also considered below.

Accordingly, the valuation of owner occupied property for the purpose of financial reporting or secured lending requires the valuer to have regard to the interaction between several IVSs, TIP's, IAS's and IFRS's simultaneously with considerable care required to comply with the requirements of each at the same time.

This section seeks to focus on IVSs, TIP's, IAS's and IFRS's in the context of the valuation of owner occupied property held by operating businesses, with the following sections considering the valuation of owner occupied property in the context of financial reporting and secured lending, respectively.

6.1.1 IVS 230 Real Property Interests

For the valuation of owner occupied property, the IVS of principal relevance is IVS 230 *Real Property Interests*. While the concepts and provisions of IVS 230 *Real Property Interests* were considered in section 5.1.1 of Chapter 5 in the context of investment property, the *Requirements* (focusing on valuation instruction, implementation and reporting) are commonly applicable to owner occupied property with IVS 230 expanding IVS 101 with regard to valuation instructions requiring the inclusion of:

- a description of the *real property* interest to be valued;
- identification of any superior or subordinate interests that affect the interest to be valued (IVS 230, para 2, page 61);
- regard to the extent of investigation and the nature and source of the information to be relied upon, as detailed in section 5.1.1 of Chapter 5 (IVS 230, para 3, pages 61–62); and
- agreed and confirmed *special assumptions*, as detailed in section 5.1.1 of Chapter 5 (IVS 230, para 4, page 62).

Similarly, the IVS 230 *Commentary* (focusing on issues that may arise in application of the Standard) detailed in section 5.1.1 of Chapter 5 in the context of investment property is commonly applicable to owner occupied property, including:

- types of property interests, such as superior and subordinate interests, rights of use and joint and several rights (IVS 230, para C1–3, page 63), as considered in section 3.2.2 of Chapter 3;
- the hierarchy of interests, including absolute interest, head lease interest, sub-lease interest and so forth (IVS 230, para C4–7, pages 63–64), as considered in section 3.2.2 of Chapter 3; and
- valuation approaches including the *market approach, income approach* and *cost approach* (IVS 230, para C12–24, pages 65–68), as considered in section 3.3 of Chapter 3.

with the *Commentary* on rent (IVS 230, para C8–11, pages 64–65) potentially being of greater relevance to the valuation of owner occupied property.

IVS 230 notes that when valuing an interest subject to a lease or an interest created by a lease, it is necessary to consider the rent under the lease and the *market rent*, if different (IVS 230, para C8, page 64) with *market rent* defined as:

> **Market rent** – the estimated amount for which an interest in real property should be leased on the valuation date between a willing lessor and a willing lessee on appropriate lease terms in an arm's length transaction, after proper marketing and where the parties had each acted knowledgably, prudently and without compulsion. (IVS 2013, page 8; RICS, 2013, page 8; IVS 230, para C9, page 64)

The definition of market rent echoes that of market value and may be interpreted similarly. In particular, *appropriate lease terms* excludes a rent inflated or deflated by special terms, considerations or concessions, being terms that would typically be agreed in the market for the type of property on the *valuation date* between market participants. As a plural, it suggests the conditions of the lease rather than a period of time and that there should be more than one condition of lease.

Valuers should take care to identify relevant conditions in a hypothetical lease of the subject property as these may vary by sector (such as between a department store or a small office suite), by geography (such as longer leases in the UK and parts of Europe or shorter leases in Asia) and by market conventions and local legislation (such as rent review clauses, alienation clauses or make good clauses). Accordingly, a valuation of *market rent* should only be provided in conjunction with an indication of the principal lease terms (or conditions, being, significantly, plural) that have been assumed (IVS 230, para C10, page 64, 65).

As the principal lease terms may vary considerably between countries, between cities within countries, between sectors and between sub-sectors, that which is *appropriate* requires careful explanation. Similarly, lease terms is plural, indicating that more than one appropriate lease term should be included such as length/period, rent review basis, outgoings basis, repair and maintenance obligations, assignment and sub-letting rights and so forth, each of which may impact upon an assessment of *market rent*.

6.1.1.1 *IVS 230* Real Property Interests *in practice*

For the valuer in practice, the valuation of owner occupied property may provide many challenges. At the outset, IVS 230 provides a framework for application to the property to be valued, allowing the valuer to develop a clear and logical approach to the valuation.

By agreeing with the client in the valuation instructions exactly what is to be valued, many challenging issues such as the nature of title, extent of boundaries, physical extent of the property, superior and subordinate interests and so forth may be clarified which will allow the valuer to identify the appropriate valuation approach for the interest to be valued.

During inspection, physical aspects may be confirmed and the areas of ambiguity diminished, saving time and reducing risk for the valuer. An expectation of physical aspects may also make the unexpected more obvious, allowing easier identification and clarification with the client, if necessary. Similarly, review of client-provided documentation will be facilitated by the knowledge of what to expect, allowing inconsistencies to be more easily visible and so reducing risk in the valuation process.

RICS VPS4 *Bases of Value, Assumptions and Special Assumptions* in the RICS Red Book Global expands on the practical application of *market rent* in IVS 230, noting that *market rent* will vary significantly according to the terms of the assumed lease contract including duration, frequency of rent reviews, responsibilities for outgoings and maintenance (RICS VPS4, para 1.3.3, page 54), being used to indicate the amount for which a vacant property may be let or for which a let property may be re-let on lease expiry (RICS VPS4, para 1.3.4, page 55).

Significantly, RICS VPS4 provides that if the market norm for lettings is to include a payment or concession by one party to the other as an incentive to enter into the lease and this is reflected in the general level of rents in the market, the *market rent* should be expressed on that basis with the nature of the incentive assumed stated along with the assumed lease terms (RICS VPS4, para 1.3.5, page 55), which Banfield (2014, page 108) notes should reflect current practice in the market in which the property is situated.

6 Valuation of OOP

6.1.2 *IVS 220* Plant and Equipment

With many owner occupied properties comprising business premises with operational plant and equipment, requiring valuation together with the real property, the IVS of principal relevance is IVS 220 *Plant and Equipment*, which comprises two sections, being *Requirements* (focusing on valuation instruction, implementation and reporting) and *Commentary* (focusing on issues that may arise in application of the Standard).

Concerning *Requirements*, IVS 220 includes modifications, additional requirements or specific examples of how the General Standards apply for the valuation of plant and equipment which are common to owner occupied property and investment property.

Within the valuation instructions, the plant and equipment asset(s) to be valued should be identified, with consideration given to the extent to which the asset is attached to or integrated with other assets, such as where it may be permanently attached and incapable of removal without demolition or where it may be part of an integrated production line with its functionality dependent on other assets, with appropriate assumptions or *special assumptions* agreed (IVS 220, para 2, page 56).

Further, additional assumptions may be required in the valuation instructions to address the state and circumstances in which the plant and equipment asset(s) are valued, such as an assumption:

- that the plant and equipment assets are valued as a whole, in place and as part of the business, considered as a going concern; or
- that the plant and equipment assets are valued as a whole, in place but on the assumption that the business is closed; or
- that the plant and equipment assets are valued as individual items for removal from their current location (IVS 220, para 4, page 57);

with care required not to omit or double count items when the *real property* interest is valued separately to the plant and equipment at the same location at the same time (IVS 220, para 3, page 57).

Consistent with the requirements of IVS 103, the valuation report shall include appropriate references to any matters included in the valuation instructions, such as those considered above.

Concerning *Commentary* (focusing on issues that may arise in application of the Standard), IVS 220 defines plant and equipment and addresses intangible assets, financing arrangements, forced sale and valuation approaches. IVS 220 *Plant and Equipment* defines plant and equipment as:

> ... tangible assets that are held by an entity for use in the production or supply of goods or services, for rental by others or for administrative purposes and that are expected to be used over a period of time

but specifically excludes real property, stock and inventory and personal property such as artwork, jewellery and collectibles (IVS 220, para C1, page 58) and intangible assets (IVS 220, para C3, page 59).

A valuation of plant and equipment may be likely to require consideration of a range of factors including:

- asset related factors, such as:
  o the asset's technical specification;
  o the remaining physical life;
  o the asset's condition, including maintenance history;
  o any costs of decommissioning or removal, if the asset is not valued in its current location; and
  o any potential loss of a complementary asset, such as the curtailing of the operational life of a machine due to a short lease of the building in which it is located;
- environment related factors, such as:
  o the location of the plant and equipment relative to raw material sources and market for product; and
  o the impact of environmental or other legislation that may restrict use or impose additional operating or decommissioning costs; and
- economic related factors, such as:
  o the actual or potential profitability of the asset based on comparison of running costs with earnings or potential earnings;
  o the demand for the product from the plant and equipment with regard to macro and micro economic factors impacting demand; and
  o the potential for the asset to be put to a more valuable use than the current use (IVS 220, para C1, page 58, 59).

Care is required when plant and equipment is encumbered by a financing arrangement where separate identification and value reporting of encumbered assets may be required depending on the purpose of the valuation (IVS 220, para C4, page 59). Similarly, care is required where insufficient time to properly market plant and equipment arises, such as due to building lease expiry, potentially leading to forced sale and requiring consideration of alternatives such as removal and sale from another location (IVS 220, para C6, C7, page 59).

Concerning valuation approaches, IVS 220 notes that all three principal valuation approaches may be applied to the valuation of plant and equipment, with the *market approach* appropriate for homogeneous classes of assets such as motor vehicles (IVS 220, para C8, C9, page 60). Where direct sales evidence is not available, the *income approach* may be appropriate if specific cash flows can be identified for the plant and equipment, though this may not be practical for individual items of plant and equipment

6 Valuation of OOP

(IVS 220, para C10, page 60). Accordingly, the *cost approach* is commonly adopted for plant and equipment through calculation of the depreciated replacement cost for an asset of equivalent utility subject to deduction for physical, functional and economic obsolescence (IVS 220, para C11, C12, page 60).

6.1.2.1 *IVS220* Plant and Equipment *in practice*

For the valuer in practice undertaking the valuation of owner occupied property, clearly distinguishing between what is *real property* and what is *plant and equipment* may be particularly challenging. From the application of practical experience, the valuer should be able to assist the client to prepare valuation instructions with attached schedules of identified *plant and equipment* capable of verification during the inspection process.

However, where *real property* stops and *plant and equipment* starts may be an interesting issue, particularly in the valuation of large manufacturing plants where it may be unclear if the building was built around the plant or the plant was created to fit the building. Discussion of such challenging issues with the client, their accountant and their auditor followed by reflection in the valuation instructions affords transparency and provides more effective risk management for the valuer.

RICS VPGA5 *Valuation of Plant and Equipment* provides further guidance on the practical application of IVS 220, separately defining plant, machinery and equipment (RICS VPGA5, para 2.2, page 92) and noting that the approach to classification, measurement and reporting of value may be influenced by:

- whether the plant and equipment is physically affixed to *real property*, in whole or in part and/or capable of being moved or relocated;
- some classes of plant and equipment depreciating at a quicker or less linear rate than *real property* due to rapid technological change;
- whether the plant and equipment is valued in combination with other assets within an operational unit or as an individual item for exchange;
- whether the plant and equipment is to be considered in situ or for removal (RICS VPGA5, para 2.1, page 92); and
- specific legislation and regulation concerning the plant and equipment in the jurisdiction in which the valuation is being undertaken (RICS VPGA5, para 7.1, 7.2, page 96).

RICS VPGA5 usefully states that the general principle is that assets installed primarily to provide services to the buildings or personnel should be valued as part of the property interest if they would normally be included in the sale of the property and/or balance sheet classification, such as (RICS VPGA5, para 2.4, page 93):

- items associated with the provision of services to the property, such as gas, electricity, water, drainage, fire protection and security;
- equipment for space heating, hot water and air conditioning not integral to any process; and
- structures and fixtures that are not an integral part of process equipment, such as chimneys, plant housings and railway tracks (RICS VPGA5, para 3.1, page 93).

Plant and equipment valued separately from the property interest may be divided into broad categories, including:

- fixed assets, such as process and production plant and machinery, fixtures and fittings, office equipment including computers, office furniture, vehicles and transport infrastructure and mobile plant;
- borderline items, such as spare parts, stores, stocks, work in progress and operating software, licenses and consents; and
- intangible assets, to which RICS VPGA5 does not generally apply (RICS VPGA5, para 4.2, 4.3, 4.4, page 93, 94).

with RICS VPGA5 providing further guidance on material considerations in the application of *market value* to plant and equipment (RICS VPGA5, para 6.1–6.6, pages 94–96).

6.1.3 *TIP 2* The Cost Approach to Tangible Assets

While considerable attention is given in this chapter to the *cost approach* to the valuation of owner occupied property, this should not be construed as suggesting that this is necessarily the most commonly used approach, indeed it may often only be used as a check approach.

With sufficient data and having regard to those issues considered in section 3.3.3 in Chapter 3, the *market approach* may be adopted and applied to owner occupied property. Similarly, having regard to those issues considered in section 3.3.2 of Chapter 3, section 5.1.3 of Chapter 5 and to the issues associated with *market rent* and hypothetical lease terms, considered above, the *income approach* may also be adopted and applied, through the income capitalisation method, discounted cash flow method or profits method, to owner occupied property.

The valuation of owner occupied property may often require the adoption of the *cost approach* for which TIP 2 *The Cost Approach to Tangible Assets* is of particular relevance. The principal objective of a TIP is to reduce diversity of practice by identifying commonly accepted processes and procedures and discussing their use, being designed to be of assistance to professional valuers through the provision of information (TIP 2, page iii). While not

6 Valuation of OOP

intended to be mandatory and leaving the responsibility for the choice of appropriate valuation methods with the valuer (TIP 2, page iii), adherence to a TIP may be likely to be persuasive in the event of a dispute over or challenge to a valuation.

TIP 2 addresses the *cost approach* to valuation of tangible assets, such as property, for a range of purposes being one of the three principal valuation approaches identified in the IVS Framework (as considered in section 3.3.3, Chapter 3) with illustrative examples of application. (TIP 2, page 1, para 1; page 2, para 7, pages 17–20, IE 1) The *cost approach* is succinctly described as:

> The approach provides an indication of value by calculating the current replacement cost of an asset and making deductions for physical deterioration and all other relevant forms of obsolescence. (TIP 2, page 1, para 2)

being formally defined as:

> A valuation approach based on the economic principle that a buyer will pay no more for an asset than the cost to obtain an asset of equal utility, whether by purchase or construction. (TIP 2, page 2, para 8)

which is based on the economic principle of substitution whereby, unless undue time, inconvenience, risk or other factors are involved, the price that a buyer in the market would pay for the asset being valued would not be more than the cost to assemble or construct an equivalent asset (TIP 2, page 1, para 3). Careful consideration is, however, required where an asset is clearly redundant or obsolete and so is of no utility, as a buyer would not substitute the asset such that its value using the *cost approach* may be very low (such as land value less the cost of demolition as considered in section 6.1.3.2, below) (TIP 2, page 4, para 17).

In the context of owner occupied property such as major logistics warehouses or investment property such as prime office towers or super-regional shopping centres, such other factors may include location and supply which preclude substitution by a buyer in the market and so render the *cost approach* to valuation inappropriate.

Conversely, for assets where location and supply are less significant, such as owner occupied country bank branches or outer metropolitan small manufacturing plants or distribution depots, unless there is a time constraint, inconvenience or risk to operations, a buyer in the market may be ambivalent as to location and so unwilling to pay more for a bank branch or small manufacturing plant or distribution depot than the cost to assemble and construct an equivalent bank branch or small manufacturing plant or distribution depot in an equally acceptable location.

While the *cost approach* may be applied to such properties as town halls, libraries, schools, hospitals and so forth, TIP 2 acknowledges that there may be special considerations in applying the *cost approach* to specialised public sector assets that are outside the scope of TIP 2 (TIP 2, page 1, para 6).

In addition to the economic principle of substitution, TIP 2 states that the *cost approach* is also applicable where there are limited transactions due to the specialised nature, design or location of the asset, or where the asset itself does not produce a cash flow or the cash flows associated with it are not separable from the business using it, noting the *cost approach* to be typically used as the primary valuation approach when the *market approach* or *income approach* cannot be applied (TIP 2, page 4, para 14).

In the context of owner occupied property such as major logistics warehouses or investment property such as prime office towers or super-regional shopping centres, transactions may not be limited such that the *market approach* or *income approach* may be applied. In the context of country bank branches or outer metropolitan small manufacturing plants or distribution depots, transactions may be so limited as to prevent the *market approach* or *income approach* being adopted, such that the *cost approach* may be applied.

While international airports and major sports stadia, which produce substantial cash flows linked to the business of the international airport or major sports stadium may be valued using a profits method, smaller airports and sports stadia may generate limited cash flow and rarely, if ever, sell on the open market rendering the *market approach* or the *income approach* inappropriate. Further, while theoretical substitution may be conceivable but possibly not practically achievable, few if any transactions may occur due to the specialised nature, design and location of airports and sports stadia so rendering the *cost approach* appropriate.

TIP 2 cautions against the automatic assumption that because an asset is specialised, the *cost approach* should automatically be adopted, advocating cross-checking by the *market approach* or *income approach* where possible (TIP 2, page 4, para 15). In the context of country bank branches or outer metropolitan small manufacturing plants or distribution depots, while transactions may be limited and the property owner occupied, a notional income may be imputed and a notional capitalisation rate adopted in a notional *income approach* to cross-check the valuation using the *cost approach*.

6.1.3.1 *Bases of value*

TIP 2 addresses the *cost approach* to valuation for tangible assets, such as property, for a range of purposes and can be used for a variety of bases – such as market value for financial reporting purposes – with application replicating the deductive process of a typical market participant based on market observations (TIP 2, page 3, para 9, 10).

When the market basis of value is required, consideration should be given to the highest and best use of the subject property, as a potentially higher value for an alternative use may render the *cost approach* inappropriate (TIP 2, page 3, para 11). Where an entity specific basis of value is required, such as investment value, regard should be had to whether the requirements of the entity may result in a higher cost because of specific factors or whether the entity could procure a replacement asset at a lower cost than other market participants (TIP 2, page 4, para 12).

6.1.3.2 Value of land

A distinctive feature of the *cost approach* is the requirement to determine the value of the land beneath the asset for which the cost is being assessed. TIP 2 requires the value of the land to have regard to the highest and best use of the property as a whole, including any interdependent assets (such as buildings, improvements, plant and equipment), with all valued on consistent assumptions for either existing use or alternative use (TIP 2, page 14, para 74).

TIP 2 specifies two methods for use in estimating the value of the land:

- an estimate of the value of the land that would be required for a modern equivalent asset; or
- an estimate of the value of the subject land;

and add to this the depreciated replacement cost of the improvements (considered further in sections 6.1.3.3 and 6.1.3.5), noting that in most cases there will be little difference where the permitted highest and best use and current use of the land are the same and sales evidence of comparable use land may be adopted (TIP 2, page 15, para 75, 76).

However, where highest and best use is greater than current use of the land or where the current use is no longer permitted, TIP 2 suggests the *cost approach* may not be appropriate but, if adopted, careful regard should be had to the depreciation rates applied to improvements (TIP 2, page 15, para 77, 78). In situations where the land value for the highest and best use is greater than the value of the entire property for current use, the value attributed to improvements may be zero or negative where demolition and clearance costs may be incurred (TIP 2, page 15, para 78).

6.1.3.3 Reproduction or replacement of buildings and/or improvements

A fundamental consideration in the application of the *cost approach* is whether that asset being valued would be recreated exactly as it exists at the date of valuation or replaced by a modern version which offers the same usefulness as a building or something in between – being the concepts of reproduction, replacement, modern equivalent asset and utility which underpin the application of the *cost approach* and are defined as follows:

- *reproduction cost* – the current cost of recreating a replica of the asset;
- *replacement cost* – the current cost of a similar asset offering equivalent utility;
- *modern equivalent asset* – an asset which provides similar function and equivalent utility to the asset being valued, but which is of a current design and constructed or made using current materials and techniques; and
- *utility* – an expression of the degree of an asset's usefulness (TIP2, para 8, page 2, 3).

For example, St Pancras Station in central London comprises a large, low rise hotel built in the Victorian Gothic style with an expansive rail terminus behind. The cost to reproduce a large, low rise hotel built in the Victorian Gothic style largely in brick with an expansive rail terminus behind largely in brick, iron and glass may be likely to be very significantly greater than the cost of replacing the asset with a modern high rise hotel and an adjacent compact rail terminus built largely in concrete and steel.

TIP 2 contemplates reproduction being unusual and 'quite rare in practice', as the theory of substitution indicates that the only cost relevant to determining the price that a market participant may pay is based on replicating the utility of the asset not the physical nature of the asset, with utility determining economic value. Reproduction cost may, therefore, only arise in such cases as heritage assets classified for historic preservation in their entirety or where an asset's exact design and features are an integral part of the benefit or utility that would accrue to an owner, such as may arise in an iconic building (TIP 2, para 20, page 5).

In the event that reproduction cost is adopted, TIP 2 states this to be:

> ... the estimated cost to construct, as of the valuation date, an exact replica of the asset insofar as possible to the same specifications using the same materials, construction techniques, quality and design including all the asset's deficiencies... where this would not be possible. . careful consideration should be given as to whether the cost of the closest available current equivalent would be more appropriate... (TIP 2, page 6, para 26)

In practice, TIP 2 notes the choice between selecting reproduction cost or replacement cost will depend on:

- the nature of the asset;
- the nature of available comparative cost data;

6 Valuation of OOP

- the purpose of the valuation; and
- whether market participants are more likely to consider a modern equivalent asset as an alternative to the asset being valued or whether they would be more likely to require a direct replica,

with replacement cost otherwise being selected where lower than reproduction cost (TIP 2, para 19, page 5).

Replacement cost seeks to estimate the cost to construct or acquire a new modern equivalent asset as of the valuation date (TIP 2, para 22, page 5), excluding redundant features (TIP 2, para 24, page 6) at the least cost (TIP 2, para 25, page 6). To estimate the replacement cost, it is necessary to establish the nature of the modern equivalent asset that the hypothetical buyer would consider an acceptable alternative to the subject property which, in turn, requires an understanding of the utility or functionality provided by the subject property as the theory of substitution requires that regard be had to the cost to a buyer of buying or creating an alternative that could provide the same utility (TIP 2, para 22, page 5, 6).

In seeking to estimate *market value* using the replacement *cost approach*, regard should be had to utility from the perspective of a market participant whereas, in seeking to estimate *investment value* using the replacement *cost approach*, regard should be had to the perspective of the specific entity, each being a measure of the economic or other benefit that can be derived from ownership of the asset (TIP 2, para 23, page 6).

6.1.3.4 Cost elements

TIP 2 requires that, for both reproduction cost and for replacement cost, all of the costs that would be incurred by a typical market participant, seeking to create an asset providing equivalent utility, be captured though they may vary depending on the basis of value and any associated assumptions (TIP 2, para 27, page 6).

Such costs may commonly include:

- direct costs, such as:
  - materials;
  - labour used in construction or installation;
- indirect costs, such as:
  - transport costs;
  - installation costs;
  - design, permit, architectural, legal, other professional costs and project management or coordination fees for complex assets;
  - engineering, procurement and construction management costs;
  - unrecoverable taxes;

o finance costs (or opportunity costs and/or risk where owner-funded) during the construction period, having regard to:
- the cost and level of debt typical for market participants, to determine the level of borrowing and interest arising;
- the typical construction period for similar construction projects, to determine the maximum period over which interest costs will be incurred; and
- the typical draw down schedule on debt facilities over the assumed construction period for similar construction projects, to determine the approximate timing of draw downs and interest then arising;
o marketing, sales or leasing commissions; and
o costs of holding the property after construction is completed but before stable occupancy is achieved (TIP 2, para 28 - 32, page 7);

with care required, when using data from actual cost of creation of the subject property or a comparable asset, concerning cost fluctuations between the date of creation and the date of valuation and any exceptional costs/savings that arose in the creation but may not arise in an equivalent replacement (TIP 2, para 34, page 8).

Similarly, care is required in the use of data relating to the cost of refurbishment or improvement as this may include adaption or alteration costs which would not be incurred in a replacement of the whole property (TIP 2, para 35, page 8). Further, costs appearing in an entity's financial records may not reflect replacement or reproduction cost, as such costs may include other costs such as a merger or other earlier purchase and should, therefore, be treated with caution (TIP 2, para 36, page 8).

TIP 2 notes that the *cost approach* may be applied to a group of assets, a single asset or to separate components of an asset depending on the purpose of valuation and availability of data, with a separate cost and depreciation calculation made where an individual asset or component could be replaced separately without major disruption to the balance and/or has a materially different remaining life (TIP 2, para 71, 72, page 14).

6.1.3.5 Depreciation

The *cost approach* seeks to estimate the costs of reproduction or replacement of a property of equivalent utility as new and then to depreciate this to reflect the impact on value of various forms of obsolescence affecting the subject property (TIP 2, para 37, page 8 – further considered in the context of IVS 300 in section 6.2.1.2, below), with obsolescence defined as:

A loss of utility of an asset caused by either physical deterioration, changes in technology, patterns of demand or environmental changes that results in a loss of value. (TIP 2, para 8, page 3)

6 Valuation of OOP

TIP 2 considers three principal forms of obsolescence being physical, functional and economic obsolescence (TIP 2, para 38, page 9), generally measured by comparison between the subject property and the hypothetical new property upon which the cost estimate is based (TIP 2, para 39, page 9).

Where a profile of depreciation can be observed from the analysis of comparable sales relative to replacement costs, TIP 2 notes a depreciation profile may be applied to determine the appropriate rate of depreciation at the valuation date such as:

- straight-line depreciation, where the same proportion of original cost is deducted each period over the estimated life of the asset;
- diminishing value deprecation, where a constant percentage rate is deducted from cost at the start of the previous period over the estimated life of the asset; or
- S-curve depreciation, where different percentage rates are deducted for each period over the estimated life of the asset (TIP 2, para 69, 70, page 14).

In the context of replacement cost, application of depreciation results in an estimate of depreciated replacement cost which TIP 2 defines as:

A method under the *cost approach* that indicates value by calculating the current replacement cost of an asset less deductions for physical deterioration and all relevant forms of obsolescence (TIP 2, para 8, page 2)

with the three principal forms of obsolescence being physical, functional and economic obsolescence.

6.1.3.5.1 Physical obsolescence
TIP 2 defines physical obsolescence as:

A loss of utility due to the physical deterioration of the asset or its components resulting from its age and normal usage that results in a loss of value. (TIP2, para 8, page 3)

TIP2 focuses on curable and incurable physical obsolescence with:

- curable physical obsolescence being often capable of correction by maintenance or repair, where the value increase is equal to or greater than the cost to cure or where curing allows other existing items to maintain their value and where the measurement of curable physical obsolescence is the cost to cure it (TIP 2, para 41, page 9); and

- incurable physical obsolescence being a condition incapable of remedy either at all or cost effectively and where measurement of incurable physical obsolescence considers the asset's age, expected total and remaining life and where the adjustment for physical obsolescence is equivalent to the proportion of the expected total life consumed (TIP 2, para 42, page 9).

   In the context of measuring physical obsolescence, physical building life may vary from economic building life. The physical life of a building represents the length of time the building could be used, appropriately main-tained but disregarding refurbishment, before it is worn out or beyond cost effective repair. The economic life of a building represents the length of time the building is anticipated to generate economic benefits (such as generating financial returns or providing non-financial benefits) in its cur-rent use, which will be influenced by the building's degree of functional or economic obsolescence (TIP 2, para 8, page 2; para 43–45, page 10).

   While the economic life of a building cannot be longer than its physical life, the physical life may exceed the economic life resulting in a value at the end of the building's economic life reflecting its potential for alternative use, reconstruction or recycling (TIP 2, para 46, page 10) with allowance for any costs of clearance, decommissioning and decontamination required to provide a floor in value (TIP 2, para 47, page 10).

6.1.3.5.2 Functional obsolescence

TIP 2 defines functional obsolescence as:

> A loss of utility resulting from inefficiencies in the subject asset compared to its replacement that results in a loss of value. (TIP 2, para 8, page 2)

TIP 2 focuses on two forms of functional obsolescence arising from changes in design, technology or both, being (TIP 2, para 50, page 11):

- excess capital cost, where changes in design, materials or technology result in a modern equivalent asset available at a lower capital cost than the subject asset (TIP 2, para 49, page 10); and
- excess operating cost, where improvements in design result in a modern equivalent asset available at a lower operating cost than the subject asset (TIP 2, para 49, page 10);

citing the example of an office building with many individual rooms separated by structural walls resulting in an inflexible layout that would limit the number of occupiers who could use the building efficiently (TIP 2, para 52, page 11).

In the context of measurement, the cost of correcting a functional inadequacy is compared with the value gained to arrive at a measure of the functional obsolescence (TIP 2, para 53, page 11).

6.1.3.5.3 Economic obsolescence

TIP 2 defines external obsolescence as:

> A loss of utility caused by economic or locational factors external to the asset that results in a loss of value. (TIP 2, para 8, page 2)

being commonly called economic obsolescence where the external factors relate to changes in supply or demand for the asset (TIP 2, para 59, page 12), with economic obsolescence defined as:

> A loss of utility caused by factors external to the asset, especially factors related to changes in supply or demand for products produced by the asset that results in a loss of value. (TIP 2, para 8, page 2)

TIP 2 specifies that the economic obsolescence adjustment be deducted after physical obsolescence and functional obsolescence because economic obsolescence is independent of the asset (TIP 2, para 61, page 12).

In the context of measurement, economic obsolescence may be assessed for a property by considering whether a going concern business could afford to pay a market rent for the property and still generate a market rate of return having regard to the value of the property (TIP 2, para 62, page 12).

6.1.3.6 Summary – Valuation of owner occupied property in IVSs

For the valuation of owner occupied property, the IVS of principal relevance is IVS 230 *Real Property Interests* which comprises *Requirements* to be followed in valuation instructions, implementation and reporting and *Commentary* which includes issues of relevance in application of which *market rent* is particularly significant.

With many owner occupied properties comprising business premises with operational *plant and equipment* requiring valuation together with the *real property*, IVS 220 *Plant and Equipment* is of principal relevance with *Requirements* to be followed in valuation instructions, implementation and reporting and *Commentary* of particular relevance concerning the classification as *real property* or *plant and equipment*.

While the *market approach* or the *income approach* may often be adopted in the valuation of owner occupied property, the *cost approach* may also be adopted with TIP 2 *The Cost Approach to Tangible Assets* being of particular relevance, addressing the assessment of land value, reproduction/replacement assessment, estimate of costs and selection of depreciation rates to reflect physical, functional and economic obsolescence, each of which may be challenging to apply in practice.

However, the valuation of owner occupied property is not only influenced by IVS 230, IVS 220 and TIP 2 but also by the provisions of IFRS, in those jurisdictions where such provisions apply for the purposes of financial reporting, which are considered in the following section.

6.1.4 Owner occupied property in IFRS

Sections 6.1.1, 6.1.2 and 6.1.3 considered those IVSs of principal relevance for the valuation of owner occupied property, being IVS 230 *Real Property Interests* and IVS 220 *Plant and Equipment*, together with TIP 2 *The Cost Approach to Tangible Assets*.

This section considers those IFRS and IAS of principal relevance for the valuation of owner occupied property, being IAS 16 *Property, Plant and Equipment*, IAS 36 *Impairment of Assets*, IFRS 5 *Non-Current Assets Held for Sale and Discontinued Operations* and IAS 17 *Leases* in the context of owner occupied property.

The following sections will then consider the valuation of owner occupied property for the purpose of financial reporting and secured lending, respectively.

6.1.4.1 IAS 16 Property, Plant and Equipment

Reflecting the importance of the appropriate measurement of property, plant and equipment in the financial statements of operating businesses, accounting standards have recognised issues associated with property, plant and equipment for around 30 years culminating in IAS 16 *Property, Plant and Equipment* which was originally adopted in 2001 (IFRS 2013, page A689).

To distinguish owner occupied property from investment property, IAS 40 *Investment Property* defines owner occupied property as:

> **Owner-occupied property** is property held (by the owner or by the lessee under a finance lease) for use in the production or supply of goods or services or for administrative purposes. (IAS 40, para 5, page A1146)

6.1.4.1.1 What is property, plant and equipment?

Property, plant and equipment is defined in IAS 16 as:

> Property, plant and equipment are tangible items that:
> (a) are held for use in the production or supply of goods or services, for rental to others, or for administrative purposes; and
> (b) are expected to be used during more than one period. (IAS 16, para 6, page A696)

6 Valuation of OOP

IAS 16 applies to all *property, plant and equipment* except (IAS 16, para 2, page A695):

- property, plant and equipment held for sale under IFRS 5 *Non-Current Assets Held for Sale and Discontinued Operations*; and
- biological assets related to agricultural activity, exploration and evaluation assets, mineral rights, mineral reserves and similar non-regenerative assets (IAS 16, para 3, page A695).

An entity using the cost model for *investment property* in accordance with IAS 40 *Investment Property* shall use the cost model in IAS 16 (IAS 16, para 5, page A695).

Accordingly, IAS 16 may be applicable to owner occupied property, plant and equipment held by most operating businesses from a small engineering business which owns its factory to a major international corporate with offices, manufacturing plants and warehouses in numerous countries around the world.

6.1.4.1.2 Property, plant and equipment recognition in financial statements
Under IAS 16, an item of *property, plant and equipment* will only be recognised if:

- it is probable that future economic benefits associated with the item will flow to the entity; and
- the cost of the item can be measured reliably (IAS 16, para 7, page A696).

However, IAS 16 recognises that items of *property, plant and equipment* may be acquired for safety or environmental reasons which, while not directly increasing future economic benefits, may facilitate future economic benefits from other assets and so are recognised (IAS 16, para 11, page A697).

IAS 16 requires general recognition of *property, plant and equipment* at its cost at the time it is incurred, including initial acquisition or construction costs and subsequent costs to add to, replace part of or service an item of *property, plant and equipment* (IAS 16, para IN6, page A692; para 10, page A697; para 15, page A698).

In determining the amount to be recognised in financial statements subsequent to initial recognition, IAS 16 requires an entity to choose between the cost model or the revaluation model and then to apply that chosen model to an entire class of *property, plant and equipment* (IAS 16, para 29, page A701). Accordingly, an operating business is precluded from measuring some of its warehouses using the cost model and the balance of its warehouses using the revaluation model, being required to select one model for application to all.

The cost model under IAS 16 states that:

> After recognition as an asset, an item of *property, plant and equipment* shall be carried at its cost less any accumulated depreciation and any accumulated impairment losses. (IAS 16, para 30, page A701)

The revaluation model under IAS 16 states that:

> After recognition as an asset, an item of *property, plant and equipment* whose fair value can be measured reliably shall be carried at a revalued amount, being its fair value at the date of revaluation less any subsequent accumulated depreciation and subsequent accumulated impairment losses. (IAS 16, para 31, page A701)

and further that:

> Revaluations shall be made with sufficient regularity to ensure that the carrying amount does not differ materially from that which would be determined using fair value at the end of the reporting period. (IAS 16, para 31, page A701)

Accordingly, the revaluation model is an interesting mix of valuation concepts and accounting concepts, with regular revaluation to fair value qualified by adjustments for depreciation and impairment losses.

Whereas owners of investment property may contemplate quarterly revaluations or, at the longest, annual revaluations, IAS 16 provides considerable flexibility for operating businesses in the frequency of revaluation which depends upon material changes in fair value with annual revaluation apparently considered necessary only where there are volatile changes in fair value and three to five yearly revaluations probably being appropriate otherwise (IAS 16, para 34, page A701). It should be noted that IAS 16 requires such revaluation to be of an entire class of *property, plant and equipment* and not the selective revaluation of individual properties or items of plant and equipment (IAS 16, Para 36, 37, page A702).

While this may pragmatically reflect the lesser significance of *property, plant and equipment* to the balance sheet of an operating business than to the balance sheet of a real estate investment trust, property company, superannuation fund and so forth, it assumes that management of the operating business has sufficient awareness of the local property market conditions for each property in its ownership to judge whether a material change in fair value may have occurred to prompt revaluation of the entire class of property. Therefore, for an operating business, a rolling programme of revaluations for a class of *property, plant and equipment* may be an effective risk management strategy and provide increased transparency in the balance sheet, as permitted under IAS 16 provided such revaluation is within a short period and revaluations are kept up to date (IAS 16, para 38, page A702).

6.1.4.1.3 Depreciation

For *property, plant and equipment* held by operating businesses, IAS 16 requires separate depreciation of each part of an item of *property, plant and equipment* that has a cost which is significant relative to the total cost of the item (IAS 16, para 43, page A703).

In the context of property, land and buildings are separable and are accounted for separately even when acquired together. While the building component is subject to depreciation as it has a limited useful life, the land component is not subject to depreciation as it has normally an unlimited useful life. Being separable, changes in the value of the land component do not affect the determination of the depreciable amount of the building component (IAS 16, para 58, page A705). Accordingly, valuation instructions for property held by operating businesses may often require an assessment of land value and the assumptions concerning same should be carefully recorded in the valuation instruction and repeated in the valuation report.

In the context of the building component, IAS 16 requires that the depreciable amount (being the cost of an asset less its residual value) (IAS 16, para 6, page A696) be allocated on a systematic basis over its useful life (being the period over which the building is expected to be available for use by the entity) (IAS 16, para 6, page A696) (IAS 16, para 50, page A704).

It should be noted that the useful life under this definition may be specific to the entity and different from the remaining economic life as would be considered by market participants generally. Although the determination of the appropriate pattern of depreciation is a matter for the entity, a valuer may be asked to advise on the residual value (being the net disposal proceeds at the end of the use period) (IAS 16, para 6, page A696) or the useful life. These are required to be reviewed at least annually (IAS 16, para 51, page A704).

It is important to note that depreciation as defined and required in IAS 16 is a different concept from the assessment of obsolescence when applying the cost approach in valuation, which is often also referred to as depreciation. Under IAS 16 depreciation is the progressive consumption of future economic benefits embodied in an asset through its use which may, secondarily, be further diminished by other factors such as technical or commercial obsolescence or wear and tear (IAS 16, para 56, page A704).

While premised on the pattern in which the asset's future economic benefits are expected to be consumed by the entity, IAS 16 does, however, recognise similar deprecation methods to those described in TIP 2 (section 6.1.3, above), including the straight line method and the diminishing value method while also adding the units of production method (IAS 16, para 60, 62, page A705).

6.1.4.1.4 Disclosure

IAS 16 requires the following extensive disclosure in financial statements for each class of *property, plant and equipment*:

- the measurement bases used for determining the gross carrying amount;
- the depreciation methods used;
- the useful lives or the depreciation rates used;
- the gross carrying amount and the accumulated depreciation (aggregated with accumulated impairment losses) at the beginning and end of the period;
- a reconciliation of the carrying amount at the beginning and end of the period showing:
  - additions;
  - assets classified as held for sale or disposal;
  - acquisitions through business combinations;
  - increases or decreases resulting from revaluations under the revaluation model and from recognised/reversed impairment losses in other comprehensive income;
  - impairment losses recognised/reversed in profit and loss;
  - depreciation;
  - net exchange differences on currency translation; and
  - other changes (IAS 16, para 73, page A707, A708);
- the existence and amounts of restrictions on title and *property, plant and equipment* pledged as security for liabilities;
- the amount of expenditures recognised in the carrying amount of *property, plant and equipment* in the course of construction;
- the amount of contractual commitments for the acquisition of *property, plant and equipment*; and
- any compensation from third parties for *property, plant and equipment* that is impaired, lost or given up (IAS 16, para 74, page 708);

and in the context of property held by an operating business and stated at revalued amounts using the revaluation model:

- the effective date of the revaluation;
- whether an independent valuer was involved;
- for each revalued class of *property, plant and equipment*, the carrying amount that would have been recognised had the assets been carried under the cost model; and
- the revaluation surplus, indicating the change for the period (IAS 16, para 77, page A709).

6 Valuation of OOP

6.1.4.2 *IAS 36* Impairment of Assets

IAS 36 *Impairment of Assets* may be applicable to any investment property carried under the cost model in IAS 40 and to owner occupied property. Under IAS 16 it is necessary to consider whether *property, plant and equipment* is 'impaired' at each reporting date, regardless of whether the cost model or the revaluation model is used.

To determine impairment, the entity applies IAS 36 (IAS 36, para 63, page A706). Under IAS 36, an impairment loss is defined as the amount by which the carrying amount of an asset or cash generating unit exceeds it recoverable amount (IAS 36, para 6).

In order to understand this definition, a number of the terms adopted require explanation:

- the 'carrying amount' is the amount of the asset currently appearing in a financial statement, normally measured as at the end of the previous accounting period. This may have been measured on the basis of cost or at fair value;
- a 'cash generating unit' is the smallest identifiable group of assets that generates cash inflows that are largely independent from the cash inflows of other assets or groups of assets;
- the 'recoverable amount' is the higher of the fair value less costs of disposal and the 'value in use'; and
- 'value in use' is the present value of the future cash flows expected to be derived from the asset or cash generating unit.

Where an asset is regularly revalued an impairment loss is less likely to arise than where the carry amount is based on historic cost less depreciation. However, the need to consider impairment at the level of the cash generating unit may mean that an individual asset may still be found to be impaired below its fair value, for example where a building is an integral part of a cash generating unit which is subject to a previously unexpected curtailment of operations.

Where an operating business property cannot be separated from other properties comprising the business for the purposes of impairment testing, such as a head office or a research centre in the middle of a major manufacturing facility, IAS 36 considers such property to be *corporate assets*, being defined as:

> ... assets other than goodwill that contribute to the future cash flows of both the cash-generating unit under review and other cash-generating units. (IAS 36, para 6, page A995)

and:

The distinctive characteristics of *corporate assets* are that they do not generate cash inflows independently of other assets or groups of assets and their carrying amount cannot be fully attributed to the cash-generating unit under review. (IAS 36, Para 101, page A1015)

IAS 36 notes that, as *corporate assets* do not generate separate cash inflows, the recoverable amount cannot be determined such that, if there is an indication of impairment, recoverable amount is determined for the entire cash generating unit (IAS 36, para 100, 101, page A1015).

The calculation of the recoverable amount requires comparison of both the fair value less costs of disposal and the value in use. Fair value less costs of disposal is self-explanatory, with the application of fair value being discussed in section 6.2.2 and in section 5.2.2.2 in Chapter 5. Although at first sight value in use appears to be a straightforward discounted cash flow exercise, IAS 36 does set out various parameters for the way in which future cash flows should be estimated and the discount rate selected (IAS 36, paras 30–57, pages A1001–A1006 and Appendix A). Before undertaking an estimate of value in use these parameters should be understood and applied as appropriate.

6.1.4.3 IFRS 5 Non-Current Assets Held for Sale and Discontinued Operations

IFRS 5 *Non-Current Assets Held for Sale and Discontinued Operations* may be applicable to surplus owner occupied property and to any investment property measured using the cost model.

IFRS 5 requires that non-current assets held for sale and discontinued operations must be disclosed separately in the financial statements and not offset (IFRS 5, para 38, page A220) in order to allow stakeholders to assess the amount, timing and uncertainty of, or prospects for, future net cash flows of the entity as the basis for decision making (IFRS 2012, page 13; IFRS 5, para 30, page A218).

IFRS 5 defines a discontinued operation as:

A component of an entity that either has been disposed of or is classified as held for sale and:

(a) represents a separate major line of business or geographical area of operations;
(b) is part of a single co-ordinated plan to dispose of a separate major line of business or geographical area of operations; or
(c) is a subsidiary acquired exclusively with a view to resale. (IFRS 5, Appendix A, Page A223)

with discontinued operations to be presented separately (IFRS, page 13).

Common to both non-current assets held for sale and discontinued operations is the prospect of the sale of property in the near future which will test any prior assessment of value.

6.1.4.4 *IAS 17* Leases

Under IAS 17 leases are classified as either finance leases or operating leases. A lease is classified as a finance lease if it transfers substantially all the risks and rewards incidental to ownership. A lease is classified as an operating lease if it does not transfer substantially all the risks and rewards incidental to ownership (IAS 17, para 8).

How a lease is classified affects its accounting treatment. A finance lease is recognised as either an asset or a liability on the statement of financial position (balance sheet). The income or outgoing under an operating lease is accounted for in the income statement (profit and loss).

Most property leases do not transfer the risks and rewards of ownership from lessor to lessee, and the right of occupation reverts to the lessor at the end of the term. Most are therefore operating leases. On the normal criteria in IAS 17 property held by an investor under a long lease as lessee on which the investor then constructs a building which is then leased to sub-lessee occupiers would be classified as an operating lease. This would have meant that many property companies would have been unable to include potentially valuable assets on their balance sheet. To avoid the difficulties and distortions this would have caused, IAS 40 provides that any property held under lease and that meets the definition of Investment Property is to be classified as a finance lease.

IAS 17 provides that when a lease is of land and buildings each element must be considered separately for classification purposes (IAS 17, para 15A, page A722). One of the tests for a finance lease is whether the lease is for the major part of the asset's economic life. Land is normally considered to have an indefinite economic life and therefore this element is normally considered to be an operating lease. However, most buildings have a finite economic life and, in the case of a long lease, it can often be argued that the lease is for the major part of that life and therefore it is a finance lease.

When a lease is identified as a finance lease, the lessee is required to account for the asset and liability based on the lower of either the fair value of the leased asset or the present value of the minimum lease payments, determined as at the inception of the lease (IVS 300, para G33, page 102). Further, the value of the asset (being the value of the benefit that a market participant would accrue from the right to use the asset for the duration of the lease) is considered separately from the value of the liability created by the lease (IAS 17, para 23, page 724). IVS 300 notes that this is different from the normal practice of valuing a lessee's interest in a property lease which reflects the present value of the asset (i.e. after deduction of liabilities).

IFRS 13 *Fair Value Measurement* does not apply to leases (IFRS 13, para 6b, page A490). Fair value is not defined in IAS 17, it being simply noted that it uses the term in a way that is different in some respects from the IFRS definition (IAS 17, para 6A, page A721).

The role of valuation in helping to determine lease classification and then in producing valuations of any finance lease assets and liabilities for financial reporting is a complex area, and one that benefits from close liaison between the valuer, client and the client's accountants.

The accounting treatment of leases continues to be under review so readers should not rely upon this book as a current statement of IFRS position and should visit www.ifrs.org to find the most recent publically stated position.

6.1.4.5 Summary – Owner occupied property in IFRS

For the valuation of owner occupied property, plant and equipment, the IAS of principal relevance is IAS 16 *Property, Plant and Equipment* which applies to most property, plant and equipment likely to be owner occupied and focuses on initial recognition in financial reporting at cost with revaluation to fair value recognising subsequent accumulated depreciation and accumulated impairment losses.

6.2 Valuation of owner occupied property for financial reporting

The previous section sought to focus on IVSs, TIP's, IAS's and IFRS's in the context of the valuation of owner occupied property held by operating businesses, with this section focusing on the valuation of owner occupied property in the context of financial reporting and the following section then focusing on the valuation of owner occupied property in the context of secured lending.

In the context of the valuation of owner occupied property for the purpose of financial reporting, the IVS of principal relevance is IVS 300 *Valuations for Financial Reporting* with IFRS 13 *Fair Value Measurement* also of relevance.

Major international corporations owning large operational property portfolios such as HSBC and Airbus are required to record the value of their property portfolios in their financial statements on the basis of IFRS. Therefore, as previously noted, the valuation of owner occupied property for the purpose of financial reporting requires the valuer to have regard to the interaction between several IVSs, TIP's, IAS's and IFRS's simultaneously with considerable care required to comply with the requirements of each at the same time.

6.2.1 *IVS 300* Valuations for Financial Reporting

IVS 300 *Valuations for Financial Reporting* comprises four sections, being *Introduction*, *Definitions*, *Requirements* (focusing on valuation instruction, implementation and reporting) and *Application Guidance* (focusing on issues that may arise in application of the Standard).

The *Introduction* to IVS 300, addressing valuations for accounting purposes for the preparation of financial statements, was considered in section 5.2.1 of Chapter 5 together with the *Requirements*.

Concerning *Commentary*, in the context of owner occupied property, IVS 300 addresses:

- fair value, as considered in section 2.4.3.4 of Chapter 2 (IVS 300, para G1–G2, pages 94–95); and
- valuation inputs and the fair value hierarchy, as considered in section 5.2.2.4 of Chapter 5 (IVS 300, para G4–G5, pages 95–96);

as well as the following which have relevance for the valuation of owner occupied property for financial reporting.

6.2.1.1 *Aggregation*

IVS 300 specifically addresses aggregation, which is generally more likely to arise regularly as an issue in the context of *property, plant and equipment* in an operating business rather than for investment property.

The value of an individual asset may be dependent upon its association with other related assets, such as:

- interdependent land, buildings, plant and other equipment employed in a business enterprise; or
- a portfolio of properties that complement each other by providing a prospective buyer with either a critical mass or a presence in strategic locations (IVSC, 2013, para 23, page 16).

Accordingly, it is important to clearly define where assets are being valued as part of a group or portfolio or individually and if the valuation of such an individual asset assumes that the other assets are available or not available to the buyer (IVSC, 2013, para 24, pages 16 and 17).

While fair value under IFRS applies to the 'unit of account' which may be an individual asset, it may also relate to a group of assets. Accordingly, when considering a potential group of assets, IFRS 13 requires determination of whether the maximum value to market participants would be to use the asset in combination with other assets as a group or to use the asset on a standalone basis, with a statement of assumption for aggregation included in both the valuation instructions and the valuation report (IVS 300, para G3, page 95).

6.2.1.2 *Depreciation*
IVS 300 notes that IAS 16 includes a requirement for an entity to account for the depreciation of *property, plant and equipment* with land not normally depreciated and valuations often being required to support the calculation of the depreciable amount (IVS 300, para G8, page 96).

Further, IVS 300 usefully notes that the term depreciation is used in different contexts in valuation and in financial reporting. In the context of valuation, depreciation is often used to refer to the adjustments made when using the *cost approach* to estimate the cost of reproducing or replacing the asset to reflect obsolescence in order to indicate value in the absence of direct sales evidence. In the context of financial reporting, depreciation refers to the charge made against income to reflect the systematic allocation of the depreciable amount of an asset over its useful life to the entity (IVS 300, para G9, page 96).

IAS 16 requires, in the context of the building component, that the depreciable amount (being the cost or carrying amount of an asset less its residual value) (IAS 16, para 6, page A696) be allocated on a systematic basis over its useful life (being the period over which the building is expected to be available for use by the entity) (IAS 16, para 6, page A696) (IAS 16, para 50, page A704) with residual value (being the net disposal proceeds at the end of the use period) (IAS 16, para 6, page A696) and useful life reviewed at least annually (IAS 16, para 51, page A704). Accordingly, while the depreciation of the building component is a matter for the reporting entity, there may be valuation inputs required such as the assessment of useful life or of residual value (IVS 300, para G10, G11, page 97).

6.2.1.2.1 Depreciation – land and buildings
As land has an unlimited life and is not depreciable, the first step in determining depreciable amount is to determine the value of the land component separate to the buildings. IVS 300 notes that this is normally done by estimating the value of the land at the date of the relevant financial statements and deducting this from the cost or carrying amount of the land and buildings combined as given in the financial statements to derive a component that can be notionally attributed to buildings (though acknowledging that this may be incapable of being realised as buildings cannot usually be sold without land) (IVS 300, para G12, page 97).

Considerable care is required to maintain consistency of assumptions when estimating the value of land. For example, if the current buildings are considered the highest and best use and such use is permitted under the relevant planning regulations, then the use of the land can be readily identified. However, if the current buildings are not considered the highest and best use and/or such use is not permitted under the relevant planning regulations, then that use of the land upon which the valuation is based should be clearly stated as an assumption or *special assumption* in both the valuation instructions and the valuation report.

Having derived a component that can be notionally attributed to buildings, the residual value of the buildings requires estimation which necessitates determination of useful life. With useful life being the period over which the building is expected to be available for use by the entity, this may differ from the economic life that may be recognised by a typical market participant. Accordingly, if the property would not be available to the entity for the whole of its economic life or the entity determines the building will be surplus to its requirements in a shorter period, then the useful life of the building may be less than its economic life (IVS 300, para G13, page 97, 98).

IVS 300 notes that residual value is the value current at the date of the financial statement but on the assumption that the asset was already at the end of its useful life and in a condition commensurate with that assumption. Accordingly, as residual value is the net disposal proceeds at the end of the use period by the entity, where the economic life of a building exceeds the useful life by the entity the residual amount may be relatively high (IVS 300, para G14, page 98).

6.2.1.2.2 Depreciation – plant and equipment
Concerning plant and equipment, IVS 300 notes that, as the useful life of plant and equipment is more likely to coincide with economic life due to higher rates of obsolescence, residual amounts may not be high but the difference in useful life and economic life should still be considered (IVS 300, para G15, page 98).

6.2.1.2.3 Depreciation – componentisation
IVS 300 notes that where the carrying amount of plant and equipment is based on historic cost, those components with a significant cost and those with a materially different useful life should be readily identifiable (IVS 300, para G16, page 98).

However, where the carrying amount is based on fair value, an allocation of that fair value between the components of the plant and equipment will be required. Where there is an active market for a component, it may be possible to determine the value attributable to the component. Conversely, where there is no active market and the value of individual components cannot be separately identified, then the value attributable to the whole is apportioned to the components for which a ratio of relative costs may be an appropriate basis for apportionment (IVS 300, para G17, page 98).

6.2.1.3 *Classification of property leases*

Finally, in the context of provisions that have greater relevance for owner occupied property than for investment property, IVS 300 addresses classification of property leases.

For most property leases, the interest in the land and buildings reverts to the lessor at the end of the lease with periodic rent reviews and make good obligations, being identifiable as an operating lease where substantially all the risks and rewards of ownership are not transferred (IVS 300, para G25, page 100).

However, a finance lease of land and buildings may arise where a lease is clearly created as a way of funding the eventual purchase of the property by the lessee, such as through an option to acquire the lessor's interest for a nominal sum after the specified rental payments have been made (IVS 300, para G26, page 100). In the event of a finance lease, IAS 17 requires the land and buildings to be considered separately for the purposes of classification with an allocation of the initial rent based on the relative fair values of the interests in the land and in the buildings at the inception of the lease (IVS 300, para G24, page 100). Where there is an active market in land rent and building rent, such allocation may be undertaken reliably. Where there is no active market in land rent, reliable allocation may not be possible with IVS 300 advising against allocation on unreliable criteria and IAS 17 then requiring the whole of the leased property to be treated as a finance lease (IVS 300, para G28, G27, page 101).

6.2.1.4 *IVS 300* Valuations for Financial Reporting *in practice*

In the context of owner occupied properties and aggregation, as considered in section 6.2.1.1 above and in the IVS Framework (IVS Framework, para 23, 24, pages 16, 17), RICS VPGA8 *Valuation of Portfolios, Collections and Groups of Properties* in the RICS Red Book Global provides further guidance.

RICS VPGA8 advocates grouping of properties in the manner most likely to be adopted in the case of an actual sale of the interest(s) being valued, having discussed the options with the client and confirmed the approach adopted in the valuation instructions and valuation report (RICS VPGA8, para 2.1, page 111). In the event of an unusual grouping, this may be dealt with using a *special assumption* (RICS VPGA8, para 2.4, page 112).

However, RICS VPGA8 cautions that offering a portfolio to the market may result in a flooding of the market reducing values or could provide a rare opportunity commanding a premium (RICS VPGA8, para 3.2, page 112). For the purposes of financial statements, RICS VPGA8 notes the purpose assumes that the portfolio will remain in the existing ownership such that a reduction or allowance would be inappropriate with a statement to such effect to be included in the report (RICS VPGA8, para 3.3, page 112). Conversely, for the purposes of secured lending, the adverse effect of market flooding should not be ignored and an assumption of orderly marketing and sequential sale should be included in the valuation instructions and valuation report. If orderly marketing and sequential sale is not possible due to extreme financial distress, a *special assumption* to that effect should be included in the valuation instructions and valuation report (RICS VPGA8, para 3.4, page 112).

6.2.2 *IFRS 13* Fair Value Measurement

While IFRS 13 *Fair Value Measurement* was considered in detail in Chapter 5 in the context of investment property, it also contains provisions of particular relevance to the valuation of owner occupied property for financial reporting purposes.

IFRS 13 *Fair Value Measurement* summarises the objective of a fair value measurement to be to estimate the price at which an orderly transaction to sell the asset would take place between market participants at the measurement date under current market conditions (IFRS 13, Appendix B, para B2, page A514).

In the context of the valuation of owner occupied property for financial reporting purposes, the following provisions of IFRS 13 *Fair Value Measurement* are of particular relevance.

6.2.2.1 *IFRS 13 highest and best use*
In an operating businesses, *property, plant and equipment* may often be held within a group of interrelated assets rather than as a separate, standalone asset.

IFRS 13 provides that the highest and best use of a non-financial asset may be through its use in combination with other assets as a group or in combination with other assets and liabilities (such as a business) (IFRS 13, para 31(a), page A494). If the highest and best use is such, IFRS 13 provides the fair value of the asset to be the price that would be received in a current transaction to sell the asset assuming that the asset would be used with other assets or with other assets and liabilities and that such assets and liabilities would be available to market participants (IFRS 13, para 31(a)(i), page A494).

Alternatively, if the highest and best use of a non-financial asset to market participants is on a standalone basis, IFRS 13 provides the fair value of the asset to be the price that would be received in a current transaction to sell the asset to market participants that would use the asset on a standalone basis (IFRS 13, para 31(b), page A495; para B3, pages A514, A515).

6.2.2.2 IFRS 13 definition of fair value

In the context of owner occupied property, while aspects of the definition of fair value will require application consistent with that considered in section 5.2.2.2 of Chapter 5, certain aspects may require more focused attention.

For example, in the context of 'to sell' considered in section 5.2.2.2 of Chapter 5, a transaction is assumed to occur in the 'principal market for the asset' or, in its absence, 'the most advantageous market for the asset' (IFRS 13, para 16, page A492). This may be an aspect requiring careful consideration for major manufacturing plants valued as part of a business as a going concern, such as car plants or bottling plants, where the 'principal market for the asset' may be considered to be a national or international market comprising other national or international car manufacturers or other bottlers, assuming that to be the market with the greatest volume and level of activity for the asset (IFRS 13, para 19, 20, page A492).

Further, for example, in the context of 'between market participants' considered in section 5.2.2.2 of Chapter 5, fair value under IFRS 13 requires the measuring entity to use the 'assumptions that market participants would use when pricing the asset... assuming that market participants act in their economic best interests' (IFRS 13, para 22, page A493). While the measuring entity is not required to identify 'specific market participants' but rather the 'characteristics that distinguish market participants generally' (IFRS 13, para 23, page A493), care is required where such a general market has few participants and the prospect of unusually strong competition may influence likely price levels.

6.2.2.3 IFRS 13 valuation techniques

As considered in section 6.1.4.1, above, in determining the amount to be recognised in financial statements subsequent to initial recognition, IAS 16 requires an entity to choose between the cost model or the revaluation model and then to apply that chosen model to an entire class of *property, plant and equipment* (IAS 16, para 29, page A701). In the context of owner occupied property, choice of the cost model is common since, in many cases, there is little advantage to the entity in opting for the revaluation model.

Echoing the IVS Framework, IFRS 13 describes the *cost approach* as reflecting the amount that would be required currently to replace the service capacity of an asset (often referred to as current replacement cost) (IFRS 13, Appendix B9, page A516). This reflects the cost to a market participant buyer of acquiring or constructing a substitute asset of comparable utility, adjusted for obsolescence with obsolescence noted to be broader than depreciation for financial reporting purposes or tax purposes and to encompass physical deterioration, functional (technological) obsolescence and economic (external) obsolescence (IFRS 13, para B9, page A516).

6 Valuation of OOP

6.2.2.4 IFRS 13 fair value hierarchy of inputs

In the context of owner occupied property, IFRS 13 provides an interesting example of a Level 2 input:

> **Building held and used.** A Level 2 input would be the price per square metre for the building (a valuation multiple) derived from observable market data, e.g. multiples derived from prices in observed transactions involving comparable (i.e. similar) buildings in similar locations (IFRS 13, Appendix B, para B35(g), page A525).

which may be of assistance to the valuer where a significant number of directly comparable sales are available.

6.2.2.5 IFRS 13 fair value measurement in practice

By way of example of IFRS 13 and IVSs in practice, the Airbus Group Financial Statements 2014 included an IFRS Consolidated Statement of Financial Position at 31 December 2014 showing 'Non-current assets' including 'Property, plant and equipment' at €16,321 million with Note 14 showing:

Land, leasehold improvements and buildings including buildings on land owned by others	€4,808
Technical equipment and machinery	€8,246
Other equipment, factory and office equipment	€1,162
Construction in progress	€2,105
Total	€16,321

(Airbus 2014, page 51)

The 'Summary of Significant Accounting Policies' stated:

> Property, plant and equipment – Property, plant and equipment is valued at acquisition or manufacturing cost less accumulated depreciation and impairment losses. Such costs include the estimated cost of replacing, servicing and restoring part of such property, plant and equipment. Items of property, plant and equipment are generally depreciated on a straight line basis. The cost of internally produced equipment and facilities include direct material and labour costs and applicable manufacturing overheads, including depreciation charges. The following useful lives are assumed: buildings 10 to 50 years, site improvements 6 to 30 years, technical equipment and machinery 3 to 20 years; and other equipment, factory and office equipment 2 to 10 years. The useful lives, depreciation methods and residual values applying to property, plant and equipment are reviewed at least annually and in case they change significantly, depreciation charges for current and future periods are adjusted accordingly.

If the carrying amount of an asset exceeds its receivable amount an impairment loss is recognised immediately in profit or loss. At each end of the reporting period, it is assessed whether there is any indication that an item of property, plant and equipment may be impaired. (Airbus 2014, page 25)

6.2.3 *Valuation of owner occupied property for financial reporting*

For the purposes of financial reporting, the valuation of owner occupied property is principally addressed by IVS 300 *Valuations for Financial Reporting* which considers various aspects of valuation in common with investment property but also focuses on aggregation, depreciation and the classification of property leases which are of particular relevance for the valuation of owner occupied property.

Similarly, IFRS 13 *Fair Value Measurement* addresses various aspects of valuation in common with investment property but requires careful consideration in the context of owner occupied property regarding such issues as highest and best use, the practical application of the definition of fair value and valuation techniques and the potential usefulness of price per square metre as a Level 2 input for valuation.

6.3 Valuation of owner occupied property for secured lending

The previous sections sought to focus on IVSs, TIP's, IAS's and IFRS's in the context of the valuation of owner occupied property held by operating businesses and in the context of valuation for financial reporting, with this section focusing on the valuation of owner occupied property in the context of secured lending for which the IVS of principal relevance is IVS 310 *Valuations of Real Property for Secured Lending*.

6.3.1 *IVS 310* Valuations of Real Property Interests for Secured Lending

IVS 310 *Valuations of Real Property Interests for Secured Lending* comprises three sections, being *Introduction*, *Requirements* (focusing on valuation instruction, implementation and reporting) and *Application Guidance* (focusing on issues that may arise in application of the Standard).

Within the *Introduction*, IVS 310 notes that lending from banks and financial institutions is often secured by the collateral of the borrower's *real property* interests (IVS 310, Introduction, page 106), which may require the bank or financial institution to obtain a valuation of the *real property* interest.

6.3.1.1 Valuation instructions and valuation reporting

Concerning *Requirements* (focusing on valuation instruction, implementation and reporting), IVS 310 expands IVS 101 with regard to valuation instructions requiring the inclusion of:

- disclosure of any material involvement that the valuer has with either the property to be valued, the borrower or a prospective borrower, with materiality of involvement being a matter for the professional judgement of the valuer guided by the test of whether the involvement would be likely to give rise to doubt in the mind of a reasonable person as to the ability of the valuer to provide an impartial valuation if it were discovered after the valuation had been carried out (IVS 310, para 2, page 107);
- identification of the *real property* interest to be used as the collateral for securing the loan(s), together with the party in whom the interest is currently vested (IVS 310, para 3, page 107);
- the *basis of value*, which will normally be *market value*, with requests for valuation on the assumption of a forced sale or imposed time limit for disposal to be addressed through a defined *special assumption* and qualified by a statement that the value will only be valid at the *valuation date* and may not be achievable in the event of future default when both market conditions and sale circumstances may be different (IVS 310, para 4, page 107);
- a defined *special assumption* where a change in the state of the property is to be reflected, such as:
  - that a proposed building has been completed at the *valuation date*; and/or
  - that a proposed lease of the property has been completed at the *valuation date*; and/or
  - that a specified occupancy level has been reached by the *valuation date*; and/or
  - that the seller had imposed a time limit for disposal that was inadequate for proper marketing (IVS 310, para 5, page 107).

Such inclusions in the valuer instructions contribute to effective risk management for both the client/lender and the valuer, making explicit and transparent each of the important premises upon which the valuation is based.

Further, with application to *property, plant and equipment*, IVS 310 expands IVS 103 with regard to valuation reporting requiring the inclusion of:

- appropriate reference to the matters addressed in the valuation instructions, above;

- comment on factors that are relevant to a lender's assessment of the performance of the security over the life of the proposed loan, such as:
  - current activity and trends in the relevant market;
  - historic, current and anticipated future demand for the type of property and location;
  - any potential and likely demand for alternative uses that exist or can be anticipated at the *valuation date*;
  - the impact of any events foreseeable at the *valuation date* on the probable future value of the security during the loan period (such as a tenant exercising an option to break a lease); and
  - where *market value* is provided subject to a *special assumption*:
  - an explanation of the *special assumption*;
    - a comment on any material difference between *market value* and *market value* subject to the *special assumption*;
    - a comment that such value may not be realisable at a future date unless the factual position is as described in the *special assumption* (IVS 310, para 7, page 108); and
- reference to the agreed sale price for the subject property, if known or ascertained, including comment on the enquiries made to establish the agreed sale price and the reasons for any difference between the agreed sale price and the valuation (IVS 310, para 8, page 108).

Such inclusions in the valuation report also contribute to effective risk management for both the client/lender and the valuer, clearly and transparently explaining potential risks and the impact of the *special assumptions* stated in the valuer instructions.

6.3.1.2 Cautionary issues in valuations of real property for secured lending purposes

Concerning *Application Guidance* (focusing on issues that may arise in application of the Standard), reflecting the importance of a valuation in the credit decision by a typically risk averse lender for real property, IVS 310 identifies a range of issues where the valuer should exercise caution.

6.3.1.2.1 Property interest, incentives and valuation approaches

The nature of the interest in the *real property* being valued should be identified, together with any other existing or creatable interests in the *real property* and the parties in whom such interests are vested, as these may impact value. If title information is not provided or not available, clear assumptions should be stated concerning title and related interests, preferably with a recommendation that these matters be verified before a loan is finalised (IVS 310, para G1, page 109).

6 Valuation of OOP

IVS 310 cites the example of a property offered for security which is subject to lease to a party related to the borrower at an income stream above market levels, which may be appropriate to disregard (IVS 310, para G2, page 109). Another example may be the valuation of a head leasehold interest in a major office building that may be impacted by issues associated with the freehold (such as rights of way or prohibitions on certain uses) or by issues associated with subsidiary leases (such as rights of first refusal to buy the head leasehold or constraints on the profile of other occupiers) which should be considered and identified, with the relevant parties, in the valuation report.

Where, in various markets around the world, incentives are offered to existing or prospective tenants these should be identified and their effect on selling price commented upon in the valuation report, but should be disregarded in an assessment of *market value* as they may not reoccur in the event that the lender has to rely on the security (IVS 310, para G3, page 109).

This may be particularly challenging where incentives are pervasive and hidden, with the effect of incentives such as motor vehicles or overseas holidays being generally harder to identify and quantify than rent-free periods or provision of fit-out. Further, in markets where a particular level of incentive has become common to the point of being assumed to occur by market participants, a focus on incentives over and above that level or upon effective rents may be prudent.

With *market value* being the appropriate basis of value for secured lending, IVS 310 notes that, while all three valuation approaches to estimate *market value* can be used for secured lending purposes, the *market approach* or the *income approach* are preferred but rely on sufficient market evidence being available. In the absence of sufficient market evidence, IVS 310 cautions against use of the *cost approach*, other than as a check approach, as it is unlikely that such a specialised property would be regarded as suitable security (IVS 310, para G4, page 109).

6.3.1.2.2 Property types – owner-occupied, trade related and specialised property

IVS 310 cautions that different types of property have different characteristics as loan security which should be addressed in the valuation of the relevant interest to provide the lender with adequate information on the suitability of the property as security and to help the lender identify any risk factors associated with the property over the duration of the loan (IVS 310, para G5, pages 109, 110).

In this context, IVS 310 addresses five property types, with investment property and development property considered in section 5.3.1.2.1 of Chapter 5, including:

- **Owner occupied property:**

  Owner occupied property will generally be valued for lending security purposes on the assumption of vacant possession, with the buyer entitled to full legal control and possession. While the owner may be considered as part of the market, any special advantage arising from the owner's occupancy should be excluded from the valuation of the property (IVS 310, para G10, page 110);

- **Trade related property:**

  Trade related property usually exhibits a strong nexus between an often specifically suited property and the income-generating business trading therein, such that the assumption of vacant possession may result in a significantly different estimate of value (due to time to re-establish, start-up costs and so forth) to that as part of an operating concern which should be addressed in the valuation report, with the value for an alternative use potentially representing *market value* (IVS 310, para G13, page 111); and

- **Specialised property:**

  By its nature, a *specialised property* may suit the business of which it is part but have limited marketability otherwise. Therefore, IVS 310 requires that (unless otherwise instructed) *specialised property* is valued for secured lending purposes on the *special assumption* that the business has ceased and the underlying security will reflect the value for an alternative use, including consideration of the costs and risk involved in achieving such alternative use. If a valuation of a *specialised property* as part of a business as a going concern is required, such value will be dependent on the ongoing profitability of the business and the valuation report should distinguish between the value of the property as part of the business and the value of the property if the business had ceased and vacated (IVS 310, para G11, G12, Page 110, 111).

Accordingly, the provisions of IVS 310 concerning property types provide sensible and practical advice to the valuer which, if followed, will contribute to effective risk management.

6.3.1.3 IVS 310 Valuations of Real Property Interests for Secured Lending in practice

RICS VPGA2 *Valuation for Secured Lending* in the RICS Red Book Global provides additional commentary on the practical implementation of IVS 310 (RICS, 2013, para 1.1, page 67), usefully listing common examples of property as security for lending, being:

- property that is, or will be, owner occupied;
- property that is, or will be, held as an investment;

- property that is fully equipped as a trading entity and valued with regard to trading potential; and
- property that is, or is intended to be, the subject of development or refurbishment (RICS, 2013, para 2.1, page 67);

echoing the property types considered in IVS 310 in section 6.3.1.2, above. Concerning valuation instructions, RICS VPGA2 concisely notes:

> The overriding objective is that the valuer should understand the lender's needs and objectives, including the terms of the loan being contemplated, and the lender should understand the advice that is given. (RICS, 2013, para 2.3, page 67)

requiring the valuer to request details of the terms of the lending facility being contemplated by the lender (RICS, 2013, para 4.4, page 69), so being consistent with the explicit and transparent approach advocated by IVS 310 which contributes to effective risk management for, as Banfield notes, valuations for secured lending have the greatest liability for the valuer with most litigation against valuers coming from banks who have lost money on property loans and are seeking to recover or mitigate their losses (Banfield, 2014, page 138).

Concerning disclosure, while IVS 310 refers to disclosure of any material involvement by the valuer, RICS VPGA2 extends this to declaration of both professional and personal potential conflicts of interest (RICS, 2013, para 3.1, page 68), any anticipated future involvement and any previous involvement with the borrower, prospective borrower, asset or party connected with the transaction within a period of 24 months preceding the date of instruction (RICS, 2013, para 3.3, 3.4, page 68) comprehensively including, for example, where the valuer or the firm:

- has a longstanding professional relationship with the borrower or the owner of the property or asset;
- is introducing the transaction to the lender or the borrower, for which a fee is payable to the valuer or the firm;
- has a financial interest in the asset or in the borrower;
- is acting for the owner of the property or asset in a related transaction;
- is acting (or has acted) for the borrower on the purchase of the property or asset;
- is retained to act in the disposal or letting of a completed development on the subject property or asset;
- has recently acted in a market transaction involving the property or asset;
- has provided fee earning professional advice on the property or asset to current or previous owners or their lenders; and/or
- is providing development consultancy for the current or previous owners (RICS, 2013, para 3.4, page 68).

Further, the RICS Red Book Global suggests that, in determining whether a conflict may exist, the valuer have regard, where material, to:

- the quantum of any financial interest in a connected party;
- the scope for the valuer or firm to benefit materially from a particular valuation outcome; and/or
- the level of fees earned from any connected party as a proportion of total fee income (RICS, 2013, para 3.5, page 69);

with the responsibility to decide whether or not to accept the instruction remaining firmly with the valuer (RICS, 2013, para 3.8, page 69). As Banfield (2014) succinctly observes:

> A final thought – it has been said that if you think you have a conflict, you most probably do. (Banfield, 2014, page 141)

Concerning valuation instructions, RICS VPGA2 cautions that the instructions for a valuation for secured lending purposes commissioned by a party other than the lender, such as the prospective borrower or a broker, should contain a statement that the valuation may not be acceptable to a lender (RICS, 2013, para 4.2, page 69).

Further, RICS VPGA2 provides comprehensive examples of *special assumptions* that may require inclusion in the letter of instruction, such as:

- that planning consent has been granted for development at the property;
- that there has been a physical change to the property, such as new construction or refurbishment;
- that a new letting on given terms, or the settlement of a rent review at a specific rent, has been completed;
- that there is a *special purchaser*, which may include the borrower;
- that a constraint which could prevent the property being either brought to or adequately exposed to the market is to be ignored;
- that a new economic or environmental designation has taken effect;
- that any unusual volatility in the market as at the *valuation date* is to be discounted; and
- that any lease or leases between connected parties have been disregarded (RICS, 2013, para 5.3, page 70);

with the RICS Red Book Global noting that any material difference in *market value* with and without the *special assumption* should be accompanied by a comment in the valuation report (RICS, 2013, para 5.4, page 70).

Concerning valuation reporting, RICS VPGA2 extends IVS 310 by requiring that the report must include:

- the valuation methodology adopted, supported (where appropriate or requested) with the calculation used;
- the extent to which a recent transaction at the subject property has been accepted as evidence of *market value*;
- comment on the suitability of the property as security for mortgage purposes, having regard to the length and terms of the loan being contemplated. If the terms are not known, a comment should be made on the general marketability of the property accompanied by a reservation of right to review when the terms of the loan are known;
- any circumstances of which the valuer is aware that could affect the price, together with provision of an indication of their effect; and
- any other factor that potentially conflicts with the definition of *market value* or its underlying assumptions (RICS, 2013, para 6.1, page 70, 71).

As with the valuation instructions, the examples are comprehensive and far reaching (such as 'any circumstances of which the valuer is aware' and 'any other factor'), so being consistent with the explicit and transparent approach advocated by IVS 310 which contributes to effective risk management.

Concerning property types, RICS VPGA2 extends IVS 310 by indicating a range of useful matters that it may be appropriate to include in the valuation process:

- **Owner-occupied property:**
  Special assumptions such as that:
  - planning consent has been, or will be, granted for development, including a change of use of the property;
  - a building or other proposed development has been completed in accordance with a defined plan and specification;
  - all necessary licenses are in place;
  - the property has been changed in a defined way (for example, removal of equipment or fixtures); and/or
  - the property is vacant when, in reality, at the *valuation date* it is occupied (RICS, 2013, para 6.2(a), page 71); and
- **Trade related property:**
  Special assumptions such as that:
  - the business has been closed and the property is vacant;
  - the trade inventory has been depleted or removed;
  - the licenses, consents, certificates and/or permits have been lost or are in jeopardy;

o accounts and records of trade are not available to a prospective purchaser (RICS, 2013, para 6.2(c)(1), page 72);

o the trading performance is at a given level; and/or

o projections of trading performance differ materially from current market expectations (RICS, 2013, para 6.2(c)(2), page 72).

with advice that it is good practice to attach the valuation instructions to the valuation report and to refer to these in the body of the report. (RICS 2013, para 6.3, page 73).

(It should be noted that RICS VPGA4 *Valuation of Individual* Trade Related Properties in the RICS Red Book Global provides specific guidance on the valuation of property on the basis of trading potential.) (RICS VPGA4, page 84)

6.3.2 Summary – Valuation of owner occupied property for secured lending

For the purposes of secured lending, the valuation of owner occupied property is principally addressed by IVS 310 *Valuation of Real Property for Secured Lending* which considers various aspects of valuation in common with investment property but also focuses on the unsuitability of the cost approach for valuation for secured lending and the particular aspects of owner occupied property, trade related property and specialised property that require careful attention, each of which contribute to effective risk management for both the client/lender and the valuer.

6.4 Summary and conclusions

Chapter 1 outlined the emergence of globalisation, the role of IFRS and the evolution of valuation standard setting, the role of IVSC and IVSs and an analysis of *market value*, being the central concept of IVSs, with an overview of other IVSs relevant to the valuation of businesses and business interests, intangible assets and financial instruments.

Chapter 2 developed a conceptual framework for valuation based on economic theory, aligned this framework with finance and capital market theory, examined the definition of the market and distinguished definitions of cost and price from defined concepts of value before reconciling these to the conceptual framework for valuation.

Chapter 3 considered various aspects of valuation within IVSs, discussed the definitions of other relevant contextual terms and identified the principal approaches to valuation within IVSs including a focus on the *market approach* to valuation.

6 · Valuation of OOP

Chapter 4 described and analysed those elements of IVSs that are of relevance to the three principal stages of the real property valuation process, being the instruction of the valuer, undertaking the valuation and reporting the valuation.

Chapter 5 focused on IVSs in the context of the valuation of investment property, IAS 40 *Investment Property*, the *income approach* to valuation and TIP 1 *Discounted Cash Flow* for the purposes of secured lending or financial reporting, though acknowledging that certain aspects of these may also apply to owner occupied property.

This chapter considered IVSs in the context of the valuation of owner-occupied property, IAS 16 *Property, Plant and Equipment*, the *cost approach* to valuation and TIP2 *The Cost Approach to Tangible Assets* for the purposes of secured lending or financial reporting, though acknowledging that certain aspects of these may also apply to investment property.

In the context of valuations concerning owner occupied property, IVS 230 *Real Property Interests* lays the foundations for the valuation of *real property* generally with the consideration of *market rent* being of particular significance. Given the probable greater incidence of plant and equipment within owner occupied property than within *investment property*, IVS220 *Plant and Equipment* lays the foundations for the valuation of plant and equipment generally, identifying the wide range of factors requiring consideration and focusing on the *cost approach*. Reflecting the importance of the *cost approach* in the valuation of plant and equipment and of owner occupied property, TIP2 *The Cost Approach to Tangible Assets* highlights the role of land value, reproduction or replacement and deprecation through physical, functional and economic obsolescence.

IVS 230, IVS 220 and TIP 2 complement IAS 16 *Property, Plant and Equipment* which defines *property, plant and equipment* and outlines it's recognition in financial statements with particular reference to depreciation and impairment. When considering the valuation of owner occupied property, regard is required to the possible impact of IAS 36 *Impairment of Assets*, particularly for plant and equipment, as well as IFRS 5 *Non–Current Assets Held for Sale and Discontinued Operations*.

Further, for the purpose of financial reporting, the IVS of principal relevance is IVS 300 *Valuations for Financial Reporting*, with IFRS 13 *Fair Value Measurement* also of relevance for owner occupied property. While principally considered in Chapter 5, in the context of the valuation of owner occupied property for the purposes of financial statements, IVS 300 *Valuations for Financial Reporting* considers aggregation, depreciation of land, buildings, plant and equipment and classification of property leases, linking to the provisions of IAS 17 *Leases*. Further, in the context of the valuation of owner occupied property for the purposes of financial statements, IFRS 13 *Fair Value Measurement* considers highest and best use, aspects of the definition of fair value in application and role of the cost model.

Concerning valuation for the purpose of secured lending for owner occupied property, the IVS of principal relevance is IVS 310 *Valuations of Real Property for Secured Lending* which clearly sets out the requirements for valuation instructions and valuation reporting and identifies cautionary issues from a secured lending viewpoint such as incentives, specialised property and trade related property.

Accordingly, the valuation of owner occupied property requires the valuer to have regard to the interaction between several IVSs, TIP's, IAS's and IFRS's simultaneously which is somewhat overwhelming, with considerable care required to comply with the requirements of each at the same time and careful discussion of valuation instructions with the client, their accountant and their auditor highly recommended as the first step.

References

Airbus Group (2014) *2014* Annual Report Financial Statements, Airbus Group NV, Leiden.

Banfield, A. (2014) *A Valuer's Guide to the RICS Red Book 2014*, RICS, London.

International Financial Reporting Council (2012) *A Briefing for Chief Executives, Audit Committees and Boards of Directors*, IFRS Foundation, London.

International Financial Reporting Standards (2013) *International Financial Reporting Standards 2013*, International Accounting Standards Board, London.

International Valuation Standards Council (2012) *TIP 1 – Discounted Cash Flow*, IVSC, London.

International Valuation Standards Council (2012) *TIP 2 – The Cost Approach to Tangible Assets*, IVSC, London.

International Valuation Standards Council (2013) *International Valuation Standards 2013*, IVSC, London.

Royal Institution of Chartered Surveyors (2013) *RICS Professional Standards, Global and UK 2014*, RICS, London.

6 Valuation of OOP

Index

International Valuation Standards: A Guide to the Valuation of Real Property Assets,
First Edition. David Parker.
© 2016 John Wiley & Sons, Ltd. Published 2016 by John Wiley & Sons, Ltd.